MULTIPLAYER
CIVILIZATION II
GOLD EDITION

First Edition, September 1998

TECHNICAL STUFF

REQUIREMENTS

For *Civilization II Multiplayer Gold Edition* to work, there are a few things your computer *must* have:

- The processor must be a 486 or better, and the system speed should be at least 33 MHz (megahertz). We recommend a Pentium running of at least 60 MHz for best results.

- You must have Windows 95 (or newer).

- There must be at least 16 MB of RAM installed in your computer.

- A double-speed (2x) CD-ROM drive or faster.

- Since the installation program will copy parts of *Civilization II Multiplayer Gold Edition* onto your hard disk, you must have sufficient empty storage space on your hard drive. How much you need depends on the installation options you choose.

- The graphics must be SVGA quality or better, capable of at least 256-color 640 x 480 mode.

- You must have a mouse attached to the computer.
- We strongly recommend (but it's not required) that you have a Windows-compatible sound card, as well.

If you intend to play multiplayer games, you'll need at least *one* of the following things:

- A Windows-compatible modem. The game should work on a modem as slow as 9600 baud, but we recommend a 28.8 kps modem or faster.
- Access to a local area network (LAN) running either the TCP/IP protocol or the IPX/SPX protocol.
- Access to the Internet with the Winsock protocol and a 28.8 kps connection (or faster).

If you think you have all of these, but still have a problem running the game, please contact MicroProse Customer Support for assistance.

INSTALLING

Before you can play *Civilization II Multiplayer Gold Edition*, the installation program must copy some files onto your hard disk. To have it do so, follow these instructions:

- Turn on your computer.
- Open the CD-ROM drive, place the *Civilization II Multiplayer Gold Edition* CD-ROM in there, and close the drive.
- This disc is a Windows "AutoPlay" CD-ROM. This means that just putting the disc in the drive for the first time starts up the installation program. If AutoPlay works as it should, you can simply click the **Install** button and skip the next three instructions.
- Double-click on the My Computer icon.
- In the window that opens, double-click on the listing for your CD-ROM drive (normally 'D').
- Finally, double-click on the file **setup.exe**. That runs the installation program.
- Choose the directory into which you want the game installed. The default directory is c:\mps\civ2.
- You have the option of doing a **Typical** installation, a **Compact** one, or a **Custom** one. If your hard drive space is limited, **Custom** allows you to decide what you want installed and leave nonessential files on the CD-ROM. Note that the game will not function unless you install the **Required** files, and there will be no sound effects unless you install the **Recommended** files.
- Once you've made your choices, the installation program copies the files you requested to your hard drive from the CD-ROM, then creates the *Civilization II* program group and icons. You also have the option of adding *Civilization II* to the Start Menu.

- Next, the installation program installs two pieces of utility software that are necessary for the game to work properly—WinG and Indeo Video for Windows.
- When the installation is done, the program returns you to Windows.

Note that even a full installation does not copy the multimedia files to your hard drive. These files take up so much space (and the access time you save by having them on your hard drive is hardly noticeable) that very few of you will actually want them installed. If you do, however, wish to have these multimedia files on your hard drive, here's how.

- Copy all of the files from the CD-ROM directory **\civ2\video** into a subdirectory of the directory into which you installed the game. This subdirectory *must* be named **video**. So, for example, if you used the default installation directory, the videos would go into **c:\mps\civ2\video**.
- Next, copy all the files from **\civ2\kings** the same way, into a subdirectory called **kings**.

Note: Once you have installed this, everything you need is in place. Do not attempt to install any previous **Civilization II** product (the original or either scenario add-on pack). It's unnecessary, and it will prevent the multiplayer edition from working.

PLAYING

Once the automated installation and setup are complete, the game is ready to play. To start:

- Make sure that there is a **Civilization II** CD-ROM in your drive. Any one—**Multiplayer Gold Edition**, **Civilization II**, **Conflicts in Civilization**, or **Fantastic Worlds**—will do. Note that which CD-ROM you put in your drive will determine what game music you hear. (If you did not install the **Recommended** files, there will be no sound effects. There will be some music.)

Now simply double-click on the **Civilization II** icon or click **Civ2** on the Windows 95 Start Menu to start the game.

TABLE OF CONTENTS

INTRODUCTION

Civilization II improves on a beloved classic. *Civilization*, its predecessor, cast you as the ruler of an infant civilization, struggling to survive and prosper in the earliest moments of history. Eventually, growth and exploration brought you into competition with ruthless, competent, but sometimes predictable computer opponents. *Civilization II* adds depth to the diplomacy and smarts to the artificial intelligence, as well as tweaking features that millions of *Civ* players had come to know too well. The result is the same compelling quality and fresh challenges for the expert player—and a wide-open world to explore for the novice.

Both you and your opponents begin with a small band of settlers surrounded by the hazards and delights of unexplored territory. Each decision you make can have important ramifications later. Should you build a city on a coast or inland? Should you concentrate on military production or agricultural improvement? Innovative displays make it easy to understand the shifting situation and implement action. If you prove an able ruler, your civilization grows larger and even more interesting to manage. The inevitable contact with neighboring civilizations opens new doors of opportunity: treaties, embassies, sabotage, trade, and war.

As time passes, you are confronted with increasingly difficult decisions. First, you must think tactically. Where is the optimum location for another city? When should you produce specific military units and city improvements? How rapidly should you explore the surrounding land? Soon, circumstances demand that you formulate strategic plans. Should you pursue war or peace with neighbors? When should you explore and expand overseas? Is it advantageous to change your type of government? Where should you focus technological research?

The success of the civilization that you build depends on your decisions. As ruler, you manage the economy, diplomacy, exploration, research, and the war machine of your civilization. Your policies must be flexible to fit an evolving world. Military units inevitably become obsolete and need replacement as you gain more advanced technologies. The balance of power among your rivals shifts often. You might have to modify your economic and governmental policies, lest you fall behind in a critical area. The empires of Alexander the Great, the Hittites, Napoleon, and Genghis Khan (to name just a few) all held pride of place on the world's stage at one time. All eventually collapsed. In *Civilization II*, the challenge is to build an empire that stands the test of time. You might succeed where great predecessors have failed. If you locate cities properly, build them soundly, defend them aggressively, and neutralize the danger from potential enemies, the descendants of your first tiny tribe might not only survive, but lead the colonization of space.

FOUR IMPULSES OF CIVILIZATION

There is no single driving force behind the urge toward civilization, no one goal toward which every culture strives. There is, instead, a web of forces and objectives that impel and beckon, shaping cultures as they grow. In *Civilization II*, there are four basic impulses that seem to be of the greatest importance to the health and flexibility of your fledgling society.

EXPLORATION

An early focus in *Civilization II* is exploration. You begin the game knowing almost nothing about your surroundings. Most of the map is dark. Your units move into this darkness of unexplored territory and discover new terrain; mountains, rivers, grasslands, and forests are just some of the features they might reveal. The areas they explore might be occupied by minor tribes or another culture's units. In either case, a chance meeting provokes a variety of encounters. As your units "map" the unknown by revealing terrain squares that once were black, they also lessen the likelihood that you will be surprised by random barbarian attacks.

ECONOMICS

As your civilization grows, you need to manage its ever more complex production and resource requirements. Adjusting the tax rates and choosing the most productive terrain for your purposes, you can control the speeds at which your population grows larger and your cities produce goods. By setting taxes higher and science lower, you can tilt your economy into a cash cow. You can also adjust the happiness of your population. Perhaps you'll make luxuries more available, or you might clamp down on unrest with a larger military presence. You can establish trade routes with other powers to bring in supplemental income every turn.

KNOWLEDGE

On the flip side of your economics management is your commitment to scholarship. By setting taxes lower and science higher, you can increase the frequency with which your population discovers new technologies. With each new advance, further paths of learning open up and new units and city improvements become available for manufacture. Some technological discoveries let your cities build unique Wonders of the World.

CONQUEST

Perhaps your taste runs to military persuasion. *Civilization II* allows you to pursue a range of postures, from pure defense through imperialistic aggression to cooperative alliance. One way to win the game is to be the last civilization standing when the dust clears. Of course, you'll face both random barbarian attacks and calculated sorties by your computer opponents.

THE BIG PICTURE

A winning strategy for *Civilization II* is one that combines all of these aspects into a flexible whole. Your first mission is to survive; your second is to thrive. It is not true that the largest civilization is necessarily the winner, nor that the wealthiest always has the upper hand. In fact, a balance of knowledge, cash, and military might allows you to respond to any crisis that occurs, whether it is a barbarian invasion, an aggressive rival, or an upsurge of internal unrest.

WINNING

To win *Civilization II*, you must follow one of two broad strategies to a final goal: Either win the space race or conquer the world. The first civilization to colonize Alpha Centauri wins; this nation most often has a large factory base dedicated to producing the specialized components of spacecraft and a head-and-shoulders lead in technological development. However, it's possible to use industrial espionage and judicious invasions to steal the necessary advances, while sabotaging the production lead of a more advanced but less well defended opponent. A leader who pursues the second option, conquering the world, is likely to focus on military strategy, though building a strong economy and financing insurrections can be pretty successful, too. See **Winning the Game** for an in-depth analysis of *Civilization II*'s scoring system.

THE VARIOUS DOCUMENTATION

It's a truism at computer game companies that most customers never read the manual. Until a problem rears its head, the average player just bulls through by trial and error; it's part of the fun. When a problem does come up, this type of player wants to spend as little time in the book as possible, then get back to the game. For those of you who just need a quick reference, the **Reference: Screen by Screen** section is the place to go.

For the rest of you, we've tried to organize the chapters in the order that you'll need them if you've never played *Civilization* or *Civilization II* before. If you're new to *Civ*, the sidebars on concepts should help you understand the fundamentals of the game.

The **Technical Stuff** (in the front of this book) is the place to find installation and startup instructions and any late changes to the game. Since it was written later, the information in it supersedes anything in the manual.

The **README** file that comes on the CD-ROM has the rundown on the very latest changes (due to printing and binding time, the manual has to be completed before the playtesters recommend their final tweaks). That info supersedes even the **Technical Stuff**.

In addition to the printed stuff and the **README**, *Civilization II* comes with a unique compendium of on-screen help. Click on the CIVILOPEDIA menu to call up a list of options describing units, improvements, governments, and even game concepts. Entries are hyperlinked so that you can jump from one entry to another with ease.

INTERFACE CONVENTIONS

You play *Civilization II* using a combination of both mouse and keyboard. Many people find that the shortcut keys on the keyboard significantly speed up their play.

Using a Mouse: Throughout the text, we assume that you understand basic mouse functions and terms, like "clicking and dragging." Since not everybody knows these things, we've provided brief definitions of how we use the most common terms. One preliminary note: *Civilization II* puts both buttons on a two-button mouse to use. If you are using a three-button mouse, the center button has no function for this game.

- "Clicking" refers to placing the mouse pointer over an area of the screen and clicking with the left mouse button.

- "Right-clicking" is clicking with the right mouse button.

- "Click-and-hold" means keeping your finger on the mouse button longer than usual (long enough that the game recognizes the "hold").

- "Dragging" means holding the left button down while moving the mouse.

- "Selecting" means clicking on something.

- "Pressing a button" with the mouse means clicking on one of the on-screen buttons.

- You can "scroll" some of the menus and boxes in the game by dragging the button along a slider bar that's on one side of the box.

Menus: The MENU BAR runs across the top of the screen. As is standard in Windows games, clicking on the name of a menu opens that menu, giving you access to the menu options. If you prefer not to use the keyboard and have enabled mouse movement of units, you can play *Civilization II* using the mouse and menus exclusively.

Shortcut Keys: Almost all of the menu options in *Civilization II* have a shortcut key ([R] for Roads, for example), which is noted on the menu. Pressing this key (or combination of keys) has the same effect as selecting the option from the menu. Another quick way to use menu options is also a Windows standard. The name of each menu has one underlined letter. Holding the [Alt] key and typing that letter opens the menu. The name of each option on the menu also has one underlined letter. Typing that letter when the menu is open activates the option.

Cursors: The mouse pointer, or cursor, has many different shapes in *Civilization II*, depending on what task you're currently attempting.

 Most often, the cursor looks like an arrow. If you have chosen a special "desktop theme" in Windows 95 or otherwise customized your cursor, you'll see your own cursor sometimes, too.

 An outline around a terrain square indicates that you are in VIEW PIECES mode. By moving the cursor with the number keypad on your keyboard, you can use this cursor to count squares from one location to another or move around the map without moving units. Toggle back to the arrow cursor by pressing the V key or choosing MOVE PIECES from the VIEW menu.

 A bold (black) arrow indicates the direction the unit on which your mouse pointer is positioned will move when you click. If you don't like this unit-movement cursor, you can disable it by unchecking the MOVE UNITS WITH MOUSE option under GAME OPTIONS in the GAME menu. *Civilization II* starts with this option disabled.

 A set of cross hairs indicates that you can click on the spot where your mouse pointer is positioned in the WORLD WINDOW to center the active VIEW UNITS window on that spot.

 The word "Go" and a bent arrow indicates that when you release the mouse button, the active unit will begin moving toward the indicated square. See **GoTo Orders** in the **Terrain and Movement** section for complete details.

 A parachute indicates that the active paratrooper unit will make a paradrop into the designated square; a "crossed-out" parachute indicates that the designated square is not a valid paradrop target. See **Paradrop Orders** in the **Terrain and Movement** section for complete details.

 As in most Windows programs, an I-beam or vertical line indicates that you can type in text from the keyboard.

 As in most Windows programs, a double-ended arrow indicates that you can resize the window frame on which your mouse pointer is positioned.

 As in most Windows programs, an hourglass indicates the program is working; please wait.

TUTORIAL

Those who have played either **Civilization** or **CivNet** are already familiar with most of the concepts presented in this tutorial. However, even if you are well acquainted with the DOS, Windows, or Macintosh version, you will find that there are many new features in **Civilization II**. Also, many of the game's existing elements, including screen layout, icons, and controls have changed from the earlier games.

The primary purpose of this tutorial is to introduce new players to the basic elements of **Civilization II**. It provides an overview of the basic game elements, and guides you through several centuries of a sample game. New actions and events are explained as they occur. The tutorial game has been set up in such a way that most of the events should be fairly predictable; however, one of the things that makes **Civilization II** exciting game after game is the element of random chance that exists. The way your computer-controlled opponents act and react to one another (and to you) might cause certain events to deviate from the path described in this tutorial. If you feel that things have gotten too far out of control, feel free to reload the saved game and start again.

To begin the tutorial, start the game and select LOAD A GAME from the GAME menu. Load the game called **tutorial.sav**. The tutorial game is set to CHIEFTAIN level, the easiest difficulty option available. The game starts on the first turn, in 4000 BC, with you taking the part of Abraham Lincoln, leader of the Americans. You might want to go to the GAME OPTIONS in the GAME menu and turn off the INSTANT ADVICE and TUTORIAL HELP options, if you find the pop-up boxes distracting.

Instructions you are to follow are set in italics. Explanations and descriptions are set in regular type. Keep in mind that this tutorial is a simple walk-through, and only touches briefly on game concepts and control features. If you want more information on anything, detailed descriptions can be found in the other chapters of this manual.

BUILDING YOUR FIRST CITY

At the start of the game, your civilization consists of a single band of wandering nomads. This is a Settlers unit. Although Settlers are capable of performing a variety of useful tasks, your first task is to move the Settlers unit to a site that is suitable for the construction of your first city.

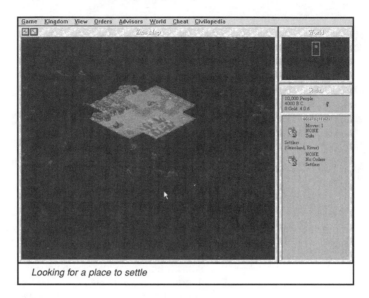

Looking for a place to settle

Finding suitable locations in which to build cities, especially your first city, is one of the most important decisions you make in the game. In order to survive and grow, each city must have access to all three resource types: food (represented by grain), production (represented by shields), and trade goods (represented by arrows). The map in **Civilization II** is divided into individual "squares," each of which contains a different type of terrain. Each terrain type yields resources in differing amounts. A good city site provides all three resource types. Normally, the lines dividing the map squares are invisible. To get an idea of how the terrain is divided, turn on the map grid by choosing Show Map Grid from the View menu, or by holding down Ctrl and pressing G.

Before you move your Settlers, take time to examine the surrounding terrain. You will note that only 21 map squares are visible. This represents the extent to which your civilization has explored the world. (This 21-square pattern is significant with regard to cities as well, as you will see later.) The surrounding black areas represent unexplored terrain. You can build a city on any terrain square except for Ocean. As mentioned earlier, each terrain type yields differing proportions of resources, so the type of terrain you choose for a city site determines the level of the city's success.

Your Settlers currently occupy a Grassland square. Normally, Grassland produces two grain when worked by one of your citizens. Note that a small shield symbol appears in the center of this particular Grassland square. That means that, in addition to its normal resources, this Grassland square also yields one shield when worked. Normal Grassland squares (without shields) appear to the northwest and northeast of your Settlers.

Directly to the north and directly to the west of the Settlers are Plains squares. The Plains terrain type produces one grain and one shield when worked by one of your citizens. Southeast, south, and southwest of the Settlers are Ocean squares, which produce one grain and two arrows each when worked. Surrounding the edge of the visible terrain are a Plains square with a river running through it, two additional Grassland squares, and four additional Ocean squares. There are also two Hills squares and a Mountains square along the northwest edge, two Forest squares to the southwest, and an Ocean square two squares to the southeast with a Whale in it. We'll look at these in a moment.

Abraham Lincoln

You have the option of moving around to find a suitable city site. If the nearby terrain is less than optimal it is worth doing so, considering the importance of proper city placement. You shouldn't waste too much time looking, however. Settlers move only one square per turn, and 20 years pass every turn this early in the game. Luckily, your starting position here is excellent: The local terrain provides a diverse resource mix, you are adjacent to a sea coast, and Grassland squares make good city locations.

Build your first city by selecting BUILD NEW CITY from the ORDERS menu, or by pressing the Ⓑ *key.* You can rename the city if you like, but we'll refer to it as Washington.

EXAMINING THE CITY DISPLAY

As soon as the city is built, a new window appears. This window is called the CITY DISPLAY. The CITY DISPLAY gives detailed information on the city's current status, including the amount of resources generated, the item currently being built by the city, and the size and attitude of the city's population.

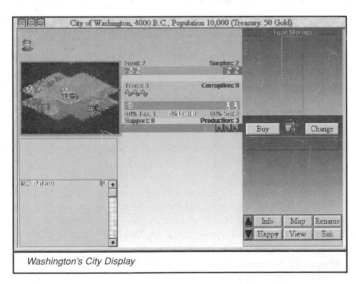

Washington's City Display

Your first priority is to check the status of the city's resources. The POPULATION ROS-TER shows that there is one citizen in Washington, and he is content. Under most circumstances, each citizen in the city is working in one of the terrain squares surrounding the city, generating resources for the city's use. As new citizens are added to the population, the game puts them to work in the terrain square it considers the most productive available. In this case, the city's single resident is producing resources in the Ocean square that contains the Whale.

You have the option of moving citizens to different terrain squares if you want to produce different combinations of resources. As you can see by the icons on the RESOURCE MAP, the Whale square is generating two grain, two shields, and two arrows. *Click the Whale square to "pick up" the citizen working there, then click on the Plains square with the river running through it, directly to the east (right) of the city.* Notice that, in the Plains square with the river, the citizen now generates one grain, one shield, and one arrow. *Click on the Plains square with the river and then click on one of the Forest squares southwest of the city.* In the Forest square, the citizen generates one grain and two shields, but no arrows. Since the Whale square is one of the most productive types of terrain, *click on the Forest square and then on the Whale square to return the citizen to his original position.*

As you can see, the combination of resources produced is based on terrain type. Under normal circumstances, each city can assign citizens to generate resources in any of the 20 terrain squares surrounding the city. The pattern of 21 squares with the city at the center that is seen in Washington's RESOURCE MAP is called the CITY RADIUS. In addition to the terrain squares in the CITY RADIUS, the city square itself always generates resources. Like the squares worked by your citizens, the number and type of resources produced in the city square is dependent on the terrain type.

Washington is currently generating four units of food. Each citizen requires two units of food each turn in order to survive. Excess grain icons accumulate in the FOOD STORAGE BOX. The more surplus food the city generates, the faster it grows. Washington is also generating three shields. Shields represent raw materials used for supporting units and building new items. Since there are currently no units to support, the shields generated each turn go directly into the PRODUCTION BOX. Finally, the city is producing three arrows, which represent trade goods. Trade goods are divided into three separate categories: Taxes (gold icons), Luxuries (goblet icons), and Science (beaker icons). Currently, one arrow is being used to generate taxes, while the other two are generating science.

Washington's IMPROVEMENTS ROSTER shows that the only building in the city is the Palace. Your Palace denotes that Washington is your civilization's capital.

FIRST PRIORITIES

Because there is so much information to assimilate at the start of the game, it's hard to know what you should do first. There are four priorities that you must keep in mind early in the game: defense, research, growth, and exploration.

Defense: Your top priority is to defend Washington from potential enemies. After all, who knows who might be lurking in all that unexplored territory? To defend the city, you must build a military unit. When the city is built, it automatically begins to construct a defensive unit. The PRODUCTION BOX shows that Washington is currently producing a Warriors unit.

Research: The science portion of your trade income is used to research new Civilization Advances. Civilization Advances are new discoveries and technologies that allow you to build newer and better military units, city improvements, and Wonders of the World.

Growth: The surplus food generated by the city eventually leads to population growth. When the FOOD STORAGE BOX is completely filled with grain, a new citizen is added to the population. Steady city growth leads to increased productivity and the ability to expand your civilization by building more Settlers to colonize the continent.

Exploration: If you don't explore the dark areas of the map, you have no way of knowing what benefits and dangers might be lurking there. By using spare units to explore the world around you, you can discover the villages of minor tribes (which often provide you with benefits such as money and new discoveries), sites for new cities, and neighboring civilizations.

When you're finished examining Washington, close the CITY DISPLAY by clicking the EXIT button in the lower right corner.

RESEARCHING CIVILIZATION ADVANCES

After closing the CITY DISPLAY, press the Enter *key to end the turn.* At the start of the next turn, you are prompted to choose the first civilization advance you want to research.

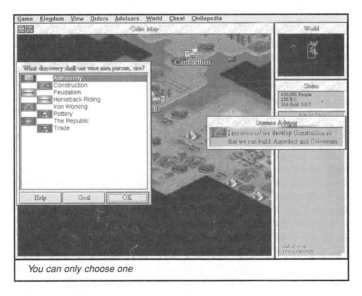

You can only choose one

When the game begins, your civilization has only minimal knowledge, usually consisting of only Irrigation, Mining, and Roads. (In some games you might be given additional advances at the start of the game, but in the tutorial this is not the case.) The bulk of your knowledge throughout the game is gained through research. There are many different strategies dictating the order in which advances are researched. For the purposes of this tutorial, we'll adopt a conservative, defensive strategy. You can experiment with research strategies of your own as you become more familiar with the game.

When the menu of possible advances appears, select Bronze Working, then click OK. We have chosen Bronze Working because the discovery of this advance allows you to build the Phalanx unit. Phalanxes are twice as effective at defending cities as Warriors.

The amount of time required to research discoveries is based on the amount of science your city is currently generating. Remember, science is one of the components of trade. *Select the TRADE ADVISOR option from the ADVISORS menu, or press the* F5 *key.* As you can see from this display, it currently takes five turns to make a new discovery. The more beaker icons you generate each turn, the faster you make new discoveries. *Click OK to close the TRADE ADVISOR window.*

As you can see by looking at the STATUS window, 20 years of game time pass. (On CHIEFTAIN level, turns start out spanning 20 years each. As the game progresses, the turns get shorter, dropping to ten years per turn, then five, two, and eventually one year per turn.)

The amount of trade allocated to taxes, luxuries, and science can be adjusted to a certain degree to suit your needs. *Select TAX RATE from the KINGDOM menu.* As you can see, there are three sliders in the TAX RATE window, each of which controls the percentage of one of the three elements of trade. Moving a slider left or right decreases or increases (respectively) the percentage of trade allocated to that element, and adjusts the other elements accordingly so that the total percentage equals 100 percent.

Unlike **Civilization** and **CivNet**, **Civilization II** limits the maximum percentage of trade that can be allocated to taxes, luxuries, and science based on your civilization's government type. You start the game in Despotism, so the maximum percentage you can allocate to any trade element is 60 percent. Note that the game automatically sets science at 60 percent and taxes at 40 percent. Since your focus should be on research at this time, and you currently require no luxuries to keep your population happy, the default settings are fine for now. *Close the TAX RATE window by clicking the OK button.*

MEANWHILE, BACK IN THE CITY...

Now, let's take a look at what happened in the city after the first turn. *Open Washington's CITY DISPLAY by clicking the city icon on the map.* Several things have changed since you last looked inside Washington. First, the information in the TITLE BAR indicates that your treasury now contains 51 gold instead of the original 50. That is because Washington is generating one gold coin of taxes each turn. Since there are currently no improvements in Washington that require upkeep, the gold is added to your treasury for future use.

Look at the FOOD STORAGE BOX. It is no longer empty. There are now two grain icons in it. This is the surplus food that was generated by the city on the first turn. It is stored in the FOOD STORAGE BOX for later use.

Finally, look at the PRODUCTION BOX. Like the FOOD STORAGE BOX, it is no longer empty. The three shields generated on the first turn were used to help build the Warriors unit currently under production.

An alternate way to close the CITY DISPLAY is to click on the ▧ button in the upper left corner. Use whichever method you find most comfortable.

Your First Unit

Until your Warriors unit is completed, you have little to do. *Press the* ⌷Enter⌷ *key three times.* It is now the fourth turn, and you have just built your first military unit. The Warriors unit is now flashing on and off in the city square. The unit is now ready to receive orders.

There are two things you can do with your first military unit. You could use the unit to defend your city. In most cases, it is unwise to leave a city undefended. This is especially true if you know that an enemy unit is nearby. However, early in the game, the world is sparsely populated, so you can take a chance and send the unit out to explore hidden terrain outside the *City Radius*.

Move the Warriors unit to the west by pressing the ⌷4⌷ *key on the numeric keypad.* Note that one of the black, unexplored terrain squares is revealed when the unit moves. Most units can "see" one square in any direction. Your turn ends automatically when your last unit finishes its movement. Since Warriors can move only one square per turn, your turn is now over.

Your First Civilization Advance

We'll go back to exploring the world in a moment. For now, something more interesting has happened. At the start of this turn, your scientists announce that they have discovered the secret of Bronze Working. Congratulations! You have discovered your first civilization advance. After the initial message of discovery, the CIVILO-PEDIA appears. The CIVILOPEDIA is an online encyclopedia of game facts. The CIVILOPEDIA screen that appears after the discovery of each advance shows the units, improvements, and Wonders you can now build as a result of the advance, as well as new lines of research available. Bronze Working allows you to build Phalanx units and the Colossus Wonder, and allows you to research Currency. Bronze Working also allows you to research Iron Working, but only after you have researched Warrior Code. *Close the CIVILOPEDIA screen by clicking the EXIT button.*

Once again the list of research choices appears, allowing you to choose the next advance you want to discover. Since Bronze Working has provided the ability to build a good defensive unit, you can now move on to a research path that enhances your exploration capability. *Choose Horseback Riding from the menu, and click OK.*

Changing Production

Before you do anything else, its time to look inside the city again. *Open Washington's CITY DISPLAY by clicking the city's icon on the map.* When you look at the PRODUCTION Box, you'll notice that the city has automatically begun to build another Warriors unit. In fact, a city goes on producing unit upon unit until it receives orders to the contrary.

Since the city is still defenseless, you need to build a unit to protect Washington from possible invaders. A Phalanx is a better defensive unit than Warriors, so that is what you should build. *Click the CHANGE button above the PRODUCTION Box.* When you do so, a menu listing the possible production options appears. *Choose Phalanx by clicking on it. Click OK to exit the PRODUCTION menu.* The Phalanx's icon now appears above the PRODUCTION Box to indicate that the city is now building a Phalanx. *Click EXIT to close the CITY DISPLAY.*

FINDING A MINOR TRIBE

Remember your Warriors unit? It's flashing again, indicating that it is once again ready to move. *Move the Warriors one square to the west by pressing the* 4 *key on the numeric keypad.* Note that, as the unit moves, any unexplored (black) terrain within one square of the unit is revealed. *Press* Enter *to end the turn.*

When the unit starts flashing again (indicating that it is the next turn), move it one square to the southwest by pressing the 1 *key on the numeric keypad.* Now here's something interesting! Your exploration has revealed a "hut," one square to the southwest of the Warriors' present position. This hut is home to a minor tribe. Minor tribes are not rival civilizations; rather, they are small villages populated with people who might be inclined to help you.

Save your game by choosing the SAVE GAME option from the GAME menu, or by holding down the Ctrl *key and pressing* S. You are about to make contact with the minor tribe. The results of such contact are random. You could receive a gift of knowledge or gold; the tribe might band together to form a mercenary military unit and join you; or the tribe might decide to honor you by establishing a new city in your empire. Of course it is possible that negative events might occur as well: The village could be empty, or populated by hostile Barbarians. By saving the game prior to contact, you have the option of reloading from the save if you don't like the results of exploring the village.

When the Warriors start flashing again, move your unit onto the hut. As stated earlier, one of a number of random events will occur as a result of contacting a minor tribe. For the purposes of this tutorial, we'll assume that you receive a gift of gold from the minor tribe.

POPULATION INCREASE

Continue your exploration for the next three turns. Move the Warriors back toward Washington, twice to the east, and once north, so you are right next to the city.

On this turn, two things happen simultaneously. First, Washington completes the Phalanx it was building. Second, the population of the city increases to two, as indicated by the number next to the city's icon. *Open Washington's CITY DISPLAY.* Notice that the FOOD STORAGE BOX has only two food in it now. Next turn it will start filling up again, accumulating grain for the next population increase.

Notice that the POPULATION ROSTER now contains two citizens. On the RESOURCE MAP, you can see that the new citizen is already at work generating resources; specifically, the citizen is generating two grain and one shield in one of the Grassland-Shield squares to the north. That's fine for now, so leave the citizen there.

As for production, it's time to change again. This early in the game, one defensive unit is more than adequate for city protection. *Click the CHANGE button, and select Settlers from the PRODUCTION menu.* It's time to start thinking about the next priority: growth. In order to expand your civilization, you need to build other cities; and for that, you need Settlers. *Close the CITY DISPLAY.*

As noted on the PRODUCTION menu, it will take Washington 10 turns to produce a Settlers unit. You can speed this up a bit through the use of your Warriors unit. Once the CITY DISPLAY is closed, the Warriors should be flashing. *Move the Warriors unit into the city, and reopen the CITY DISPLAY.* In the center section of the CITY DISPLAY you should see two icons: a Phalanx unit and a Warriors unit. *Click on the Warriors unit icon. From the menu of options that appears, choose DISBAND and click OK.*

Now, look at the PRODUCTION BOX. Five shields appear as soon as the Warriors unit is disbanded. When a unit is disbanded inside one of your cities, half of its original cost in shields is added to the production currently in progress. *Close the CITY DISPLAY.*

Now, back on the map, the Phalanx is flashing. In order to protect the city, the Phalanx must remain inside Washington. Units provide the best protection when they are fortified. *Fortify the Phalanx by choosing FORTIFY from the ORDERS menu, or by pressing the* F *key.* Fortified units remain in their defensive position until you manually reactivate them. For now, the Phalanx should be left alone to guard Washington.

INTERIM

Because you have so few units and cities early in the game, there are often periods of time that pass without your having to take any action. *After fortifying your Phalanx, press* Enter *two times.* At this point, your wise men discover Horseback Riding. In addition to allowing the research of several new advances, Horseback Riding allows you to build Horsemen, fast-moving military units that are great for exploration.

Choose Code of Laws as the next advance to research. For the purposes of this tutorial, our goal now is to develop Trade. In order to do so, you must research both Code of Laws and Currency. Code of Laws also leads to Monarchy, a more advanced form of government that helps to increase your productivity. *Continue pressing* Enter.

About six turns later, you are notified that Washington has completed the Settlers it has been building. *Choose the ZOOM TO CITY option on the notification menu to open the CITY DISPLAY. Once there, change production so that Washington is building a Horsemen unit.* You'll be using the Horsemen to do some more exploration as soon as it's built.

You'll notice that Washington's population has dropped to one. That is because Settlers units represent citizens that leave the city in order to improve the surrounding terrain or to establish a new city. Also, one of the three shields generated by the city is now being used for support. That is because, under Despotism, any units beyond the size of the city's population require one shield each turn to support them. Right now, you have two units, but only one citizen. At any rate, the FOOD STORAGE BOX shows that the population is about to increase again, so these situations are only temporary. *Close the CITY DISPLAY.*

EXPANDING YOUR EMPIRE

Now it's time to expand your empire. *Move your Settlers directly west until they reach the sea coast, then move them one square to the southwest. Use the BUILD CITY command on the ORDERS menu, or press* B *to build a new city.* Again, you can name the city anything you want, but we'll refer to it by its default name, "New York."

When New York's CITY DISPLAY opens, you'll notice a couple of differences from Washington when it was first built. Although New York is generating just as much food as Washington did, raw materials and trade goods generation are both significantly lower. That's because there are no special resources, like Whales, to take advantage of within New York's CITY RADIUS at this time. This brings us to another oddity: the entire CITY RADIUS of New York is not visible. That's because there is still some unexplored terrain nearby. In order for the city to take advantage of its entire CITY RADIUS, all the terrain therein must be explored. You'll have to take care of that as soon as possible; you never know what useful resources might be lurking in the dark.

Notice that New York is currently producing a Phalanx. Since this city needs to be protected too, a Phalanx is just what you want. *Close the City Display.*

After a couple of turns pass, the Horsemen unit is completed in Washington. *When the Horsemen unit appears, open Washington's City Display, and click the Change button.* Since you have enough units for the time being, and you aren't quite ready to incur the upkeep expense of a Barracks, let's build your first Wonder of the World. *Choose Colossus from the Production menu, and close the City Display.*

Meanwhile, let's go and explore that hidden terrain near New York. *Move your Horsemen west, toward New York.* Notice that Horsemen have twice the movement capability of the other units you've used so far. That's why they are so good for exploring.

As you move toward New York, your wise men make another discovery: Code of Laws. *When you are offered the choice of what to research next, choose Currency.*

On the next two turns, move the Horsemen southwest. Halfway through the second turn's movement, the Horsemen should reach the coast just south of New York, revealing several new terrain squares. One of these is a Whale. (Remember how productive that was back in Washington?) Maybe it is inside New York's City Radius...

Open New York's City Display. The entire City Radius is now visible; and you're in luck! The Whale square is inside the City Radius. *Click the Grassland square northeast of the city to "pick up" your worker, then click the Whale square to put him to work again.* Note that New York's resource generation has now significantly increased. *Close the City Display.*

Move your Horsemen directly east until you reach the Forest on the coast west of Washington. Notice that your unit only gets to move once when moving into a Forest. That's because it takes two movement points to move into Forest squares. Because of their rugged features, many terrain types require more than one movement point in order to move through them. *Now, move your Horsemen east, past Washington, until you get to the River. Then, proceed roughly east-southeast, following the coast.*

After your Horsemen unit is several squares past Washington, the Phalanx in New York is completed. *Fortify the Phalanx, just as you did in Washington, and change the production in New York to Settlers.*

As you continue to explore, your Horsemen might encounter one or two minor tribes. *When you discover Currency, select Trade as your next research project. Save the game again, and enter these villages just as you did the first time you met a minor tribe. Restart from the saved game if you don't like the results.*

Meeting Another Civilization

If you continue along the coastline as instructed, you eventually meet your nearest neighbors, the Sioux. Their capital city, Little Bighorn, is located some distance away, on the opposite coast directly southeast of Washington. As soon as you enter Sioux territory, their leader, Sitting Bull, requests an audience with you. *Accept Sitting Bull's invitation by clicking OK.*

Establishing effective communication with your neighbors is vital to your success. Early in the game, you should take any reasonable actions to ensure that nearby civilizations enjoy your company. Not only does this keep your civilization reasonably safe from attack, it can also lead to profitable exchanges of money and information.

Sitting Bull

You can see your opponent's attitude toward you when you make contact with one another. The attitudes of rival leaders are based on your past behavior when dealing with other civilizations. Since this is your first contact with any civilization, Sitting Bull should have a fairly good attitude when you first meet ("cordial" at the very least).

The most likely result of this encounter is that Sitting Bull will offer to exchange knowledge or sign a peace treaty. *Whatever Sitting Bull offers, accept his proposals.* Notice that each time you agree to his proposals, Sitting Bull's attitude steadily improves. This is important, because you want to make friends at this stage in the game. *If Sitting Bull's attitude is particularly good ("enthusiastic" or "worshipful"),* SUGGEST A PERMANENT STRATEGIC ALLIANCE *with the Sioux.* A permanent alliance is better than a treaty, because it allows both civilizations to move freely through one another's territory. *Whether the alliance is accepted or rejected, end the meeting by choosing* CONSIDER THIS DISCUSSION COMPLETE *and clicking OK. If the alliance was rejected, move your Horsemen unit away from Little Bighorn as soon as possible to avoid violating the peace treaty.* If you establish a reputation of violating peace treaties, your opponents are less likely to sign agreements and treaties with you in the future.

After this encounter, you have gained a friend (for now), and possibly one or two free civilization advances as a result of technology exchange with the Sioux. Now that you have made contact, you can chat with Sitting Bull at any time by selecting the FOREIGN MINISTER option from the ADVISORS menu, and sending an emissary to the Sioux. Sitting Bull can also contact you at any time. You shouldn't pester your opponents too frequently, however, because rival leaders quickly grow weary of interruptions.

If you are contacted by the Sioux at any time during the remainder of this tutorial, agree to their demands. During the tutorial game, you want to keep the Sioux happy so they won't attack you. During a real game, use your own judgment as to how to respond to an opponent's demands.

IMPROVING THE TERRAIN

Continue exploring with your Horsemen to the northeast of Little Bighorn. Avoid entering Little Bighorn's CITY RADIUS, *because this will be viewed as a violation of your peace treaty.*

After a number of turns, your wise men discover Trade. *Select Ceremonial Burial as your next advance. If you already have Ceremonial Burial (as a result of knowledge exchanged with the Sioux), select Monarchy.*

Several turns later, New York finishes building its Settlers. *Open New York's* CITY DISPLAY *and click the* CHANGE *button.* Notice that there are now several more options on the PRODUCTION menu; the discovery of Code of Laws allows you to build a Courthouse, and the discovery of Trade allows you to build Caravan units. *Select Caravan, and close the* CITY DISPLAY.

When the Settlers unit becomes active, move it one square to the northeast of New York (using the 9 *key on the numeric keypad) onto the Grassland-Shield square. For the next few turns, keep exploring with the Horsemen, but skip the*

Settler's turn by pressing the Spacebar. *Continue to do this until New York's population has increased to two. When this happens, open New York's* CITY DISPLAY.

When you look at New York's RESOURCE MAP, you see that the Grassland-Shield square northeast of the city is currently generating one shield and two grain. That's not bad, but you can use your Settlers unit to improve the production in that terrain square. *Close the* CITY DISPLAY. *When the Settlers becomes active, choose* BUILD ROAD *from the* ORDERS *menu, or press the* R *key*. For the next couple of turns, the Settlers unit spends its time building a road. When the Settlers become active again, you see on the map that there is now a road leading out of New York to the northeast. *Now, open New York's* CITY DISPLAY *again and look at the* RESOURCE MAP. Notice that, after the construction of the road, the same Grassland-Shield square is now generating one trade good icon in addition to its former resources. Not only do you get this benefit, but roads also increase movement speed; units only expend one-third of a movement point to move along a road, no matter what type of terrain the road occupies.

Close the CITY DISPLAY. Believe it or not, the terrain can still be improved further. *When the Settlers become active again, choose* BUILD IRRIGATION *from the* ORDERS *menu, or press the* I *key.*

Building irrigation takes a bit longer than building roads. While you're waiting for the Settlers to complete their task, you discover another civilization advance. *If you just discovered Ceremonial Burial, select Monarchy as your next advance. If you just discovered Monarchy, select Writing as your next advance, and choose* NOT JUST YET... *when you are offered the chance to start a revolution to change governments.*

Several turns later, the Settlers complete their irrigation project; the terrain square is now marked to show that it is irrigated. *Open the* CITY DISPLAY *for New York*. Notice that the resource production has not changed as a result of irrigation. Normally, this would not be the case; irrigation usually increases the grain output of Grasslands by one. However, under Despotism, your current system of government, any terrain square producing three or more of any resource type has its production reduced by one. So, instead of three grain, the square still produces only two. This illustrates the drawbacks of Despotism, and explains why your research is now proceeding toward Monarchy, where such penalties do not exist. *Close the* CITY DISPLAY.

While you're waiting for the next advance to be discovered, use the Settlers unit to build a road between New York and Washington. Move one square toward Washington and build a road. Continue until you have connected the two cities. This will facilitate fast travel between your cities. *After the road is built, use the Settlers to start improving the terrain around Washington.*

ESTABLISHING A TRADE ROUTE

Shortly after you start building your inter-city road, the Caravan in New York is completed. You'll be using this Caravan to establish a trade route between New York and Little Bighorn. Trade routes increase the amount of trade goods generated in both their home city and the city with which the trade route is established. Trade routes also give the Caravan's home city a cash and science bonus on the turn when the route is established. Each city can operate up to three separate trade routes.

After you are notified of the Caravan's completion, a menu appears listing the possible trade goods that the Caravan can carry. *Select each commodity in turn, and click the* SUPPLY AND DEMAND *button to review what cities traffic in that item. If Little Bighorn demands one of the items on your list, select that item and click OK. Otherwise, select any item and click OK.* You get both the trade increase and a cash and science bonus no matter what your Caravan carries, but the cash and science bonuses are bigger if you supply goods demanded by the destination city. *Confirm your choice by clicking CONFIRM AND ZOOM. When New York's CITY DISPLAY appears, change the city's production to Marketplace.* The Marketplace improvement increases both tax and luxury output in New York.

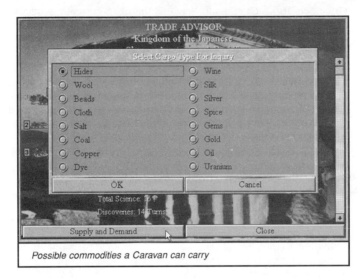

Possible commodities a Caravan can carry

As soon as the Caravan becomes active, start moving toward Washington. It takes a while to get to Little Bighorn, because a Caravan moves at a rate of one square per turn. It's worth the trip, though. The farther away the destination, the higher your cash and science bonus.

En-route to Washington, you discover another civilization advance (Monarchy or, if you're ahead of the game, Writing). *For now, don't declare a revolution. Select your next advance: Writing (if you don't already have it) or Map Making.* We'll come back to Monarchy shortly. You will, in fact, discover another advance before your Caravan reaches Little Bighorn. *This time, choose Map Making (if you don't have it) or Warrior Code.*

Meanwhile, back on the trade route, your Caravan reaches Washington. *Move the Caravan into the city.* When the Caravan enters Washington, you get a list of options. You can establish a trade route with Washington (which you don't want to do). You are also given the option to HELP BUILD WONDER. (Remember, Washington is still in the process of building the Colossus.) If you were to choose this option, the Caravan would be disbanded, and 60 shields would be added to the production of the Colossus. This is an excellent way to accelerate the construction of Wonders of the World which, obviously, take quite a long time to build. For now, however, your goal is to establish a trade route with Little Bighorn. *Choose KEEP MOVING and click OK.*

Continue moving the Caravan until you reach Little Bighorn, then move the unit into the city. Choose ESTABLISH TRADE ROUTE from the menu. You have now established your first trade route! A message appears telling you how much money you receive as an immediate bonus. An equivalent number of beakers is added to your current research project at the same time. *Open New York's CITY DISPLAY.* Note that the trade route is now listed in the bottom center portion of the CITY DISPLAY, and that New York's arrow production has increased as a result of the trade route.

CHANGING GOVERNMENTS

By now, you have established a small, but thriving, civilization. You are doing well, but you could do better. The last thing you'll learn in this tutorial is how to improve your civilization by switching to better forms of government.

Open New York's City Display. Note that the city is currently generating six grain, five arrows, and four shields (assuming that the trade route with Little Bighorn is generating one arrow. Your actual number of arrows might vary slightly.) *Close the City Display.*

Now, it's time to change governments. *Select the Revolution! option from the Kingdom menu and confirm your choice to overthrow the government.* Within a few turns, a menu appears listing the systems of government currently available to you. *Choose Monarchy and click OK.* Your civilization is now ruled through a Monarchy. The Tax Rate window appears, giving you the opportunity to reset your division of trade between taxes, luxuries, and science. *Note that your maximum rate is now capped at 70 percent and close the window.* Now, you'll make discoveries more quickly.

Let's take a look at the effects of the government change. *Open New York's City Display and look at the production changes.* The city's grain production has increased from six to eight. Note that the Grassland-Shield square you irrigated earlier is now generating three grain instead of two. The other extra grain is coming from the city square itself (it is automatically irrigated when the city is built). Trade has also increased as a result of the change in government. The Whale square is now generating one additional arrow. This has the effect of increasing the number of beakers from three to four. Shield generation has remained the same, because none of the terrain currently in use around New York is capable of producing more than two shields under the present circumstances. If you look at the City Display for Washington, you'll notice similar increases in that city as well.

CONCLUSION

So ends the tutorial. You should now be familiar with many of the basic concepts of *Civilization II*. Feel free to continue playing the tutorial game and see how you do, or go back and start a new game on a randomly generated world. Remember, you have only scratched the surface when it comes to learning the game. Use the rest of this manual and the online Civilopedia in the game to help you with new concepts as you encounter them.

Have fun, and good luck! May your reign be long and fruitful.

SETTING UP A GAME

Beginning a game of **Civilization II** means choosing the circumstances in which you want to play. Your options include specifying the number and location (physical starting point) of your opponents and manipulating the environmental and physical parameters of the world you'll explore.

YOUR FIRST DECISION

To launch the game, click on the **Civilization II** icon. After the game has initialized itself, the opening animation begins (if you chose to install it). You can wait for it to end or press any key to cut it short. Setting up a game means making easy decisions on a series of options screens. At the first of these, you decide whether to start a new game or continue a previous one, among other things. The full list of options is described below. Once you've chosen an option, you'll need to click OK to continue.

Start a New Game: Begin an entirely new game. Choosing this option means going through the basic pre-game options screens, as we explain below.

Start on Premade World: Play on a custom map created with the MAP EDITOR utility or a map extracted from a saved game. A dialog box lists all of the saved maps and games available in the current directory. Choose the map you wish to load. You can switch directories to find maps you've saved in other locations.

Customize World: Build a world, right down to the picky details of land form, climate, and geologic age. When you choose this option, you see all of the setup screens, not just the important ones.

Begin Scenario: Choose this option to load a scenario. A dialog box lists all of the scenarios available in the current directory. You can switch directories to find scenarios in other locations. When you begin, you choose which civilization you want to rule.

Load a Game: Load and continue a previously saved game. A dialog box lists all of the saved games available in this directory. Choose the game you wish to load. You can switch directories to find games you've saved in other locations.

Multiplayer Game: Begin a new game against any combination of up to 6 human and AI rulers. The pre-game options are a bit different for this type of game; the differences are explained in **Multiplayer Games**.

View Hall of Fame: See the standings of previous conquerors and despots.

View Credits: Find out who's responsible for creating the game.

Use the OK button to confirm your choice, or CANCEL to quit *Civilization II*.

CUSTOMIZING GAME SETUPS

These option screens progress from whole-world effects down to the name of your tribal leader. If at any point you realize that you'd like to reset an earlier parameter (you suddenly wonder what a jungle planet would be like, but you're past that screen), you can click the CANCEL button located on each screen to "turn back the page" to a previous screen, then make another choice. When you are happy with the choices you have selected, click the OK button to continue on to the next screen. If you want to be surprised, you can click the RANDOM button to let the game select a parameter for you.

SELECT SIZE OF WORLD

By choosing the size of the map, you can determine how much territory there is, and to a large degree, how long the game takes to play.

Small: This size map leads to short, intensely contested games. Tribes find each other quickly.

Normal: This is the standard size map.

Large: This sprawling map takes longer to explore and exploit. Consequently, games go on longer.

Custom: Choose this option to specify the height and width of your map. The dialog box explains the limits of your choices.

CUSTOMIZE: LANDMASS

This parameter sets the percentage of terrain squares that are land.

Small: Choosing this option gives your world a small number of land squares and a larger number of ocean squares.

Normal: This option yields about equal numbers of land and ocean squares.

Large: This option produces a large number of land squares and a small number of ocean squares.

CUSTOMIZE: LAND FORM

This parameter determines the way in which your world's land is shaped into land masses.

Archipelago: This option produces relatively large numbers of relatively small continents.

Varied: Choosing this option gives your world an average number of average sized continents.

Continents: This option yields one or two large land masses.

CUSTOMIZE: CLIMATE

This parameter sets the relative frequency with which particular terrain types occur.

Arid: Choosing this option gives your world a larger number of "dry" terrain squares, such as Plains and Desert.

Normal: This option yields about equal numbers of "wet" and "dry" terrain squares.

Wet: This option produces a larger number of "wet" terrain squares, such as Grassland, Forest, and Swamp. It also increases the number and length of rivers generated.

CUSTOMIZE: TEMPERATURE

This parameter determines the relative frequency with which particular terrain types occur.

Cool: This option produces larger numbers of polar terrain squares, like Tundra and Glacier.

Temperate: Choosing this option gives your world an average number of each terrain type.

Warm: This option yields a larger number of tropical terrain, like Desert, Plains, and Jungle.

CUSTOMIZE: AGE

This parameter determines whether like terrain squares clump together or are widely scattered.

3 Billion Years: This option yields a young world, one in which terrain squares seem to occur in clusters.

4 Billion Years: This option yields a middle-aged world, one in which glaciation and plate tectonics have been acting to diversify terrain.

5 Billion Years: This option produces an old world, one in which the forces of nature and chaos have almost wholly randomized the terrain features.

DIFFICULTY LEVELS

Choose the level of difficulty at which you wish to play. Although *Civilization II* is not necessarily more difficult as a whole than its predecessor, there are new features and adjustments that will not be familiar to players of previous versions. (New players don't need to worry, as they have no bad habits to break.) If you are used to playing *Civilization* at a particular level, we recommend that you start your first *Civilization II* game at one level easier difficulty.

A number of factors are adjusted at each difficulty level, including the general level of discontent among your citizens, the average number of barbarian units encountered in a surprise attack, the pace of technological advancement, and the total number of turns in the game.

Chieftain: This easiest level is recommended for first-time players. The program provides advice when a player must make decisions.

Warlord: Civilization advances take longer to acquire at this level of play. Warlord level best suits the occasional player who doesn't want too difficult a test.

Prince: At this difficulty level, advances come much more slowly. You need some experience and skill to win.

King: Experienced and skilled players often play at this level, where the slow pace of advancement and the unstable attitude of citizens presents a significant challenge.

Emperor: This level is for those who feel the need to be humbled. Your opponents will no longer pull their punches; if you want to win, you'll have to earn it.

Deity: The ultimate *Civilization* challenge, for those who think they've learned to beat the game. You'll have to give a virtuoso performance to survive at this level. And yes, some of us can actually win (sometimes). Good luck!

LEVEL OF COMPETITION

Choose to have between three and seven civilizations running loose in the world. More opponents do not necessarily mean more danger, although more opponents means earlier contact and an increased risk of war. Of course, contact with other civilizations also offers opportunities for trade, alliances, and the rewards of the spoils of war when you emerge victorious. The fewer your opponents, the more time you have to peaceably expand and develop before encountering rivals. Barbarians are a factor in either situation, and do not count as a rival civilization.

Note that in multiplayer games, you also have the option of having only two civilizations— a one-on-one game versus another person.

Your civilization counts as one of the cultures, so if you choose a world with three civilizations, you only face two rivals. Seven civilizations (you and six others) is the maximum number for any *Civilization II* game.

LEVEL OF BARBARIAN ACTIVITY

A new feature in *Civilization II* is your ability to set the aggressiveness of barbarian units in the game.

Villages Only: Players who really hate barbarians can choose to play in this "ideal world." There is a significant scoring penalty, however, so you'll have to make the most of it.

Roving Bands: Barbarian bands and pirates occasionally appear, but half as frequently and in smaller numbers than at higher levels. There is a slight scoring penalty at this level.

Restless Tribes: Barbarians, in moderate to significant numbers, appear at intervals. This represents the "standard" level of barbarian activity found in the original *Civilization*. Your score is unaffected at this level.

Raging Hordes: You asked for it! The world is full of barbarians, and they appear in large numbers. If you survive, you receive a scoring bonus.

SELECT GAME RULES

The default option here is USE STANDARD RULES. If you want to tweak the parameters of the game, choose the CUSTOMIZE RULES option to change the whole flavor of the challenge. The SELECT CUSTOM FEATURES screen offers several different possibilities.

'Mahatma' Gandhi

Simplified Combat: When this box is not checked, units have hit points and firepower statistics. When it is checked, combat is absolute—the unit that wins is completely whole, and the unit that loses is demolished.

Flat World: When this box is checked, the map edges are the boundaries of the world, and no ships can cross from the east margin of the map to the west margin (or from west to east, either).

Select Computer Opponents: The location of your first unit and the proximity of your rivals is usually determined randomly. However, you can choose to specify the identities of your opponents. For each rival position, a dialog box gives you three tribes from which to choose and a RANDOM button if you have no strong preference. You can select the starting locations of some or all of your opponents if you create a custom map of the world. See CREATING YOUR OWN WORLDS for the details.

Accelerated Startup: When this box is checked, you can choose from a starting date one or two millennia into the game. The computer settles your first city (or two) for you, builds initial units, and completes initial research into advances, all in the blink of an eye.

Bloodlust (no spaceships allowed): When this box is checked, no player can build spaceship parts, and the only way to see the winner's animation is to conquer the world.

Don't Restart Eliminated Players: Normally, when a civilization is wiped out, the computer looks to see if conditions are right to settle another civilization carrying shields the color of the eliminated culture. When this button is checked, no colors are resurrected, and each opponent eliminated is one less power in the world.

SELECT YOUR GENDER

You can choose to play a male or a female leader. Each civilization has one default leader of each gender, and of course, you can customize your leader's name.

Select Your Tribe

Select the name of your tribe from the options available, or click on the Custom button. The Customize Your Tribe dialog box includes spaces for you to enter the name of your Leader, your Tribe, and an Adjective, the adjectival form of your tribe's name (for messages and announcements). The default options give examples of each entry.

Use the Titles button to specify the titles by which you prefer to be addressed for each form of government in the game.

When you're satisfied with your choices in each screen, click the OK button.

Select Your City Style

Here you can choose the style in which your citizens build. The default style is chosen to reflect your tribe's national origins as closely as possible.

Bronze Age Monolith: In the style of the Mayan and Sumerian empires, your city icons build from simple stone boxes to complex clusters of megalithic proportions.

Classical Forum: Following the Greek and Roman styles, your city icons progress from neat marble structures to gleaming colonnaded vistas.

Far East Pavilion: In the Oriental tradition, your city icons build from red-tiled gables to elaborately layered pagodas.

Medieval Castle: Following European models, your city icons grow from narrow thatched cottages to tightly packed labyrinths of humanity.

READY, SET, GO

After you are satisfied with your settings, click OK to start the clock ticking on your civilization. A screen pops up welcoming you to your position as leader and detailing the accomplishments of your culture thus far. When you have finished reading the screen, press any key or click the OK button on the screen to begin the game.

CHANGES FROM CIVILIZATION TO CIVILIZATION II

If you're already familiar with **Civilization** in one of its previous incarnations—the Macintosh version, the DOS version, the Windows version, or the multiplayer version (**CivNet**)—there are a lot of features in **Civilization II** that are familiar. However, that familiarity can lead you into some pitfalls, because the game has evolved and grown, so that this new version is substantially different. Take a few moments to peruse this section for a summary of the changes you can expect.

CIVILIZATION'S NEW LOOK

As **Civilization** has matured as a game, the quality of graphics has also matured. **Civilization II** has high resolution graphics now, scaleable fonts and windows, and whole new units and improvements. Settlers units are no longer represented by those old, familiar covered wagon icons. But more is new than simply different pictures.

THE MAP

Civilization II uses an isometric grid instead of the old, square grid. This means each square (what we call a *terrain square*, or just *square*) is now a diamond shape, as if you are viewing it from an angle. Movement still proceeds along the compass points as it always did. Some players may have difficulty getting used to this new view, finding it hard to tell where a city's radius begins and ends, for instance. If you have this problem, we recommend you select SHOW MAP GRID from the VIEW menu or press [Ctrl] [G]. This activates a grid overlay that outlines each map square.

THE UNITS

Every unit icon in the game now carries a shield. The color of the shield body indicates the civilization to which that unit belongs. As in *Civilization*, barbarian units are always red. The colored strength bar at the top of the shield indicates the overall health of the unit. We'll go into detail in **New Combat Concepts**, but for now you should know that green indicates a healthy unit, yellow means the unit is somewhat damaged, and red shows a critically injured unit.

THE CITIES

You can choose what style of architecture your civilization prefers to build when you set up a game. As your cities increase in size, the icons that represent them on the map also change, reflecting the increasing urbanization and population of the site. Whenever you capture a city, its icons change to reflect your preferred style of architecture. Once your civilization reaches the industrial era, the architecture of your cities begins to reflect your new level of technology.

THE DISPLAYS

Many screens and displays have been redesigned to better present new information and to take advantage of the more sophisticated graphics now available. Most of the information should be self-explanatory; all the major game windows are illustrated in **Reference: Screen by Screen**.

NEW COMBAT CONCEPTS

Players of *Civilization* were occasionally disconcerted when a "lucky" veteran Phalanx unit, fortified in an enemy city, destroyed an attacking Battleship unit. Mathematically it was possible, but the image conjured up just didn't sit right. How could ancient spearmen take out a modern steel warship? To smooth out such freakish reaches of probability, *Civilization II* has added two new statistics for each unit: *hit points* and *firepower*.

HIT POINTS & FIREPOWER

Hit points are graphically indicated by the colored *strength bar* across the top of each unit's shield. Both the length of the strength bar and the color are significant. As a unit loses hit points in an attack, its strength bar gets shorter. In addition, when the unit is reduced to approximately two-thirds of its full strength, the strength bar changes from green to yellow. When a unit's hit points are reduced to around one-third of its full strength, the bar changes from yellow to red.

Hit points represent a unit's relative durability in combat situations. Ancient and unarmed units generally have 10 hit points. Units with firearms have 20, and units with steel armor have 30. Battleships, with their extraordinarily thick armor, are unique in having 40 hit points. A unit with 10 hit points can have ten points of damage done to it before being destroyed. This does not necessarily mean that ten units each hit it one time. Units also have a new statistic, firepower, which indicates the number of points of damage that unit does each time it successfully scores a hit.

These new statistics widen the gap between primitive technologies and modern weaponry. A Musketeers unit with a strength of three attacking Pikemen of strength two has an "effective strength" of far greater than three, simply because its increased hit points (20, representing its firearms) allow it to sustain twice as much damage as the Pikemen. A veteran Phalanx unit might still damage a Battleship, but the chance of utterly demolishing it is negligible.

RESTORATION

The new stats also bring with them the need for *restoration*. When combat was all-or-nothing, defeated units were always destroyed, and victorious units emerged unscathed. Now, victory is not always without cost. A damaged unit might suffer curtailed movement points and is vulnerable to counterattacks by further enemy units. So how do you regain full strength?

A damaged unit can partially restore itself by skipping its entire turn (you press the Spacebar). Units regenerate faster when they remain in cities for a full turn. If the city they occupy has certain improvements, they can heal even more rapidly. Along with its former capacity for turning out veteran units, a Barracks can repair ground units. The new Port Facility city improvement can repair naval units, and the new Airport city improvement can repair air units—in all three cases, the damaged unit is restored to full strength in a single turn.

NEW AND CHANGED UNITS

People have been suggesting new units to include in **Civilization** since the initial release of the game. For **Civilization II**, we wanted a more continuous progression of development in the three types of ground troops: the basic, all-purpose Infantry, the swift-moving Cavalry, and the heavy-weapon Artillery. In addition, there are more gradations in ships and in air units. Modern units often fulfill specialized roles, and more units have special abilities and unique capabilities. Finally, each non-combat unit of old gains an advanced version, so that Settlers are followed by Engineers, Diplomats by Spies, and Caravans by Freight. Engineers work and move twice as quickly as Settlers, and can *transform* terrain using modern technology. Spies can perform normal diplomatic missions more effectively than Diplomats, and have several new missions available, including poisoning water supplies and even planting nuclear devices! Freight units move more quickly than Caravans, and provide greater economic bonuses for trading.

The existence of all of these new units gave rise to the opportunity to rebalance some old ones. Chariots have been toned down to an ADM of 3/1/2, for instance, while Legions have been beefed up to an ADM of 4/2/1. You'll find the full details in the CIVILOPEDIA entries for each unit.

SPECIAL COMBAT CASES

To better reflect their real-world abilities and handicaps, many units have unique combat rules and abilities. For instance, when a ship bombards a ground unit on shore, the firepower of both units is reduced to one. This simulates the low accuracy of shore bombardment. Similarly, ships defending in port have their firepower reduced to one, because of the limitations of maneuverability. Air units attacking ships in port have their firepower doubled, to represent the vulnerability of their targets. The **Combat** section of **Units** gives the full details for each exceptional case.

NEW PRODUCTION CONCEPTS

We've tweaked the economics of the game a little to help fill in some gaps and to make playing more of a challenge for experienced loophole dodgers.

WASTE

In previous versions of **Civilization**, trade is modified by corruption. When an empire sprawls over a great area, and its form of government is low on the scale of sophistication, corruption lowers the total trade goods intake in cities on the fringes and frontiers. The more sophisticated the government and the smaller the sprawl, the less effect corruption has.

Civilization II extends this concept of modification to include another resource. Now shield production is also affected by the level of government and the sprawl of empire. In fringe locations, some proportion of the shields that workers generate each turn is lost as *waste*.

PENALTIES FOR SWITCHING PRODUCTION

A city can produce three different types of things: units, improvements, and Wonders. To close several loopholes that players had been exploiting, **Civilization II** introduces a significant penalty for switching production between different types (changing a city's production from City Walls to Knights, for instance, or from City Walls to a Wonder of the World). Switching from one type of production to another in mid-stream (or mid-build) costs a 50 percent reduction in the number of shields already accumulated. Switching production within a type—from one unit to a different unit, for instance—incurs no penalty.

NEW AND CHANGED IMPROVEMENTS

Along with new units, **Civilization II** also includes new city improvements. These improvements address needs that have arisen because of other changes in the game. For instance, the new concept of restoration (mentioned under **New Combat Concepts**) led to the development of facilities where restoration could take place in one turn. Port Facilities repair naval units, Airports repair air units, and Barracks restore ground units (as well as continuing their "old" function of producing veteran units). The new Superhighways improvement grants a 50 percent increase in trade to citizens working land within a CITY RADIUS, and the new Supermarket improvement allows workers on irrigated land to produce 50 percent more food. To compensate, laying railroad track in a square now only increases workers' shield production in the underlying terrain, instead of increasing all resources. All of these details are listed in full in the CIVILOPEDIA entries for each improvement.

In addition, some classic city improvements have been adjusted to fit the new demands of play. Colosseums (which in **Civilization** made three citizens content) now make four citizens content once your tribe discovers the Electronics advance. This represents the effects of television on the masses. On the other hand, a Cathedral is less effective as an improvement (making only three citizens content instead of four). Further, other discoveries can improve or undermine a Cathedral's influence. Achieving the advance of Theology increases the effectiveness by one citizen; however, the discovery of Communism reduces it by one citizen. This represents the diminished influence of organized religion in the modern world. Courthouses, under a Democracy, now make one content person happy in addition to their classic effect.

Under other forms of government, Courthouses now also make a city more difficult for opponents to bribe. You cannot build a Manufacturing Plant in a city that does not yet have a Factory. Further, plants in cities where the Factory has been sold or lost increase output 50 percent (not 100 percent) until the Factory is rebuilt.

The same loss of bonus applies to the Bank & Marketplace combination and to the University & Library pairing. City Walls are cheaper and no longer cost maintenance. Aqueducts are now required for cities to increase beyond size eight; they used to be required to get above size 10. The full details are listed in the CIVILOPEDIA entries for each improvement, so be sure to check them out.

NEW TERRAIN CONCEPTS

Redrawing the squares as isometric diamonds doesn't affect the gameplay in *Civilization II*. However, there were some elements of terrain that we decided could be jazzed up, including new special resources and upgrades for city squares.

RIVERS

In *Civilization*, rivers were considered their own terrain type. Now, they are features that can be found running through almost any terrain, making their appearance more true-to-life. To simulate the beneficial effect rivers had on trade, especially in ancient times, any ground unit can follow a riverbed (either upstream or down) for a cost of only one-third of a movement point per square. The presence of a river in an adjacent terrain square still indicates access to water for irrigation, if that adjoining terrain can be irrigated. Rivers still convey a defense bonus of 50 percent, and squares through which they run can still be worked for trade goods in addition to the yield of the basic terrain.

NEW SPECIAL TERRAIN

To spice up your world, special terrain resources have been re-allocated in *Civilization II*. Now each terrain type (except Grassland) has two associated special resources, each with its own developmental bonuses. Each special resource has an icon that rests on top of the basic terrain square. To allow for these new resources, some of the special icons with which you are familiar have been renamed and adjusted—for instance, the special resource for Swamp used to be Oil. This resource yielded an extra four shields, along with the one food that basic swamps could generate. Now the Peat resource allows workers to produce four extra shields. In addition, Swamps might also be enhanced by Spice, which allows citizens working them to produce four extra trade arrows, but does not yield any shields. The **Special Terrain Chart** on the **Poster** summarizes all special terrain resource icons, names, and statistics.

UPGRADING CITY SQUARES

It makes sense that city squares (the terrain square under the city itself) should improve as civilizations become more advanced. In *Civilization II*, city squares are automatically improved from roads to railroad once your tribe discovers the Railroad advance. Now units can slide through them without losing one-third of a movement point. Once you have discovered Refrigeration, each city square in your empire is automatically improved to farmland.

NEW MOVEMENT CONCEPTS

To simulate the effect of river transport, which was particularly important to early civilizations, ground units moving along rivers only use one-third of a movement point for each square (i.e., as if they were moving along a road). Note that the unit must follow the main river channel to receive this benefit: simply hopping from one bend to another doesn't count.

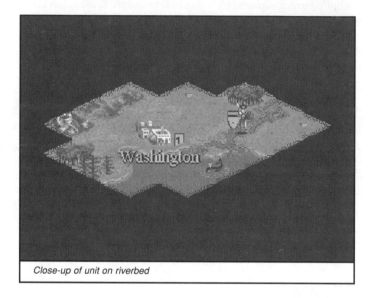

Close-up of unit on riverbed

In addition, some new units (like Alpine Troops, Explorers, and Partisans) have the ability and equipment to move quickly through even the most difficult terrain. In game terms, they *treat all terrain as roads*. This means that it never costs them more than one-third of a movement point to enter any square—regardless of the terrain type or the actual existence of roads. Units with the ability to treat all terrain as roads can still use railroads for free movement, just as any other unit.

Sailing experience accumulates with new advances. In the early days, your Triremes have a 50 percent chance of being lost at sea each time they end their turn in a square that is not touching the shoreline. However, once your civilization discovers Seafaring, your crews' experience of the coastal waters is vaster, and they are less likely to panic, only foundering 25 percent of the time; the chance of a Trireme being lost at sea is correspondingly reduced. Once you discover Navigation, the crews' knowledge and confidence is greater still, and their likelihood of unexpected foundering is reduced to one in eight. (If you possess the Lighthouse Wonder, the chance of foundering is eliminated altogether—but we'll tell you more about that in **New & Improved Wonders** later on).

Finally, teamwork counts in *Civilization II*. Two Settlers (or Engineers) improving a square (irrigating, building railroads, or whatever) will work as a team and finish the job twice as fast. You can add even more Settlers or Engineers on a tough task, like draining and irrigating a Swamp. The full details are explained under **Settlers & Engineers**.

There are three new orders available to Settlers and Engineer units once you've discovered the appropriate advances. The new Engineer unit (which becomes available with discovery of Explosives and works twice as quickly as a regular Settlers unit) can TRANSFORM terrain into a vastly different type. Which terrain results from transformation is noted in the **Terrain Chart**.

Once you have discovered Radio, Settlers or Engineer units can BUILD AIRBASE in any square in which they could ordinarily build a fortress. An airbase allows friendly planes to land and refuel.

Once you've discovered Refrigeration, Settlers or Engineer units can IMPROVE FARMLAND to prepare high-yield market gardens.

GOVERNMENT IMPROVEMENTS

There have been significant changes in the way different government types function. In addition, a new type of government, Fundamentalism, has been added to round out your choices. A quick rundown of the most important adjustments follows; for complete details, see **Governments**.

Monarchy has been vastly improved in that the first three units from each city cost no shield support. We now strongly suggest switching to Monarchy as soon as it becomes available.

Similarly, *Communism* does not have to support the first three units from each city, and units are twice as effective at imposing martial law (so up to six unhappy citizens can be suppressed). No corruption occurs under Communism, and all Spy units produced by Communist governments are considered veterans.

Republic has been improved in that the first unit away from a city does not cause unrest and the Senate only concludes unwanted peace treaties 50 percent of the time.

And perhaps most importantly, units in *Democracies* and *Republics* do not cause unrest *if they are in a fortress square within three squares of a friendly city*. This is intended to allow realistic defensive frontiers.

You can no longer avoid Senate interference in your foreign policy by simply refusing to meet foreign emissaries. However, in the Senate of a *Republic* the "Doves" are in power about 50 percent of the time (in a *Democracy* the Doves are always a force to be reckoned with).

When you undertake a Revolution to change your government, you experience the usual period of Anarchy. However, once the menu appears allowing you to select a new form of government, you may freely and instantly change your government for the rest of that turn (by selecting REVOLUTION from the KINGDOM menu). This allows you to compare the effects of various government types.

Note that science, tax, and luxury rates are now restricted by your government type. Under *Despotism*, for instance, no single rate can be set higher than 60 percent. Under

Monarchy the maximum rate rises to 70 percent. The other government forms all allow up to 80 percent, except for *Democracy*, which allows complete control with rate caps only at the 100 percent mark.

NEW CONCEPTS IN DIPLOMACY

Diplomacy has expanded significantly in **Civilization II**. The AI (Artificial Intelligence) has been improved so that rival civilizations remember your actions and can learn from their past dealings with you, adding a topic to your FOREIGN MINISTER's report known as *reputation*. To complement this concept, there are finer gradations of hostilities between the extremes of peace and war, and a variety of new ways to progress between them. No longer are you considered at war with a rival merely because you have no treaty with him or her.

Once you make contact with a rival, you can speak to him or her at any time by calling up the FOREIGN MINISTER's report and clicking the SEND EMISSARY button. You are no longer limited by having to set up an embassy with a rival civilization first. However, constantly chatting up opponents makes them weary, and you can exhaust their patience with too many requests.

REPUTATION

Rumors of your past transgressions will proceed you! Breaking a treaty or an alliance carries a slight but permanent diplomatic penalty in all future negotiations with all other players. The more treaties you break, the less other players trust you. If you break treaties systematically, the other players learn from their mistakes and become as ruthless as you. If you have an excuse for breaking a treaty (the rival in question uses a Diplomat to steal technology from you, for instance, or another opponent offers you money to break an alliance or treaty), the diplomatic penalty is eliminated or reduced.

Since keeping your word is more important than behaving peaceably, refusing to sign a peace treaty or opting for a temporary cease fire instead are honorable alternatives. It is possible to maintain a spotless reputation while waging a war of conquest.

DIPLOMATIC STATES

New to **Civilization II** are the states of *cease fire, neutrality,* and *alliance*; they fill out the classic **Civilization** states of *peace* and *war*. If you don't want to be friends for all time, but you'd like time to regroup, or to pull a city back from the brink of disaster, you now have the option to propose a temporary cease fire. In game terms, cease fires expire after approximately 16 turns, and they are automatically extended when tribute is paid by either side. You are informed when a cease fire has expired.

Neutrality is the state your civilization adopts by default. Neutrality exists when you have not yet encountered a culture and when you decline to enter into a cease fire or permanent peace agreement.

If you'd like an even closer relationship than simple peace, you have the option to propose a permanent alliance. In game terms, alliances allow you to ignore your ally civilization's zones of control. This means your units can move freely through his territory and his can move through yours. Your ally's nearby units will not disrupt production in your cities, and vice versa.

Finally, peace treaties now recognize territorial borders. Moving into the city radius of an enemy city might be taken as a violation of your accord and used as an excuse to declare war. Rivals will warn you when you are violating their territory.

COUNTERESPIONAGE

In addition to their foreign service tasks, envoys can engage in counterespionage when they stay home. Diplomats and Spies stationed in friendly cities have a chance to thwart "steal technology" attempts by enemy Diplomats and Spies.

NEW & IMPROVED WONDERS

Along with adding and rebalancing units, improvements and advances, we couldn't resist the chance to dress up the Wonders of the World. In fact, there are seven new Wonders sprinkled in the Renaissance and Industrial ages. More important to veteran *Civilization* players, several of the old Wonders have changed considerably in effect, and many have had expiration dates tweaked. Some Wonders no longer expire at all. A quick summary follows.

Elizabeth I

The *Pyramids* now act as a granary in every one of your cities. In addition to the old plus-one movement effect, the *Lighthouse* now allows Triremes to move across open ocean without fear of swamping, and all new ships start with veteran status. The *Great Wall* doubles your units' combat strength against barbarians in addition to forcing your opponents to offer peace *and* acting as a City Wall in every one of your cities.

Magellan's Expedition now confers a plus-two movement bonus on all your ships. *Michaelangelo's Chapel* now counts as a Cathedral in every one of your cities, instead of its previous ability of increasing the effect of existing Cathedrals. The *United Nations*, in addition to its classic effect, also counts as an embassy with every player and gives Democracies a 50 percent chance to override the Senate's interference in foreign policy negotiations. Finally, the *SETI Program* now counts as a Research Lab in every one of your cities, which reduces its science benefit from the previous 100 percent increase to a more balanced 50 percent.

The effect of the *Colossus* expires once any tribe discovers Flight. The *Great Library* expires once any tribe discovers Electricity. The *Great Wall* expires once any tribe discovers Metallurgy. And finally, *J.S. Bach's Cathedral* now requires the advance of Theology to build.

For the full scoop on these and all the other Wonders, see WONDERS OF THE WORLD in the CIVILOPEDIA.

MISCELLANEOUS CHANGES

Some civilization advance prerequisites have changed slightly, mostly to eliminate redundancies. Physics, for example, used to require Navigation and Mathematics; however, Navigation already presumes that your culture discovered Mathematics (via Astronomy). Physics now requires Navigation and Literacy. Since some people find the **Advance Chart** (found on the **Poster**) difficult enough to follow without memorizing the additional changes, we've provided help in a variety of places. When deciding which next civilization advance to research, you can use the GOAL button to help you find your way through the chart. In addition, each CIVILOPEDIA entry includes the relevant segment of the "advance tree."

Many civilization advances which used to be dead ends (e.g., Chivalry, Feudalism, Conscription, Pottery) now lead to bigger and better things. Chivalry, Feudalism, and Conscription, for instance, are all directly on the prerequisite chain for Mobile Warfare (Armor unit).

Computer players are no longer "given" Wonders of the World. They must build them. You will be told whenever a computer player has begun construction of a Wonder.

When you disband a unit in a city square, it contributes half of its production cost in shields to the city's current project. This represents your ability to "retrain" old troops with new weapons, or to make an all-out effort to complete a city improvement or Wonder. Caravans and Freight units retain their special ability to add their *full* production value to Wonders of the World when they enter a city which is producing one.

ULTIMATE CHANGES

If you're already familiar with *Civilization II*, there are a few things you should know. In the time between the original release way back when and today, we've upgraded the game just a little. Take a few moments to browse this section; it's a summary of the changes.

Engineers no longer ignore zones of control. This change was put in one of the earliest updates (patches) we released. It helps prevent computer-controlled engineers from slipping into your territory and building cities within your borders.

You can now automate Settlers. Automated Settlers and Engineers behave exactly as if a friendly AI were controlling them, except that they will not build cities. They will improve the terrain around existing ones.

There are a few new menu options, and the ones that were changed after the original manual was printed have been properly documented. Read **The Menu Bar** in **Reference: Screen by Screen** to find out about them all.

A few units have been modified. The attack strength of the Cruise missile is now 18, not 20. The defense strength of Fighters, Stealth Fighters, and Stealth Bombers have been increased slightly.

There is a way to view all the Wonder movies without actually building the wonders. The Wonder movie cheat is described in **Graphic Options** (under the **Game** menu).

The Colossus now affects sea squares as well as land squares.

The scenario-building tools have been significantly enhanced. The details are spread around in **Reference: Screen by Screen** and the new **Playing Scenarios** section.

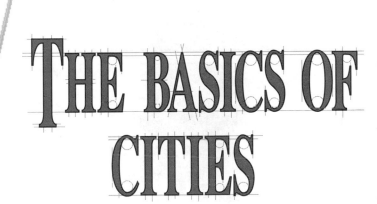

THE BASICS OF CITIES

When you start a game of **Civilization II**, your Settlers
unit stands on a terrain square surrounded by the darkness
of the unknown. Though you can choose to let this single group
of Settlers (if you're really special, you could possibly have two Settlers
units) wander the world alone, that's not the point of the game. As soon as you've
found a decent site, you want your Settlers to build a permanent settlement—a city.
You must build at least one city, because only cities can produce new units, allowing your civilization to grow and develop. You'll probably build a dozen or more cities
over the course of the game.

Cities are the residences of your population, the sources of tax dollars, and the
homes of your scientists. Each city organizes the development of the area surrounding it, harvesting the nearby agricultural land, natural resources, and potential trade goods, then converting these resources into food, industrial production,
technology, and cash.

One way to measure the success of your civilization is by the number and size of the
cities you have built or captured. Larger cities collect more taxes, conduct more technological research, and produce new items faster. Civilizations with small numbers of
cities and small city sizes risk being overrun by larger and more powerful neighbors.

CITY CONCEPTS

To comprehend the CITY DISPLAY in *Civilization II*, you must understand the symbolism the game uses to represent the concepts relevant to population growth and urban dynamics. Take a look at the CITY DISPLAY while you're reading—it'll make things a lot clearer.

Cities arose when stationary populations banded together to produce not only enough food to feed themselves day to day, but sufficient leftovers to store for later use. Once food storage developed, not every citizen had to produce food all day, and some people specialized in producing other goods. Eventually, cities accumulated enough surplus food and goods that they could trade their excess with nearby populations.

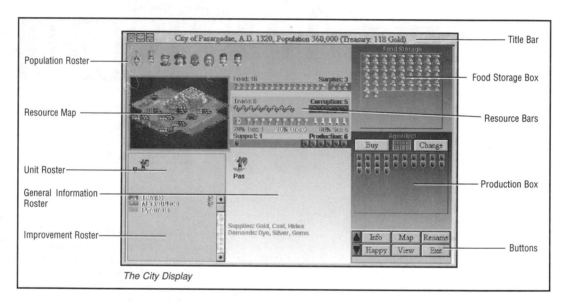

The City Display

To represent the accumulated population in a game city, *Civilization II* maintains a POPULATION ROSTER. Each citizen *icon*—a small symbol—stands for a segment of that city's population (the exact number of people he or she represents changes as the city grows). The roster displays both citizens who work the land around the city and citizens whose specializations produce other effects. The POPULATION ROSTER tells you more than just how large your city has grown (you'll find lots more details under **Population Roster** in **Reference: Screen by Screen**), but there are other points of interest in this display, so we're moving on.

Other icons in the CITY DISPLAY represent a city's production of food, raw materials, and trade goods. We're going to call these materials the *resources* of the city. Production is linked to terrain in the game, just as it is in the real world (for example, deserts are not the best food-producing areas in either case). A full discussion of the types of terrain available in *Civilization II* and their resources is outside the scope of this chapter (you'll find it under **Terrain & Movement**). For now, you need to know that citizens working on terrain squares (or "map squares") can produce three different types of icons: *grain*, which represents food; *shields*, which represents raw materials the city can use to produce goods; and *arrows*, which represent trade goods. On some terrain squares, workers produce a larger proportion of one than of the others. On some squares, workers can't produce any of one type (a citizen working on Tundra produces no shields, for instance).

The resource icons—grain, shields, and arrows—that appear on the map are recapitulated in other displays, where they reveal further details of your city's economy and growth. We'll explain all the details in the reference sections that describe those displays.

GAINING NEW CITIES

You can acquire new cities in three ways. Most frequently, you build them with Settlers units. If you are aggressive, you can conquer the cities of your neighbors. Occasionally, you can gain a city when a minor tribe discovered by your units elects to join your civilization.

FOUNDING NEW CITIES

The most common way to gain new cities is to send out Settlers to tame the wilderness. In fact, you start the game with a Settlers unit whose primary task is to found your first city. The terrain under and around your city is important, so if you want to select the best possible place for your metropolis, skip down to **Choosing Your Location**. If you want to jump right in, choose a square with rivers, plains and/or grasslands near it.

When your active Settlers unit stands on the square where you wish to build a new city, choose the option BUILD NEW CITY from the ORDERS menu. If you accidentally build a city by mistake, you can select the CANCEL button on the NAME CITY screen to retrieve your Settlers unit.

Your advisors propose a name for the new city; you can type in a different name if you prefer something else. When you are satisfied with the name, press [Enter] or click the OK button. The CITY DISPLAY opens so that you can arrange the city's initial production and economic development. When the display closes, your new city appears on the map. The Settlers unit disappears, having converted into the first citizens of your new city.

CHOOSING YOUR LOCATION

When building a new city, carefully plan where you place it. Citizens can work the terrain surrounding the city square in an X-shaped pattern (see **City Radius** for a diagram showing the exact dimensions). This area is called the CITY RADIUS (the terrain square on which the Settlers were standing becomes the city square). The natural resources available where a population settles affect its ability to produce food and goods. Cities built on or near water sources can irrigate to increase their crop yields, and cities near mineral outcroppings can mine for raw materials. On the other hand, cities surrounded by desert are always handicapped by the aridness of their terrain, and cities encircled by mountains find arable cropland at a premium.

Choose a location carefully

In addition to the economic potential within the city's radius, you need to consider the proximity of other cities and the strategic value of a location. Ideally, you want to locate cities in areas that offer a combination of benefits: food for population growth, raw materials for production, and river or coastal areas for trade. Where possible, take advantage of the presence of special resources on terrain squares (see **Terrain & Movement** for details on their benefits).

PROXIMITY OF CITIES

Another consideration when planning new cities is the current or potential location of other cities. You want to minimize the chance that one city's radius overlaps another's. Since a map square can only be used by one city at a time, radius overlap restricts the potential growth of one or both cities. Explore nearby lands as soon as possible to begin planning the placement of future cities. You want to take best advantage of the terrain. Of course, the geography of your particular continent will limit your choices. If you find yourself on a small island, your potential city sites will necessarily be more crowded than if you can sprawl across a vast continent.

STRATEGIC VALUE

The strategic value of a city site is a final consideration. A city square's underlying terrain can increase any defender's strength when that city comes under attack. In some circumstances, the defensive value of a particular city's terrain might be more important than the economic value; consider the case where a continent narrows to a bottleneck and a rival holds the other side. Good defensive terrain (Hills, Mountains, and Jungle) is generally poor for food production and inhibits the early growth of a city. If you need to compromise between growth and defense, build the city on a Plains or Grassland square with a river running through it if possible. This yields decent trade production and gains a 50 percent defense bonus.

Regardless of where a city is built, the city square is easier to defend than the same unimproved terrain. In a city you can build the City Walls improvement, which triples the defense factors of military units stationed there. Also, units defending a city square are destroyed one at a time if they lose. Outside of cities, all units stacked together are destroyed when any military unit in the stack is defeated (units in Fortresses are the only exception; see **Fortresses**).

Placing some cities on the seacoast gives you access to the ocean. You can launch ship units to explore the world and to transport your units overseas. With few coastal cities, your sea power is inhibited.

CAPTURING CITIES

Other civilizations normally defend their cities with one or more military units (armies for short), and sometimes with the city improvement City Walls. A defended city flies a pennant showing its owner's color. A walled city is surrounded by a short wall. There are two ways to acquire enemy cities: force and subversion. If you choose force, you must destroy the defenders by successfully attacking with your military units. Once the city is undefended, you can move a friendly army into the city and capture it. If you prefer subversion, you must successfully bribe dissidents in the city with your Diplomat or Spy unit (and sufficient funds—see **Diplomats & Spies** for all the details on such espionage). The dissidents capture the city for you, as their armies automatically convert to your side. Once captured, the city becomes yours to control and manage as you would any other.

Capturing an enemy city can also lead to side benefits, such as the discovery of a new technological advance and plundered cash to add to your coffers. Capture, however, eliminates one point of population (unless the City Walls, which can prevent this loss, are still standing). Therefore, when your units enter a city with only one point of population remaining, it is destroyed instead of captured. Diplomats and Spies can incite dissidents (see **Diplomats & Spies**) to capture a city without reducing its population below one.

Occupation of an enemy city destroys roughly half of the improvements the city has built, including all Temples and Cathedrals. Certain military units, such as Fighters and Bombers, are also destroyed rather than captured. Capture does not affect Wonders of the World (though, of course, destroying a city does—see **Wonders of the World** for more details). Inciting revolt creates less damage to the city, as the dissidents rely less on bombardment, and their familiarity allows them to pinpoint targets more accurately. A city captured by revolt loses only the Temple and Cathedral improvements (if it had them).

CONVERTING MINOR TRIBES

As your units explore the world, they might encounter the villages of minor tribes—civilizations too small or too peripatetic to count as "settled" (see **Minor Tribes** for the scoop on these situations). Minor tribes react to contact with a range of emotions, from delight to hostility. Occasionally, a minor tribe is sufficiently awed by your emissaries to immediately form a new city and become part of your civilization.

Move your exploring unit onto the village icon to discover the tribe's attitude towards your civilization. If they choose to form a new city, you need do nothing: Your advisors propose a name for the new city (which you can change if you prefer something else). When you are satisfied with the name, press Enter or click the OK button. The CITY DISPLAY opens so that you can arrange the city's initial production and economic development. When you close the display, your new city appears on the map. The village icon is replaced by the new city square, and members of the tribe settle in as the first citizens of your new city.

THE PARTS OF A CITY

THE CITY SQUARE

The terrain a city occupies is especially important because it is always under development. You cannot take workers off of this square when adjusting resource development on the RESOURCE MAP (see **Resource Map** in **Reference: Screen by Screen**). If this area is not useful, especially for producing food, then population growth in the new city is handicapped. For this reason, you'll find new cities do best when they are built on Plains or Grasslands squares or squares with rivers. These terrain types provide the best food production and, thus, faster population growth.

Note that all beginning civilizations possess the technologies of building Roads, Mining, and Irrigation. When you found a city on a Plains, Grassland, Hills, or Desert square, (or the special terrains based on those types) including squares with rivers running through them, the city square is automatically improved by roads and irrigation. When you found a city on any other type of terrain, the city square is automatically improved by roads and, if applicable, mining. You cannot assign a Settlers or Engineer unit to further improve a city square by, for example, adding mining or railroads, regardless of terrain, although you can change the terrain to another type (Forest to Plains, for example). Move a Settlers or Engineer unit into the city square and check the ORDERS menu to see what changes are possible. City squares do automatically improve with the discovery of certain advances.

The City Radius

The potential area of development, called the *City Radius*, extends two map squares out from a city in every direction except vertically or horizontally. Since the development area only extends one square from the city square in these directions, the resulting "radius" actually looks like a fat X, not like a circle. If the city grows large enough, its citizens can bring all of this area into development. When planning a new city, consider the long-term benefits of all the terrain squares within this radius.

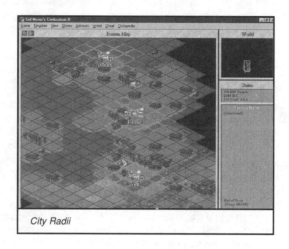

City Radii

For the city's population to increase, the radius must encompass terrain that workers can cultivate to produce food. Your (potentially) most important cities also have raw materials available. These cities can quickly build and support military units and Wonders. Hills and Forests allow your citizens to produce good quantities of raw materials, as do squares containing special terrain icons (pheasants, buffalo, coal, fish, and others—see **Special Terrains** for complete details).

The importance of trade in generating taxes and civilization advances makes river squares especially good sites for cities early in the game. Where you have no rivers or coastal areas, you can generate trade by building roads on Plains or Grasslands.

When a square within your City Radius is outlined, it indicates that another city is claiming that terrain's resource production. It could be one of your cities, if the city radii overlap. If you own both cities, you can flip between Resource Maps to adjust production in each to the best benefit of both locations. It could also be a rival city that one of your opponents has built close to you. Finding an outlined square in your city's radius might even lead you to discover a rival city in unrevealed territory or outside of your units' observation range.

MANAGING YOUR CITIES

Once you've founded, captured, or gained a city, you need to direct its growth and production. Each city has different assets and demands, so each should be managed individually. You must keep several goals in mind when managing a city: maintaining population growth, maximizing a useful mix of economic development (food, raw materials, and trade), producing tax revenue, producing technological research, and producing useful units and improvements, all the while maintaining an attitude of contentment and thereby avoiding civil disorder. For cities to grow and prosper, they need to balance economic output with the citizens' needs for infrastructure and services.

CITY MANAGEMENT CONCEPTS

As your city increases in size, its population expands, and it produces more and more food, shields, and trade. These represent your city's basic resources: edibles, raw materials, and trade goods. In city management, you add another layer of concepts which address how you turn these materials into products you can use. Refer to the CITY DISPLAY as you read.

Grain feeds your population and supports the city's units. When a city produces more food than its population and units consume each turn, the excess accumulates in the FOOD STORAGE BOX. When the box is full, another citizen is added to the POPULATION ROSTER, and the city increases in size. If your city is not producing enough food each turn to feed its population, the shortfall is noted, and stores are removed from the FOOD STORAGE BOX. If the box empties, any units that require food for support are disbanded, one by one, until a balance is achieved. If your city still experiences a shortfall, one citizen is removed from the POPULATION ROSTER, and your city decreases in size.

Shields power your industrial capacity and support the city's units. When a city produces more shields than your units expend each turn, the excess shields accumulate in the PRODUCTION BOX each turn. When the PRODUCTION BOX is full, your city produces something. It can "build" one of three kinds of things: *units*, which move around the map (like Settlers and Chariots), *city improvements*, which are tied to specific cities (like Libraries and Aqueducts), and *Wonders of the World*, which give unique benefits to the civilization that builds them (like the Pyramids or Magellan's Expedition)—but more about these details later. The type of government your people develop and the distance remote cities are located from your palace affect your shield production. Sometimes raw materials can be lost to waste. You can read all about the details of waste under **Trade Management Concepts**. If your city runs short of the raw materials it requires each turn, one or more units (that it supports) are forced to disband. The units farthest from home are disbanded first.

Based on the tax rates you set, trade arrows are further divided into three commodities that your civilization acquires: luxuries, taxes, and science. These commodities each have their own icons: Luxuries are represented by goblets, taxes are represented by gold, and science or research is represented by beakers. The type of government your people develop and the distance remote cities are located from your palace affects your trade income. Sometimes trade can be lost to corruption. You can read all about the details of trade transactions under **Trade Management Concepts**.

POPULATION GROWTH

Keeping a city's population growing is important because each additional citizen contributes something to your civilization. Each new citizen brings a new terrain square under production in your CITY RADIUS until there are no empty squares to work. After this point, each new citizen becomes an Entertainer (see **Specialists** for details on what Entertainers do). Thus, population growth increases your economic power, and concurrently, the strength of your civilization. The size of your population is a major factor in determining your civilization score, and is a measure of how well you have ruled.

RESOURCE DEVELOPMENT

The citizens of a city that work the surrounding countryside harness the economic resources within the city's radius. Depending on the needs of your civilization, there might be times when you prefer increased industrial output from a particular city over population growth. At other times, you'll want increased trade revenues. Still other times, sheer population growth might be the most important goal.

You can manipulate the output of a city by reassigning workers on the RESOURCE MAP. Each terrain square that shows resource icons is being worked by a citizen. Click on one of those squares, and you take the citizen off work. An Entertainer icon (a little Elvis) appears at the end of the POPULATION ROSTER. Now click on an empty terrain square. Elvis disappears from the POPULATION ROSTER and resources appear in that square, indicating that a citizen is now working there. By experimenting with the placement of workers on the RESOURCE MAP, you can find the optimum production ratio of food to raw materials to trade for that city.

Having an Entertainer on your POPULATION ROSTER might change the attitude of one or more of your citizens. For more information on this reaction, see **Happiness & Civil Disorder**.

TAX REVENUE

The percentage of your trade that is converted into tax revenue, or gold icons, is determined by the tax rate you set—see **Trade Rates** for information on how to manipulate the ratios of taxes, science, and luxuries. Why do you need tax revenue, anyway? You need revenue, or cash, because most improvements you build within cities require a stipend of gold for maintenance. Gold is also useful for speeding industrial production (see **Rush Jobs**), bribing enemy armies or inciting revolts in enemy cities (see **Diplomats & Spies**), and for negotiating peace with your neighbors (see **Diplomacy**).

The combined tax revenues of all your cities must exceed their combined maintenance requirements before gold can accumulate in your treasury. It is not necessary

Mao Tse-tung

for each city to have a positive cash flow. However, enough cities must do so to cover your civilizations' expenses, or your treasury will be depleted to cover the deficit. You can watch your STATUS window or check with your TRADE ADVISOR to see if you have a surplus or a deficit, as we'll explain under **Advisors** in **Reference: Screen by Screen**.

Some cities might not be especially suited for industrial production because of terrain or other factors, but they might still be good trading centers and capable of generating lots of income. Develop these locations with roads (and later, railroads), trade routes (see **Caravans & Freight** for the lowdown on trade route bonuses), city improvements like Marketplace, Bank, and Stock Exchange, and Wonders to be your civilization's cash cows. If you get to the point where you are no longer interested in building new items in a location, you can use the Capitalization improvement to convert a city's shields into gold—see the CIVILOPEDIA entry for details.

TECHNOLOGICAL RESEARCH

The greater the research contribution each city makes toward new civilization advances, the faster your people discover each new advance. The science rate you set determines the amount of research done in each city (see **Trade Rates** for the essentials of adjusting the ratios of science, taxes, and luxuries).

A city's research contribution can be influenced by adjusting the city's total trade income—research is a fraction of trade—by creating Scientists (see **Specialists**), and by building certain city improvements. Improvements that can help are the Library, University, and Research Lab, which all increase research, and several Wonders. The **Civilization Advances** chapter goes into detail about how to read the advance tree, so if you want the nuts and bolts, flip there next.

INDUSTRIAL PRODUCTION

Your most valuable cities can be those with the greatest industrial capacity—those whose workers produce the greatest number of shields. These cities can quickly produce expensive military units with which you can extend the power of your civilization. They are also best at producing Wonders of the World, as Wonders generally cost immense numbers of shields. But city management is dynamic. You must regularly monitor the production of your cities to ensure you are building the items you most need.

Several factors influence a city's production of shields: The terrain within your CITY RADIUS is most important, as citizens working on some types of terrain produce no shields at all (see **Terrain & Movement** for further explanations). You might find it worthwhile to set Settlers (and later, Engineers) to improving the terrain squares within your CITY RADIUS so that they yield more or different resources (see **Settlers & Engineers** for examples of what improvements they can make).

Beyond terrain, the form of government your civilization chooses can cause each city to spend some of its raw materials as maintenance for the military units that call the city home. It is possible that you can have so many units drawing raw materials from a city that there are no surplus shields. In a city where this is the case, progress on the item under construction (unit, improvement, or Wonder) stops until the situation is resolved.

A number of strategies allow you to adjust industrial capacity. The simplest is to shift citizens working on the RESOURCE MAP so that they produce more shields (see **Resource Development** for instructions). You can also use Settlers or Engineers to improve a terrain square within the CITY RADIUS so that it yields more shields. Or, order Settlers units to build a new city (they'll no longer draw support from the city that sponsored them when they've settled their own town). You might also try reassigning units so that they are attached to a different city (see **Homing Units** for the lowdown on how to do this).

Within each city, you can order the construction of improvements such as a Factory, Hydro Plant, or Offshore Platform that increase shield production. Several Wonders also affect shield output. Consult the CIVILOPEDIA for the complete list of possible city improvements and Wonders. It shows the construction and maintenance cost of each item, its purpose, and what advance is required to make it available.

CITY PROTECTION

Great economic management of a city is worthless if the city is captured by rivals or barbarians. Therefore, part of your management plan must concern the defense of each city. The minimum city defense is one army, preferably one with a good defense factor. A second defender can provide back-up in case the first is taken out (see **Military Units** for details of combat). An army with a strong attack factor is also useful. This unit can strike at enemies that move adjacent to the city, perhaps destroying them before they can launch an attack. Fortify any armies that you expect to defend a city (choose the Fortify option from the Orders menu or press the F key) because fortified units gain an increased defense strength—as we'll explain more fully under **Military Units**.

A city's defense can be substantially increased by building City Walls, an improvement that triples any defender's strength against most attackers (although not against Howitzers or air units). Veteran status and terrain bonuses are figured in before this tripling takes effect. City Walls also prevent population loss when defending units are destroyed (see **Combat**).

When civilization advances make available new army types with better defense factors, take the first opportunity to replace old defenders with better units. Since the offensive capability of your enemies improves as they acquire new advances, your defenses must improve to keep up.

Linking cities with roads and railroads can be very helpful in speeding the movement of units from one end of your empire to trouble spots elsewhere. This puts your defensive armies on "interior lines," allowing them to move rapidly to where they are needed.

IMPROVEMENTS

City improvements represent the commercial, bureaucratic, educational, and public works infrastructure that make large and efficient cities possible. In the real world, New York City's dense population depends on the extensive subway system for transportation, and buys electrical power generated by distant grids. Los Angeles is located in a desert and pipes in much of its water from sources hundreds of miles away.

Vladimir Lenin

In *Civilization II*, improvements are also critical to the growth and importance of cities. Inadequate provision of these facilities can limit the potential size of a city. Each improvement provides some service or otherwise makes a city work more efficiently. You must choose which improvement to implement at what time—does your city need a Marketplace or a Library more? Would a Courthouse provide more benefit than a Colosseum? City improvements are listed alphabetically in the Civilopedia. It explains the building costs, benefits, and maintenance fees of each improvement, along with any conditions which make the improvement obsolete or non-functional.

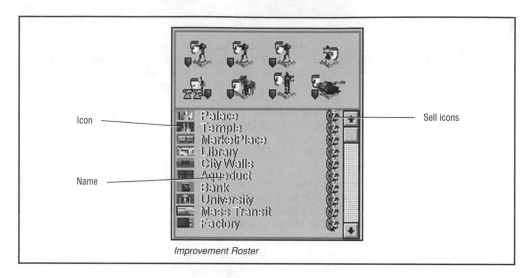

Icon

Name

Sell icons

Improvement Roster

LOSING IMPROVEMENTS

Improvements are not invulnerable, nor are they guaranteed to be permanent fixtures in an ever-dynamic city. The Barracks improvement, for instance, has a planned obsolescence. Once your civilization discovers the advance of Gunpowder, your old Barracks is rendered obsolete, and it disappears. (The same result attends your discovery of Mobile Warfare. These military installations are sensitive to changes in technology.) To regain its benefits each time, you must rebuild a Barracks improvement in each city you desire to have one.

Most improvements don't disappear over time, but they can be vulnerable to capture, fire sale, and sabotage. If you're really strapped for cash, you can even sell a city's improvements.

CAPTURE

Some, all, or none of a city's improvements might be destroyed when it is captured by another civilization. When a city is completely destroyed, all improvements are destroyed as well.

FIRE SALE

If you have less money in your treasury than is needed to pay a city improvement's maintenance cost at the beginning of your turn, *Civilization II* automatically sells the improvement for cash. Deficit spending is not allowed—even if by the end of the turn you would have had a positive cash flow again.

SABOTAGE

Foreign Diplomats or Spies can enter one of your cities and attempt industrial sabotage (of course, your envoys can attempt to sabotage your rivals' cities, too). This might result in the destruction of an existing improvement (or it might scrap the item that city is currently producing—see **Diplomats & Spies** for complete details on diplomatic actions). There are two defenses against this type of attack—destroying the Diplomat or Spy before he or she can enter your city, or stationing Diplomats or Spies of your own in the city for counterespionage.

SELLING IMPROVEMENTS

To raise cash, click on the improvement in the IMPROVEMENTS ROSTER of the CITY DISPLAY. A dialog box shows how much gold you could receive for selling the improvement. Normally you can gain one gold per resource invested in construction. If you sell, the improvement disappears from the city and the money is added to your treasury.

Selling improvements can be useful when you are short of money and are threatened with the random sale of an improvement. It can also be useful when you are under attack with no reasonable chance of defending or recovering a city. By selling off its improvements, you reduce its value to the enemy and salvage something. You can sell only one improvement per turn in each city. You cannot sell Wonders of the World.

RUSH JOBS

There are also times when you need the specific benefits of an improvement right now, and not 20 turns down the line. If you have sufficient funds, you can rush completion of a partially built item by paying cold, hard cash. However, speeding construction in this manner costs a premium. When workers are rushed, they receive overtime wages, and must pay surcharges on material delivery and fabrication. The surcharges for a rush job depend on what proportion of the work is already completed, whether the job is civil or military or a Wonder, and can cost up to eight times as much gold as the normal accumulation of shield icons.

To rush a job without paying cash, you have two options. When any Caravan or Freight unit enters a city where a Wonder is under construction, you can have it deliver its goods specifically to the project by choosing the HELP BUILD WONDER option when it arrives. The unit contributes its cost in shields directly to the RESOURCE BOX. Alternatively, any unit that you disband *in a city* contributes one-half its unit cost in shields to the current construction, whether it is a Wonder, an improvement, or another unit. This represents the retraining of troops and redisbursement of their supplies.

Items completed by rush jobs are available at the beginning of your next turn, so there is no advantage for rushing items that would be complete on the next turn anyway. To judge whether an item can be completed next turn without rushing, compare the surplus raw materials the city is generating to the number needed for completion. For very expensive items, it might be useful to consult your CITY STATUS advisor from the ADVISORS menu for an exact count of the remaining cost.

RENAMING YOUR CITY

You may rename any of your cities whenever you wish. This feature is useful when you capture a city and wish its name to be consistent with the names of cities you have founded, or when you discover that you're confusing units from two cities because their names are too similar.

Open the CITY DISPLAY and then click on the RENAME button. A dialog box opens in which you can type in the new city name. Press Enter or click the OK button to accept the name. If you decide not to change it, click CANCEL.

MANAGING YOUR TRADE

Trade is a fundamental force driving civilizations. It introduces unique and exotic valuables, stimulates the economy, and fires the imaginations of a culture's foremost thinkers. The effects of trade permeate society in many surprising and subtle ways, and your ability to direct trade's impact is likewise varied.

TRADE MANAGEMENT CONCEPTS

Taking up where we left off in **City Management Concepts**, these are the further divisions that result from trade income (arrow icons): luxuries (goblets), taxes (gold), and science funding (beakers).

Luxuries make your population more content. The availability of luxuries means that some citizens can enjoy a more pampered existence. Every two goblets make one contented citizen happy. We'll talk more about happiness a little later.

Taxes maintain city improvements and add to your treasury. Taxes support basic city services, and surplus funds accumulate in your treasury. There are plenty of useful ways to spend money in *Civilization II*, as we'll explain in a little while. If funding dries up, your city might be forced to sell off improvements.

Research funding powers your technological research. Each new advance requires the accumulation of a certain number of beakers to achieve. The **Civilization Advances** chapter explains the details of the search for knowledge, but for now, you just need to know that new discoveries often allow you to build new units and city improvements, and sometimes open up the possibility of building Wonders of the World. In addition, each discovery leads to further discoveries, creating a chain of progress. If your cities don't produce many beakers, your civilization doesn't progress very fast.

Which of these three is the most important? That varies according to what you want to achieve right now. To give trade management the most flexibility, *Civilization II* lets you adjust the proportion of trade income that is devoted to each of these three areas. The TAX RATE option on the KINGDOM menu lets you change the ratio of taxes to science to luxuries by 10 percent increments, and also shows you how these rates affect your funding and the speed at which your knowledge increases.

In **City Concepts**, we mentioned that the POPULATION ROSTER can tell you more than just the number of citizens in your city. It can also tell you your citizens' general level of contentment. Citizen icons appear in three different attitudes: *happy, content,* and *unhappy.* When you start building cities, you start with content citizens. The type of government your civilization develops and the level of difficulty at which you chose to play affect how rapidly unrest begins to trouble your populations. Unhappy citizens must be balanced by happy citizens, or your city falls into *civil disorder.* Not only does civil disorder sound bad, it has all sorts of nasty consequences, as we'll explain shortly.

For now, you need to know that you can increase the happiness of your citizens several different ways, among them: *building specific city improvements* like Temples and Marketplaces (we'll explain all about **Improvements** shortly), *reassigning military units* (the dirt about martial law and foreign service effects appears under **Military Units**), *adjusting the tax rates* (as we'll discuss under **Kingdom Menu** in **Reference: Screen by Screen**), and *pulling citizens off production work to make them specialists* (see **Specialists** for the skinny on this).

Phew! That's a lot of stuff to digest all at once. Just one more thing—we mentioned types of governments two paragraphs ago. Discovering new advances encompasses more than just new gadgets to improve sanitation and military might. The game counts philosophical concepts and theories as "new technologies," too. Every civilization starts out as a Despotism, but you can develop new forms of government. These might, in turn, have a profound effect on the happiness of your citizens and the rate at which your citizens produce raw materials, food, and trade.

TRADE RATES

When you start a new game of **Civilization II**, none of your trade benefits are tied up in luxuries—instead, 40 percent of your trade goes toward revenue from taxes, and 60 percent of it is funneled into science. To change the proportion of tax and science income, pull down the KINGDOM menu and choose the option TAX RATE. Choose a new rate by sliding one or more of the buttons along the slider bars. A notation at the top of the box mentions the maximum any one percentage can be, given your current form of government. Another notation lists the income and outflow as gold per turn, and finally, an entry calculates how many turns it will take to achieve a new advance. If you are interested in focusing on civilization advances, you might want to increase the amount of science being conducted. If you rapidly build city improvements, you might want to increase your taxes to cover the maintenance costs. If you are concerned about the attitude of your citizens, you might want to increase the availability of luxuries to make your citizens happier (we'll explain all about happiness in a few moments). Experiment with different rates to see what levels of income and science you can achieve.

If it is difficult to adjust all three sliders at once, you can click the box at the right end of any bar to lock that value in place. Now only the other two sliders move when you drag on one.

GOVERNMENTS

Another tool of city—and trade—management is the type of government under which your culture operates. Every civilization starts out as a Despotism, but some of the advances you can research are intellectual in nature, rather than technological, and these include five new governmental concepts. Once you have discovered a new form of government, you can choose to sponsor a revolution in order to change government types. (You can also gain access to new forms of government by building the Statue of Liberty Wonder.)

Anarchy, or the lack of government, occurs only when you lose control, either because civil unrest topples your current government, or immediately following a revolution. Civil unrest continues as long as conditions are ripe for it. In the case of a revolution, your people's attitude naturally stabilizes. After a few turns, once your civilization settles down, a dialog box appears listing all the possible forms of government your culture has available. Choose the one you like, and that regime takes effect immediately.

A new feature in **Civilization II** lets you change governments instantaneously and without penalty for the remainder of this turn. If your first choice turns out to be unsatisfactory, pull down the menu again and select a different government. Once you press [Enter] to end your turn, you must go through the entire revolution process (including several turns of Anarchy) if you want to change governments again.

There are three "ancient" forms of government—Despotism, Monarchy, and the Republic—and three "modern" ones—Communism, Fundamentalism, and Democracy. The Republic and Democracy are the most sophisticated from an economic point of view, but they impose severe restrictions on your military forces. The other forms offer trade-offs between economics and increased military flexibility. In essence, you could summarize governmental variants this way: The more freedom you give your people, the less they will want to fight for you, but the stronger your economy will become. We've collected the details of each form of government's bonuses and drawbacks in regard to trade, support provided to units, production, and the attitude of the citizenry. Depending on your style of play, you might not develop each advance in order of sophistication.

ANARCHY

You have temporarily lost control of the government. You continue controlling the movements of your units, and cities continue to operate on their own, but some important functions of your civilization grind to a halt until control is restored.

Attitude: Up to three troops in each city can institute martial law; each makes one unhappy citizen content (see **Happiness & Civil Disorder**).

Corruption & Waste: Corruption is rampant. Although no maintenance is charged for city improvements, no tax revenue is collected and no scientific research is accomplished while Anarchy continues.

Resource Support: Military units do not require raw material support until the number of units making a city their home (see **Unit Roster**) exceeds the number of citizens on the POPULATION ROSTER. Each military unit in excess of the city's population points requires one shield for industrial support. Settlers require one food for support each turn.

Special Conditions: While Anarchy continues, citizens cannot work up to their potential. The penalty for this atmosphere of tension is that workers produce one fewer resource icon in any terrain that can generate more than two icons of any one kind. Mines, for example, which might normally be worked for three shields, only produce two under Anarchy.

DESPOTISM

You rule by absolute fiat. The people just have to live with it because your will is enforced by the army. Due to the severe limits on economic and personal freedom, production is at a minimum. But total control makes conducting war relatively easy.

Attitude: Up to three troops in each city can enforce martial law; each makes one unhappy citizen content (see **Happiness & Civil Disorder**).

Corruption & Waste: Corruption and waste are both major problems under Despotism. Trade income losses due to corruption and shield production losses due to waste increase with the distance a city is located from its capital.

Resource Support: Under a Despotism, military units do not require resource support until the number of units making a city their home (see **Unit Roster**) exceeds the number of citizens on the POPULATION ROSTER. Each military unit in excess of the city's population points requires one shield for support each turn. Settlers require one food for support.

Special Conditions: Citizens cannot work up to their potential. The penalty for this atmosphere of tension is that workers produce one fewer resource icon in any terrain that can generate more than two icons of any one kind. Mines, for example, which might normally be worked for three shields, only produce two under Despotism. In addition, the maximum rate at which you can set tax, luxury, or science production is 60 percent.

MONARCHY

Your rule is less than absolute, and an aristocracy of upper-class citizens influences your decisions. The aristocratic classes, at least, have a certain amount of economic freedom, and this results in the potential for greater production. Your feudal vassals are partially responsible for helping to defend your kingdom, but they may in some cases deduct a share of your civilization's production as maintenance for military units.

Attitude: Up to three troops in each city can institute martial law; each makes one unhappy citizen content (see **Happiness & Civil Disorder**).

Corruption & Waste: A certain amount of your economic output is siphoned off by your aristocrats, particularly those farthest from your watchful eye—corruption and waste are significant problems under a Monarchy, though not as severe as they are under Despotism. Trade income losses due to corruption and shield production losses due to waste increase with the distance a city is located from its capital.

Resource Support: Your feudal vassals support up to *three* units from each city at no cost to you. Each additional unit requires one shield per turn. Settlers require one food per turn for support.

Special Conditions: Under a Monarchy, the maximum rate at which you can set tax, luxury, or science production is 70 percent.

REPUBLIC

You rule over an assembly of city-states formed from the cities that your civilization controls. Each city is an autonomous state, yet also is part of the republic which you rule. The people feel that you rule at their request. They enjoy substantial personal and economic freedom, and this results in greatly increased trade. A Senate reviews your diplomacy, and has a chance to override your decisions. Military conflict is unpopular among the masses, and your government must bear the full cost of supporting its army.

Attitude: Each ground and naval unit *beyond the first* that is not stationed in a friendly city or in a Fortress within three squares of a friendly city (except units whose attack strength is zero), and each Bomber, Stealth Bomber, Helicopter, or missile unit—regardless of the city it occupies—makes one citizen unhappy each turn.

Note: In *Civilization II*, units are not penalized based on their *home* city; they need only be in *any* friendly city.

Corruption & Waste: Corruption and waste remain a problem under a Republic, though not as severe as they are under a Monarchy. Trade income losses due to corruption and shield production losses due to waste increase with the distance a city is located from its capital.

Resource Support: Each military unit requires one shield for support each turn. Settlers require two food per turn.

Special Conditions: Under a Republic your workers produce an extra arrow icon in any square where they are already producing at least one. Your Senate can force you into accepting a peaceful resolution to any negotiation, though it will only choose to do so roughly 50 percent of the time. Finally, the maximum rate at which you can set tax, luxury, or science production is 80 percent.

COMMUNISM

You are the head of a communist government, and you rule with the support of the controlling party. Although this form of government allows more production than Despotism, the orthodoxy of the party restricts personal and economic freedom, limiting trade. On the positive side, corruption is negated by the action of the local party apparatus, the army and secret police suppress most dissent, and your large security forces recruit excellent spies.

Attitude: Up to three troops in each city can enforce martial law; each makes two unhappy citizens content (see **Happiness & Civil Disorder**).

Corruption & Waste: Under Communism, state control of the economy eliminates organized crime, and none of your cities suffer corruption or waste.

Resource Support: Regardless of city size, each military unit beyond the *third* a city supports requires one shield each turn. Settlers require two food for support.

Special Conditions: All Spy units produced under Communist governments are Veterans. Under Communism, the maximum rate at which you can set tax, luxury, or science production is 80 percent.

FUNDAMENTALISM

Fundamentalism is a form of government based on the literal, forceful, and uncompromising interpretation of religious dogma. Fundamentalist societies maintain that their own beliefs are the only true path to salvation, and tend to be rigidly intolerant of any dissenting view—a fact which tends to choke off intellectual development. On the other hand, the people in such societies are often fanatically devoted to their beliefs and may be willing to die, use force, or commit great atrocities to preserve them. This unthinking devotion, often obnoxious to neighboring societies, can be harnessed by a clever and cynical leader.

Attitude: Under Fundamentalism, no citizen is ever unhappy! Improvements that normally convert unhappy citizens to content citizens produce "tithes" (gold) equivalent to the number of people they would normally convert, and require no maintenance.

Corruption & Waste: Fundamentalism has very low rates of corruption and waste.

Resource Support: Because of your people's zeal, each city can support *10* military units at no cost to you. Settlers eat two food per turn. Only fundamentalists can build Fanatic units, which never require support.

Special Conditions: Under Fundamentalism, tax/luxury/science rates cannot be set higher than 80 percent. In addition, the rigidity of mindset and emphasis on doctrine means that all scientific research is *halved*. The diplomatic penalties for "terrorist acts" (such as bombing city improvements, poisoning wells, and so forth) committed by Diplomats and Spies is reduced, since the world comes to expect no better.

DEMOCRACY

You rule as the elected executive of a modern Democracy. The people feel that you rule because they chose you. The degree of freedom allowed under this government results in the maximum opportunity for economic production and trade. However, the people also have a very strong voice in determining how much economic production is devoted to improving the standard of living. Any diplomatic decisions you make are subject to review by your Senate—and the Senate always opposes actions that would lead to war. Maintaining a military force in the field comes with great political and economic costs.

Attitude: Each ground and naval unit not stationed in a friendly city or in a Fortress within three squares of a friendly city (except units whose attack strength is zero), and each Bomber, Stealth Bomber, Helicopter, or missile unit—regardless of the city it occupies—makes *two* citizens unhappy in its home city.

Note: In *Civilization II*, units are not penalized based on their *home* city; they need only be in *any* friendly city. In addition, Democracy is fragile. If even one of your cities remains in civil disorder for more than a turn, your government collapses into Anarchy.

Corruption & Waste: One of Democracy's greatest advantages is its ability to squelch corruption and waste. Neither exists in your cities.

Resource Support: Each military unit appropriates one shield for support each turn. Settlers require two food for support each turn.

Special Conditions: Under Democracy, your workers generate an additional arrow icon wherever at least one already exists. Patriotism and strong democratic traditions make your cities and units *immune to all forms of bribery*. Finally, the Senate can force a peaceful resolution to any negotiation, and will do so whenever possible.

HAPPINESS & CIVIL DISORDER

Happiness and its inverse state, civil disorder, are indirectly related to trade. Lack of trade leads to stagnation, and a slow economy means a lack of goods and services. The citizens in your cities have one of three different attitudes or emotional states: happiness, contentment, or unhappiness. The first citizens of your first city start out in a contented state. As the population of the city grows, competition for jobs, commodities, and services increases. Eventually, depending on the difficulty level at which you play, the form of government your civilization employs, and the economic conditions in your city, some citizens start to grumble and display unhappiness. If you don't take an active role in city management as population increases, the natural trend of citizens' attitudes is toward unhappiness.

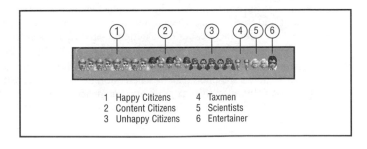

1 Happy Citizens	4 Taxmen
2 Content Citizens	5 Scientists
3 Unhappy Citizens	6 Entertainer

So what can you do to counter this trend? If your population is already suffering civil disorder because of an attitude imbalance, you need to take immediate steps, as we suggest under **Restoring Order**. However, you needn't wait until a crisis occurs; you can keep citizens content by taking a longer outlook and providing services as the demand becomes imminent, or even ahead of demand.

The temperament of your citizens depends on the level of difficulty at which you play. At Chieftain level, your people are so even-tempered that the first six citizens on the POPULATION ROSTER start out content. Each new citizen above this number starts with a bad attitude, and must depend on improvements, luxuries, martial law, and/or Wonders of the World to improve his or her state of mind. The number of citizens who start content decreases by one with each successive level of difficulty, until at Deity level, your people are so temperamental that only one citizen starts out content. The second and subsequent citizens show their unhappiness and must be cajoled into better humor with any of the management tools at your disposal.

SPECIAL UNHAPPINESS FACTORS

There are two special conditions that cause further unhappiness in some populations. Under a Despotism, and to a progressively lesser degree under other types of government, citizen unhappiness increases with the number of cities. This can lead to very unhappy citizens who must be converted first to unhappy citizens before they can become content.

In Republics and Democracies, each ground or naval unit not in a friendly city or fortress within three squares of a friendly city, and each bomber, Helicopter, or missile unit regardless of where it is located, might create unhappy citizens. You can think of it as units "in the field." Because of their routine flight training, most air units are always "in the field," but the protective role of fighters makes them an exception to the rule.

In a Republic, the first unit in the field *does not* cause discontent. Each subsequent army in the field creates one unhappy citizen. If your civilization is a Democracy, each unit in the field causes two unhappy citizens. Units with an attack strength of zero (that is, an ADM rating that starts with zero, like Transports and Engineers) do not cause unhappiness in this manner. When a city is in disorder, disbanding distant military units, returning them to their home cities, or changing their cities can make some unhappy citizens content and might restore the city to order.

CIVIL DISORDER

As we mentioned in **City Management Concepts**, cities that don't maintain a favorable balance of happy people over unhappy people go into civil disorder. Cities in civil disorder produce no tax revenue, technological research, or food surpluses, and the condition suspends production. Prolonged civil disorder might bring down a government and throw your civilization into Anarchy. A nuclear reactor in a city suffering civil disorder might experience a meltdown due to lax safety controls (see **Nuclear Meltdown**). Keeping a city stable is a very high priority.

A city suffers civil disorder when unhappy people outnumber happy people. Content people and Specialists are ignored in the calculation. When order is restored, the city returns to normal operation the next turn. You can restore order in several ways.

Restoring Order

You can pay to complete an improvement, such as a Temple, that can convert sufficient unhappy citizens to contentment (or content citizens to happiness) to restore the balance. See **Rush Jobs** for instructions on how to do this.

You can also change the tax rates of your civilization. Increasing the availability of luxuries might convert some content people into happy citizens, allowing them to balance the unhappy populace. See **Trade Rates** for information on economic manipulation.

You can take one or more citizens out of the work force, and make them Specialists. This increases the number of happy people. For information on how to do this, see **Specialists**. When creating Specialists, be careful not to also cause shortages of food or resources that trigger starvation of the population or the scrapping of armies.

If your civilization operates under Anarchy, Despotism, Monarchy, or Communism, you can use martial law to restore order to a city. Up to three military units, each with an attack factor of one or more, can be stationed in a city to enforce martial law. Each military unit makes one unhappy citizen in a city content under the first three types of government. When you are operating under Communism, martial law is doubly effective, and each army makes two citizens content. If you have enough military units to enforce it, and a low enough level of unhappiness, martial law might be enough to restore order.

We Love the _____ Day

If a city's population becomes sufficiently happy, it (not your whole civilization—just this one location) spontaneously holds a celebration in honor of your rule. The people declare a "We Love the (title of the leader) Day" in thanks for the prosperity your management has made possible. While the circumstances that support this celebratory mood continue, the city enjoys certain benefits, depending on your civilization's type of government. You will see the effects of celebration begin on the first *full turn* that a city celebrates, that is, the turn *after* the party is announced.

The people love you!

To trigger a celebration day, a city must fulfill certain conditions: there can be no unhappy citizens in the city, there must be at least as many happy citizens as content citizens, and the Population Roster must number at least three citizens. Specialists are considered content citizens for this calculation. For example, a city with five happy citizens, four content citizens, and no unhappy citizens celebrates. A city with ten happy citizens, three content citizens and one unhappy citizen does not.

ANARCHY

The celebration has no effect when your government is in Anarchy.

DESPOTISM

The celebrating city collects resources as if its government is a Monarchy (see **Governments**). This can increase the amount of food and raw materials your citizens can produce in certain improved (irrigated and mined) terrain types.

MONARCHY/COMMUNISM/FUNDAMENTALISM

A celebrating city currently ruled by any of these governments collects resources as if its government is a Republic (see **Governments**). This increases the amount of trade your citizens can produce in any terrain that generates trade goods.

REPUBLIC/DEMOCRACY

A city currently ruled by either of these governments increases in population by one point each turn it celebrates, so long as sufficient food is available. This can result in dramatic growth of the city.

TERRAIN AND MOVEMENT

TERRAIN & MOVEMENT CONCEPTS

The game map in *Civilization II* is divided into small independent parts, or terrain squares, as we mentioned in **City Concepts**. For simplicity, each square consists of a single type of terrain, even though the real world is not as perfectly organized as that. To represent that some types of terrain are easy to walk across and others require slogging through mud or hacking through thick underbrush, your units spend *movement points* to enter each new square. Every unit has an ADM rating (the acronym stands for Attack/Defense/Movement); the M, or third number in the rating, indicates how many movement points it can spend in a turn. You can find out all about units and their ADM ratings under **Military Units**.

Each terrain type has its own *movement point cost* (and they're all conveniently listed in the **Terrain Charts** on the **Poster**). Your Settlers or Engineer units can improve (that is, lower) these movement point costs by laying roads and later railroads in terrain squares (see **Settlers & Engineers** for the lowdown on how they do this). When a unit moves into a new square, it pays that square's movement point cost. If it has any movement points— or fractions of movement points—left after moving one square, a unit can attempt to move again until it reaches the limit of its movement points. Attacking counts as movement— that is, your units spend movement points to attack. You can read about the details under **Military Units**; what you need to know here is that a unit's attack strength might be reduced if it has less than a full movement point remaining at the time of combat. You'll get a message asking if you want to continue with the attack.

The proximity of enemy units or cities can also restrict a unit's movement options. Units and cities have what in military circles is called a *zone of control*; their influence extends into the eight squares that immediately surround them. Your units cannot move directly from one rival's zone of control into another's zone of control unless you have an alliance with the second tribe. This represents a unit's ability to threaten or pin down enemy troops nearby. When an enemy Legion is nearby waiting to pounce, your troops cannot afford to expose their vulnerable flanks. The blockers don't have to be units or cities of the same civilization. The **Movement Restriction** diagram should make it clearer, so give it a look-see. Some units (such as Diplomats and Caravans) have special abilities that allow them to ignore these restrictions. Zones of control are not relevant to air units and naval units.

TYPES OF TERRAIN

The differences in terrain are deeper than a variety of artwork and colors to make the game map more visually interesting. Each type of terrain has its own economic usefulness, effect on movement, and effect on combat. Detailed information about the types is provided in the TERRAIN CHART on the **Poster** and in the CIVILOPEDIA.

To get terrain information from the CIVILOPEDIA, click on the CIVILOPEDIA menu, and select the TERRAIN TYPES option. A list of both standard terrain types and their special resources appears. If you don't recognize the icon for a special resource, click on the standard terrain type to see what special resources are possible.

A Note About Rivers

In *Civilization II*, rivers are not a type of terrain unto themselves. Instead, they can flow through any type of terrain. Rivers make movement easier for ground units that follow the line of the river bed either up- or downstream, because each square costs only one-third of a movement point, regardless of the underlying terrain. Settlers and Engineer units cannot build roads across rivers until your tribe discovers the Bridge Building advance. Rivers count as sources of water for the purposes of irrigation. Citizens working terrain through which a river flows gain a bonus arrow icon, representing the ease with which rivers facilitate trade. Finally, a river's presence enhances the defense bonus of the terrain through which it flows.

Standard Terrain Squares

The standard types of terrain can be divided along climactic lines. Here's a short summary. Glacier and Tundra squares are both cold terrain. Neither produces much in the way of raw materials, and neither can be converted into more profitable terrain. Swamp and Jungle are both wet terrain. Neither is easy to move through, and it costs a considerable investment of time to convert either into more profitable terrain. Plains and Grassland squares are both open terrain. Both are easy to travel across, and when improved, both produce substantial amounts of food as well as other raw materials. Hills and Mountains squares are both vertically challenging. They take some effort to travel across and yield more raw materials when developed by mining. Ocean squares generate substantial amounts of trade, and appropriate types of terrain bordering them can be irrigated. Ground units can move at a rate of one-third of a movement point per square if they follow a riverbed up- or downstream. Desert squares are dry terrain that can be developed for marginal production. Forest squares are difficult to travel through, but yield decent raw materials.

Special Terrain Squares

Each standard terrain square might be enhanced by one of two types of special resource. Where special resources appear, they add significantly to the economic value of the terrain. Distinct symbols mark the location of these resources. If your Settlers or Engineer units convert a square containing a special resource icon into another terrain type, the original specialty is lost. If the new terrain type can be enhanced by special resources, it is; if the new terrain is Grassland, it remains a standard terrain. Right now, we'll give you a brief summary.

Glaciers can be enhanced by *Oil* deposits, representing increased mineral wealth, and therefore yielding extra shields when worked. Alternatively, the presence of Walruses indicate the availability of *Ivory*, with its greatly enhanced trade goods yield.

Musk Ox stand in some Tundra squares, indicating excellent food sources or the potential for good grazing; workers in these squares can produce additional food. Other Tundra squares display *Fur*, indicating the high potential for arrows because of desirable trade goods.

Swamp squares can contain *Peat*, whose usefulness as fuel is indicated by the enhanced shield yield, or perhaps *Spice*, exotic flavorings which are prized the world over, and therefore represent bonus yields in both food and arrow icons.

Gems shine in Jungle terrain to indicate the presence of precious stones, ivory, spices, salt, or other valuable commodities. These are good trade items and, therefore, the square in which they appear generates substantial arrows. Jungles also have the potential to produce exotic *Fruits* which naturally increase the food output.

Buffalo trotting across the Plains represent raw materials on the hoof; workers in these squares generate extra shields. On the other hand, *Grain* represents a particularly fertile piece of open ground, and a rich source of food.

Coal deposits, shown as black lump icons in Hills terrain, represent rich locations of coal or metal ores. These areas produce greatly increased shields, especially when mined. On the other hand, some hills are *Wine* country, especially suited for growing grapes. Wine terrain yields greatly increased trade.

Gold gleams in Mountains terrain, representing a bonanza of precious metal ore. The value of these deposits produces tremendous trade goods. Alternatively, workers might discover *Iron* deposits in mountainous areas, yielding a substantial number of shields.

Fish swimming in Ocean terrain represent the location of underwater banks and reefs where currents and nutrients create excellent fishing grounds. Fishing grounds produce increased amounts of food. On the other hand, *Whales* indicate the bounty of the deeps, and an increase in raw materials and trade goods as well as foodstuffs.

An *Oasis* is a very fertile island in Desert terrain where workers can harvest substantial quantities of food. Conversely, *Oil*, representing the presence of mineral wealth, especially petroleum, can also be found in Desert squares. As they do in Glaciers, Oil squares in Desert terrain yield extra shields when worked.

A *Pheasant* peers through some Forest terrain. The presence of game indicates excellent food sources available. On the other hand, *Silk* represents a luxurious product of mulberry Forests that brings increased yield from trade goods.

OPTIMAL CITY SITES

The economic usefulness of the various terrain types is important when selecting city sites. Citizens work the terrain within a city's radius to produce the food, raw materials, and trade that the city needs to grow and be productive (see **The City Radius**). Some terrain types are more valuable than others, in that citizens working them produce more resources. Other terrains start out yielding little, and only develop their full potential when they are improved. These squares can be irrigated, mined, or surfaced for increased economic value. Other squares are important because they can be converted into more valuable terrain, as we'll discuss soon (for instructions on how to irrigate, mine, surface, and convert terrain, see **Settlers & Engineers**). The best city sites offer immediate food, raw material, and trade production, plus the potential for long term development.

TERRAIN CONVERSION

When surveying sites for a new city, keep in mind the potential for terrain squares within the city's radius to be improved. Hills and Mountains squares can be mined so that citizens working them produce increased raw materials. Plains and Grassland squares, whether or not rivers run through them, can be irrigated so that citizens working there produce more food. Swamp and Jungle squares can be cleared to yield Grassland or planted to yield Forest. Forest can be cleared to yield a Plains. Plains and Grassland squares can be retimbered to yield Forest if you need raw materials. An area dense with Jungle and Swamp squares looks barren at first, but has the potential to become a very rich city site.

Improvements are not limited to agricultural effects. Settlers and Engineers also improve terrain by laying roads across terrain squares. Roads allow better access to a city, and therefore, increase the trade goods citizens working some squares produce. Plains, Grassland, and Desert squares all produce trade once penetrated by roads. Railroads eliminate the movement point cost of the terrain across which they are laid and might increase resource production as well. For more information on terrain improvements, see **Settlers & Engineers**—they're the units that do the work.

PLANETARY CARETAKING

Manipulating terrain to produce the maximum number of shields has a downside, of course. One cost of heedless industrial growth is a gradual polluting and poisoning of the environment. Of the many dangers posed by pollution in the real world, the greatest might be global warming. Theorists believe an unchecked rise in the planet's atmospheric temperature threatens catastrophic geographic changes, including melting polar ice caps, rising sea levels, and parched farmlands. Different threats of poisoning occur if nuclear weapons are detonated or a nuclear reactor melts down.

Civilization II models pollution from industry and nuclear disaster as a balancing factor for growth. As you steer your civilization into the industrial age, you must manage your cities and monitor your terrain to minimize pollution and prevent the disaster of global warming.

POLLUTION

Every turn, the game assigns a probability of pollution occurring within the economic radius of each city. The likelihood of this contamination depends on two factors: the number of shields produced (industrial pollution) and the population supported (smog). In some cities, industrial pollution is the major factor in the calculation, and in other cities smog is a bigger hazard. Below a certain level, the chance of pollution is negligible, but as industrial output builds, so does the likelihood of its darker side effects. Smog has no effect on pollution calculations until your civilization acquires the advance of Automobile.

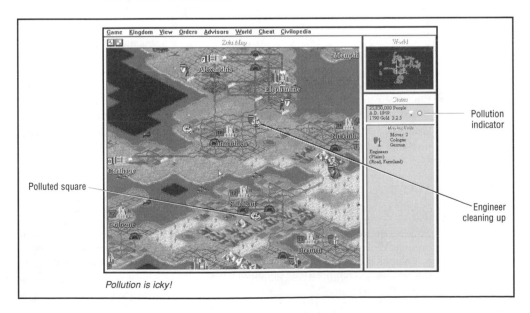

Pollution is icky!

Pollution warning symbols (yellow triangles with little skulls) begin appearing on the CITY DISPLAY in the GENERAL INFORMATION window when the combined pressures of smog and industrial pollution begin to create a significant threat of contamination. The number of symbols roughly indicates the probability each turn of a square within the city radius becoming polluted. For example, a city generating a large number of raw materials each turn (say 20) and inhabited by a large population might show several of them in its CITY DISPLAY. The exact probability of pollution being produced by industrial pollution and smog depends on the difficulty level at which you set the game.

Certain city improvements can help the situation. A Nuclear Power Plant, Hydro Power Plant, Solar Plant, or Recycling Center improvement in a city reduces the impact of industrial pollution, in turn decreasing the accumulation of warnings. Solar Plants also help prevent global warming by absorbing excess heat in the atmosphere. The Hoover Dam, a modern Wonder of the World, acts as a Hydro Power Plant for all friendly cities. The Mass Transit improvement eliminates smog.

NUCLEAR CONTAMINATION

The detonation of nuclear weapons or the meltdown of a Nuclear Power Plant can also cause contamination. For game purposes, *Civilization II* treats this as identical to industrial pollution, though in real life the effects might be considerably different (and longer term).

NUCLEAR WEAPONS

A Nuclear unit not only destroys the army or city it targets, but all units stacked with the target and those in adjacent squares as well. It also pollutes a number of map squares around the impact square. Enemy units' zones of control (which are discussed under **Movement Restrictions**) might make it impossible for your Settlers or Engineer units to clean up this contamination in a timely fashion, and your rival might not spend the time or manpower. Unchecked pollution significantly raises the risk of a global warming disaster.

NUCLEAR MELTDOWN

If a Nuclear Power Plant melts down, half of the city's population is destroyed. Additionally, some random number of squares near the city become polluted.

The risk of meltdown always exists when a city which has a Nuclear Power Plant goes into civil disorder. Civilian unrest might result in safety procedures becoming so lax that a catastrophic accident occurs. If you build Nuclear Power Plants in any of your cities, take special care not to allow those cities to go into disorder.

When your civilization achieves the technological advance of Fusion Power, the risk of meltdown disappears. Your Nuclear Plants automatically convert to fusion-powered facilities once you have achieved this advance.

POLLUTION'S EFFECTS

Pollution is represented graphically by a skull on the terrain square in which it occurs. It reduces the production of food, raw materials, and trade to one-half (rounded up) of pre-pollution levels. For example, a square where workers produced four food, one shield, and two trade before pollution blighted the square yields only two food, one shield, and one trade after contamination. Once the terrain is detoxified, workers' production returns to pre-pollution levels.

Polluted terrain can be detoxified by any Settlers or Engineer unit. The working unit's shield is marked with a "P" to note it has been ordered to detoxify a polluted square. After four turns of work (an Engineer can clean up in two), the pollution disappears. Adding more Settlers or Engineer units to a polluted square speeds the cleanup. If you use the GoTo City order, your city list marks which locations suffer from pollution. Note that a polluted square within the radius overlap of two cities is listed once for each city; if your cities are close together, this might give you an alarming overstatement of the total pollution your civilization suffers.

MONITORING POLLUTION

Your environmental advisors inform you immediately when any map square within your territory becomes polluted. A skull appears on the polluted square.

You can monitor the extent of pollution throughout your civilization by watching the pollution indicator, a small icon in the Status window. The color of the icon depends on the number of currently polluted terrain squares and the number of turns they have remained contaminated. It indicates the extent of the risk of global warming.

GLOBAL WARMING

Global warming might occur at any time that at least nine map squares, anywhere in the world, are polluted. The probability that it will occur increases with the length of time contamination on this scale is left untreated. If polluted terrain is left unattended for too long, environmental damage occurs, as detailed under **Disasters**.

Once an environmental disaster has occurred, the cycle starts over again. The planet achieves equilibrium at the new, higher temperatures. If pollution continues or increases once more to high levels, another bout of environmental problems might occur. This cycle can repeat endlessly if pollution is not controlled.

MINOR TRIBES

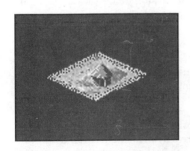

Thatch-roofed hut icons scattered about the map of the world indicate the presence of minor tribe villages. These populations are too isolated, too unorganized, or too migratory to develop into major civilizations. Minor tribes react to contact with a range of emotions, from delight to hostility. There is no way to predict a village's response, but most potential responses are favorable. There is one unique situation: air units cannot encounter minor tribe villages. Instead, their overflight scares the villagers, and the hut icon vanishes as the tribe abandons their territory in terror.

Playtesters and *Civilization* fans alike call these hut icons "goody huts." Here's what might happen when you move a ground unit onto terrain that a minor tribe occupies.

- Occasionally a minor tribe is sufficiently advanced, yet awed by your emissary, to immediately form a new city and become part of your civilization.

- On the other hand, your unit might have stumbled upon a village which has discovered an advance unknown to your civilization. Graciously, they share their knowledge.

- To placate your emissary unit, a village might give your civilization valuable resources (gold) as a gift. The gift is added to your treasury.

- Your emissary unit stirs up the young bloods in the village with his tales of valor and victory. All the impressionable warriors run off to join your army, creating a new military unit "carrying your colors."

- Your emissary makes a horrible *faux pas*, and the minor tribe turns vicious. A random number of barbarian units comes boiling out of the terrain squares that adjoin the village. Duck (or run, if you can)!

- Your emissary arrives at a spot rumored to contain a village only to find the inhabitants long gone and the dwellings empty. Nothing occurs.

- Your unit catches up with a particularly peripatetic tribe, and impresses them with his or her goods and possessions. The minor tribe is willing to join your civilization, though not necessarily interested in settling in their present location. The villagers become a Settlers (or Engineer) unit carrying your shield.

MOVEMENT

There are two basic methods of moving units a square or two at a time: by keyboard commands or (if you have enabled mouse movement) by mouse clicks. The keyboard method uses the eight edge keys of the numeric keypad. The 5 key in the center is inactive; think of it as your unit's position. The keys surrounding the 5 represent the points of a compass. For example pressing 7 sends your unit northwest, while pressing 6 sends your unit east.

The mouse method involves placing your mouse cursor near the edge of the unit in the direction you want it to travel. When the cursor turns into an arrow pointing in the appropriate direction, click the left mouse button to make the unit move. Note that this method works only if you turn on the MOVE UNITS W/ MOUSE option in GAME OPTIONS. You can also use the GoTo order to send a unit over long distances, as we explain in detail under **GoTo Orders**.

Units can move up to the limit of their movement factors, with a few caveats. The most important exception is that a unit can always move at least one square in a turn, regardless of the movement point cost of the terrain. Are we saying a unit can always move? Not quite. An enemy unit or city's presence can hamstring any unit with the zone of control restriction, as you'll see in a moment. There are other, common-sense restrictions on where units can move and where they can't, which are elaborated under **Movement Restrictions**.

Back to movement factors. A unit with a movement factor greater than one must compare its movement factor with the movement point cost of the terrain square you wish it to enter. The unit pays the movement point cost (subtracts the movement point cost from its remaining movement factor) for each new square it enters, until you choose to stop advancing, or the unit's movement factor is smaller than the movement point cost of the terrain square. There's a small chance that a unit can enter a square even if its movement factor is lower than the movement point cost of the terrain, which is why sometimes Chariots can cross Mountains squares, and sometimes they can't. When an army is unable to complete a movement order because it doesn't have enough movement points to proceed, its movement is finished for the turn. The map then centers on the next active unit.

Roads and railroads speed the movement of ground units. They do this by lowering the movement point cost of the terrain over which they are built. Any terrain square with a road across it costs just one-third of a movement point to cross. Any terrain square with a railroad costs no movement points to cross—zero! Cities automatically have roads in their city squares, so entering a city square always costs one-third of a movement point. Once your civilization discovers the Railroad advance, city squares are automatically upgraded to railroads, so your units can slide through them for free.

THE ACTIVE UNIT

How do you know whose turn it is? Every turn, *Civilization II* activates each unit in turn by centering the map around the unit and making it blink. You can give orders to each unit as it becomes the active unit (see the **Orders Menu** in **Reference: Screen by Screen**). Five special orders deserve fuller explanations here.

No Orders

To skip a unit for the turn, press the Skip Turn (Spacebar) key or choose the option from the Orders menu. Once you've skipped a unit's turn, the troops are on liberty for the day—you can't recall them to duty again this turn.

GoTo Orders

To send a unit on a long trek, you have two options. You can click-and-hold on any square on the map until your cursor turns into a crooked "Go" arrow. If the destination square isn't visible in the Map window, you can use the Zoom Out button to enlarge the area you are viewing, click on the World window to shift your view to another area of the map, or switch to View Pieces mode by pressing the V key or choosing the option from the View menu, and move the cursor with the number pad keys. If you'd rather send a unit to a city, you can press the GoTo G key or choose the option from the Orders menu. A screen pops up listing all of your cities; click on the All Players button to see every destination city in the world.

Once a destination is established, the unit automatically "goes to" that square, whether it takes only one turn to complete its orders, or many turns. If the unit is attacked, or an obstruction prevents the unit from completing its journey, it becomes active once again. Ground units cannot travel between continents on a GoTo order.

Wait Orders

To skip a unit temporarily, press the Wait W key or choose that option from the Orders menu. This passes you on to the next unit and sends the skipped army to the end of the line. You'll see this unit again after all the others have had a chance to move.

Paradrop Orders

Paratroopers that have not moved this turn have the special ability to make paradrops when in a city or Airbase. Press the Paradrop P key or choose the option from the Orders menu. Your cursor turns into a parachute. You can make a paradrop in any land square within 10 of the origination square, as long the target square is not occupied by enemy troops. As you run the mouse over the map, the cursor changes from a parachute to a crossed-out parachute to indicate "illegal" destination squares. Click on a square to make the drop. Paratroopers have one movement point after they drop to attack or change position.

AIRLIFT ORDERS

Once your civilization has discovered the Radio advance, you can build Airport improvements. Once you have two or more Airports, you can airlift one unit per turn into or out of each Airport. Activate a unit in a city, then press the AIRLIFT key [I] or choose the option from the ORDERS menu. A list of cities with Airports appears, and you can select your destination. Enemy Fighters and Stealth Fighters within range of either the target or destination city have a chance to scramble and interdict the airlift.

ACTIVATING FORTIFIED AND SLEEPING UNITS

Fortified and sleeping units do not become the active unit. If you want them to move or change position, you must activate them first. Click the mouse pointer on the square in which fortified or sleeping units are stationed. This opens a box displaying all units in that square. Click again on the icons of all units you wish to activate. Fortified or sleeping units within a city must be activated from within the CITY DISPLAY—see **City Display** for instructions on how to do this. Sleeping units automatically activate when enemy units move into an adjacent square.

NAVIGATING THE MAP WINDOW

We've talked about moving your units around the map, but there are several tools which allow you to look at different map areas and move around the game world. First, let's describe the two modes of *Civilization II*. In MOVE PIECES mode, the active unit blinks, and you can use the number pad keys or cursor arrows to move it across the map. In VIEW PIECES mode, the square-outline cursor blinks, and you can use the number pad keys to move it across the map. You are automatically placed in MOVE PIECES mode at the beginning of each turn, and automatically switched to VIEW PIECES mode when "end of turn" is flashing. Toggle between the modes by pressing the [V] key, clicking on the lower portion of the STATUS window, or selecting your choice on the VIEW menu. You cannot switch to MOVE PIECES mode unless there are units still waiting to move.

Of course, you can simply click on a map square to center the MAP window there. If you want to move a long distance, you can use the ZOOM buttons to increase the acreage shown in the window, or click on the WORLD window.

If your cursor is over a unit, stack of units, or city square in VIEW PIECES mode, you can press the ACTIVATE UNIT [A] key to activate some or all of the units in that square. If there is more than one unit, a pop-up box allows you to choose among them. If the active unit in MOVE PIECES mode happens to be standing in a city, the ACTIVATE UNIT key also works to activate any fellow units in the city, without opening the CITY DISPLAY.

MOVEMENT RESTRICTIONS

Most of the restrictions placed on unit movement are a matter of common sense, as we mentioned earlier. We're spelling them all out here, in case you try to order a unit somewhere that seems possible and the game won't let you do it.

GROUND UNITS

Ground units (all non-ship and non-air units) normally move only on land. To traverse the wide (or narrow) oceans or even to get across lakes, they must board naval transport. Not all ships take passengers; see **Naval Units** under **Mobile Units** for a list of those that do.

Boarding a ship uses up all a unit's movement points for the turn and puts it to sleep. If you attempt to move a naval unit into a land square that does not contain a port city, any passengers are offered the option to MAKE LANDFALL and disembark. If a naval unit carrying ground troops makes port, all passengers automatically wake up.

NAVAL UNITS

Ships normally move only on the ocean, although they can also sail across inland lakes. Ships cannot navigate rivers, deltas, or swamps in the game, though of course some do in real life. Instead, river navigation is represented by the reduced movement point cost for ground units following riverbeds. City squares that touch a shoreline along one side or at one corner are the only "land" squares that ships can enter—here they make port. Making port costs one movement point.

AIR UNITS

Air units can cross both land and sea squares at a cost of one movement point per square, but they must land in a friendly city, at an Airbase, or on a Carrier unit to refuel every turn or two. Though planes can sometimes fly above rival ground units in real life without causing an incident, they are always required to encounter enemy ground units that they overfly in *Civilization II*. To avoid attacking rival units by accident, carefully guide your planes around them. Air units have the advantage in maneuverability. Neither ground nor ship units can attack air units that appear "next to them" because of the disparate vertical locations. The one exception is the Diplomat or Spy unit's ability to bribe adjacent units into switching sides. See **Diplomats & Spies** below.

ZONES OF CONTROL

Ground units cannot move directly from one square adjacent to an enemy army or city to another such square. The squares that surround a unit are in that unit's zone of control—the same holds true for a city. Neither ground troops nor Settlers units can move directly from one rival's zone of control into another square within a rival's zone of control. The prohibited square might be adjacent to the first enemy army, to another army (even one from a different civilization), or to any enemy city. Ground units can only move into such a controlled square if a friendly unit or city already occupies the square, or if you have formed an alliance with a rival player (which we'll explain fully in **Diplomacy**).

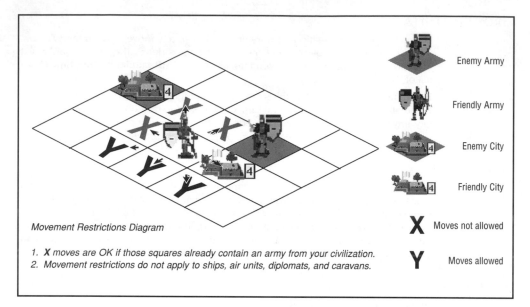

Movement Restrictions Diagram

Enemy Army

Friendly Army

Enemy City

Friendly City

X Moves not allowed

Y Moves allowed

1. **X** *moves are OK if those squares already contain an army from your civilization.*
2. *Movement restrictions do not apply to ships, air units, diplomats, and caravans.*

Some units have special abilities which allow them to ignore zones of control. Air units have the whole sky in which to maneuver; naval units have the open sea. Diplomats and Spies use social convention and diplomatic immunity with equal aplomb, and Caravans and Freight units can argue neutrality and engineer special deliveries. Partisans use intimate knowledge of the local terrain to good effect. Explorers' solitary nature and singleness of purpose get them out of tight places. The **Movement Restrictions** diagram offers a graphic representation of a unit confronted by enemy zones of control.

CIVILIZATION ADVANCES

The major dynamic of change throughout the history of civilization has been the continuing advance and accumulation of knowledge. As humankind progressed by fits and starts through the ages, civilizations rose and fell, their success or failure due to what knowledge they acquired and how they employed it.

Those who first acquire new knowledge are often able to employ it to build a more powerful position, but there are many cases of civilizations that obtained some new invention first, then failed to use it to their advantage. The pace at which a society develops and implements new knowledge depends on many factors, including its social organization, economic organization, geographic location, leadership, and competition.

The concept of progress being not only inevitable, but even a good thing is a relatively recent phenomenon. Only in the last several hundred years have we actively studied history and considered the evidence of the historical record. For most of human history, the pace of progress was so slow as to be barely detectable, but since the Industrial Revolution, the pace of advance and change has dramatically increased. Rapid change is now considered normal. For much of the world, new discoveries are continually expected and are not a surprise.

THE CONCEPT OF CIVILIZATION ADVANCES

As we said in **City Management Concepts**, scientific research is what drives your civilization's scientific and intellectual growth. The science (beaker icons) each city generates every turn represents a percentage of the total trade that city brings in. You can adjust the amount of science generated with the TAX RATE option on the KINGDOM menu. A low science ratio generates advances slowly; a high ratio generates them more quickly.

You want to accumulate research, in the form of beakers, to gain advances—new technologies. Each new advance allows your civilization to build new units or city improvements; sometimes a new advance makes possible the construction of a new Wonder of the World. Each new civilization advance also opens up a path to researching further technologies. You could look at the connections between advances as a flow chart (see the **Poster** for an example), as a web, or as a tree. The important concept is that each technology is a building block that allows research into further advances. You can even research into the realms of science fiction; each futuristic advance you discover adds bonus points to your final score, as we'll explain in **Future Technology**, coming right up.

Accumulated research isn't the only way to gain advances. Contact with a minor tribe might also net you a new civilization advance—see **Minor Tribes** for all the possible outcomes of an encounter. Finally, parley with other civilizations can result in an option to exchange technologies, and war offers the opportunity to wrest them by force from cities you subjugate. We'll give you the full details under **Diplomacy**.

The scientific research performed in each city you own is totaled in the SCIENCE ADVISOR's Report (see **The Advisors menu** in **Reference: Screen by Screen** for more about the Science Advisor and his duties). Each new advance that your civilization discovers "costs" a certain amount of science (accumulation of beakers). As time progresses, new advances require more funding to research. The SCIENCE ADVISOR's Report also lists the technologies you have already discovered or been given, and the current advance your scientists are researching.

CLIMBING THE TECHNOLOGY TREE

Once your civilization begins to accumulate scientific research, your Science Advisor asks you to choose a new civilization advance to research. Before making your choice, you can immediately get help concerning the available technologies. Press the GOAL button to see a list of all the advances in the game. Select the one you're most interested in pursuing, and click OK to find out which of the options you now have will further your research toward your goal. A message informs you if none of the options is suitable. Technologies you should be able to research but that are not on the current list of possibilities eventually show up (at a later choice-point). Once you have chosen a direction for your research, you cannot change your mind. Your scientists pursue that topic until they learn the new civilization advance. If you are unfamiliar with the advantages of a particular advance, highlight it and click on the HELP button to see the CIVILOPEDIA entry.

Advances are divided into five broad categories: Military, Economic, Social, Academic, and Applied. The icons in front of each advance show which category each advance belongs to. They can help you decide which advance will further your general strategy if you are, for instance, following a militaristic path, rather than an economic one. These icons also appear in the diplomatic screens, to help summarize the technology paths of your opponents.

When research is complete, your chief investigator announces the discovery. The CIVILOPEDIA screen appears, detailing the impact of the advance, including any new units, city improvements, and Wonders that have become available. The PRODUCTION menus in each CITY DISPLAY are immediately revised to include these new items wherever they are appropriate (for instance, inland cities can never build ships, so ship units never appear on their PRODUCTION menus, even if you have discovered Navigation or later seafaring advances).

As each new advance is acquired, your advisor appears again to ask for a new topic to research. The list of choices is updated with each new discovery to reflect your growing knowledge base. Technologies you acquire through means other than research (see **Diplomats & Spies** and **Minor Tribes** for details) no longer appear on the list of choices—you've already discovered them. If by chance you're given the civilization advance your scientists are currently researching, your Science Advisor immediately switches the research effort to a new topic of your choice—the accumulated beakers that represent research into the gift advance are transferred to the new topic.

THE POSTER

The **Poster** contains a graphic technology tree, or flowchart, that lists every civilization advance in *Civilization II*. For easier reference, advances are subdivided into the same four ages as Wonders of the World. The age of your civilization does not limit the advances you can research in any way.

Each entry on the chart gives the name of the advance and any new units, improvements, Wonders, or spaceship parts your civilization can now build as a result of this discovery. Some advances also allow your Settlers or Engineer units to undertake new orders.

Many technologies are the synergy of two diverse threads of inquiry. As a result, a second prerequisite advance might be listed in parentheses below the name of the current advance. By following the arrows along the chart, you can see that Alphabet leads to Mapmaking. By reading the second prerequisites, you can see that Mapmaking (along with Astronomy) leads to Navigation.

You can use this flowchart as a quick reference to what you want to discover next, or to plan an extensive research effort that culminates in an important technology like Railroad or Nuclear Fission. It can also remind you of advances you are ignoring.

FUTURE TECHNOLOGY

After your scientists discover the Fusion Power and Recycling advances, they can begin researching futuristic advances. These not-yet-imagined civilization advances are collectively known as "Future Tech." When your civilization accumulates enough scientific research (beakers) to finish one unit of Future Tech, you can research another. Each Future Tech you discover adds five points to your final score (see **Scoring** for other ways to boost your final total).

SPECIAL ADVANCE EFFECTS

A number of the advances in *Civilization II* have effects independent of the new units and improvements you can build. We'll summarize these effects here. Each advance's CIVILOPEDIA entry reminds you of these effects.

- Achieving the Corporation advance allows you to focus a city's production on revenue. The discovery of the Corporation advance allows your citizens to "build" the Capitalization improvement, and market a city's research to produce high-tech consumer goods that generate tax income.

- The discovery of the Democracy advance allows each Courthouse improvement to make one content citizen happy.

- Once your civilization discovers the Electronics advance, your Colosseums can make four unhappy people content in each city, not just three.

- The discovery of Fusion Power eliminates the possibility of a meltdown in your Nuclear Power Plants. In addition, it gives the Thrust Components of your spaceship 25 percent more power.

- Both Navigation and Seafaring reduce the chance of your Trireme units being lost at sea.

- Once your culture has embraced the Nuclear Power advance, all of your naval units gain one extra movement point.

- If you discover the Philosophy advance before any other civilization has done so, you earn a "free" advance.

- Once your civilization has achieved the Railroad advance, all your city squares are automatically upgraded from roads to railroads. It no longer costs any movement points to enter cities.

- Once your civilization has achieved the Refrigeration advance, all your city squares are automatically upgraded from irrigated land to farmland, if the terrain is suitable. Once you build the Supermarket improvement, your workers can harvest 50 percent more food from these spaces.

- The discovery of Theology makes your Cathedrals more influential. Instead of making three unhappy people per city content, a Cathedral now relieves four.

There is one disadvantageous special effect. Once you discover the advance of Communism, the effect of the Cathedral improvement (which discovering the Monotheism advance allows you to build) is lessened. Instead of making three unhappy people per city content, a Cathedral now only relieves two.

If your culture has discovered both Theology and Communism, the special effects cancel each other.

WONDERS OF THE WORLD

A Wonder of the World is a dramatic, awe-inspiring accomplishment. It is typically a great achievement of engineering, science, or the arts, representing a milestone in the history of humankind. As your civilization progresses through the years, certain advances make building Wonders of the World possible. Twenty-eight Wonders are included in *Civilization II*, seven each representing the four great epochs of civilization: the Ancient World, the Renaissance (including the High Middle Ages), the Industrial Revolution, and the Modern World (present and future). These Wonders are the extraordinary monuments of a civilization, bringing everlasting glory and other benefits to their owners.

THE CONCEPT OF WONDERS

Wonders of the World are like extraordinary city improvements, in that they are structures (or achievements) that your civilization can undertake to "build." Unlike city improvements, *each Wonder is unique, existing only in the city where it is constructed.* Each one confers a specific, unique benefit on the civilization that owns it (you can find the specifics in the CIVILOPEDIA listing for each Wonder). If one of your cities is captured by a rival power, and you had built a Wonder there, that Wonder no longer benefits your civilization. Instead, its bonuses now apply to the conquering civilization. The same holds true if your units capture a city containing a Wonder from a rival player.

If a Wonder is destroyed by the decimation of the city in which it stood, it can never be rebuilt. Its benefits are lost to the world forever. Further, some of the glories of the ancient and Renaissance Wonders dim over time. Objects and accomplishments that awed the ancients lose their luster for people of the Modern Age. *The achievement of later advances can negate the benefits of older Wonders,* regardless of whether your civilization or another discovers the canceling advance.

CONSTRUCTING WONDERS

You can build a Wonder only if you have discovered the advance that makes it possible, and if it does not already exist somewhere else in the world (if it exists in another

city, it won't appear as an option on your PRODUCTION menu). However, you can start construction of a Wonder even if another civilization is working on the same project—you just race to see who gets done first. A message warns you if another civilization's completion of a Wonder is imminent.

If you are building a Wonder in one of your cities and the same Wonder is completed elsewhere before you finish, you must convert your production to something else. Any excess shields you have accumulated beyond the number required to construct your new project are lost, so be careful what you choose. As you click on each potential project, you see a graphic representation of the shortfall or excess of shields you currently have with respect to the new project's requirements.

Wonders are not destroyed when an enemy captures the city in which they exist. However, if a city possessing a Wonder is destroyed (that is, if its population is reduced to zero by siege or bombardment), that Wonder is lost forever and cannot be rebuilt.

Wonders of the World are often long-term projects (as befits their magnificence). If you want to accomplish construction of a Wonder faster than the city that is building it can generate shields, you have several options. You can divert trade goods into the Wonder's coffers by moving a Caravan or Freight unit into the city of construction and accepting the choice HELP BUILD WONDER—see **Caravans & Freight** for details about Caravan interactions. You can also spend cash directly from your treasury. Click the BUY button at the top of the PRODUCTION menu; if you have enough cash on hand to purchase the Wonder, you can choose to pay, and the Wonder will be completed next turn. In addition, you can disband troops currently in the city that is constructing the Wonder. Each disbanded unit contributes shields equal to one-half its construction cost directly to the RESOURCE BOX, representing the reallocation of support from the unit to the construction.

Wonders can be built in any city and more than one may be built in the same city. Each Wonder has both specific and general benefits. You can read about the specific benefits in the appropriate CIVILOPEDIA entry. The glory that accrues to your civilization for possessing a Wonder is one of the general benefits conferred by such great works; more importantly, this glory continues to accrue even if new advances make the Wonder's specific benefit obsolete. In addition, each Wonder that your civilization possesses adds to your *Civilization II* score. The presence of Wonders is significant to the calculations determining the top five cities in the world. Further, the presence of Wonders influences historians, such as Gibbon, who periodically rate the world's civilizations. Finally, Wonders also sway your people to improve your throne room (see **Throne Room** for the particulars).

UNITS

Units are groups of citizens, soldiers, and envoys that can move around the world of *Civilization II* and interact with other units and civilizations. Some non-combat units, like Caravans, Explorers, and Settlers, have special functions which are explained separately.

UNIT CONCEPTS

Units are the pieces you move around on the map in *Civilization II*. Each civilization's units carry a different color shield. Units carrying red shields are always barbarians.

Units can be divided into types according to the way they move: ground (or land) units, air units, and naval (or sea) units. Each unit has statistics for attack strength, defense strength, and movement points. These stats are listed in a shorthand, code-like set of numbers, which we've already mentioned is called the ADM—this stands for Attack/Defense/Movement. You can find each unit's ADM numbers in the CIVILOPEDIA. In addition, each unit—even non-combat units—has statistics for hit points and firepower, which are also found in the CIVILOPEDIA. The strength bar at the top of a unit's shield indicates how many hit points that unit currently has, both by its length and by its color.

Attack strength shows the likelihood of inflicting damage when attacking an opponent. Units with a high attack strength are useful for offensives in which they are attacking.

Defense strength represents the ability of a unit to defend itself when attacked; it is the likelihood that damage will be inflicted on an attacking unit. Units with high defense strength are useful for defending cities and other positions against enemy troops. The terrain on which a unit stands can increase its defensive strength, as you'll find in **Terrain & Movement**.

Movement points indicate how far a unit can travel—or how many times a unit can attack—in a turn; they're explained in detail in **Terrain & Movement**, too.

Hit points indicate how much damage a unit can withstand before it is destroyed. Units with a greater number of hit points can absorb more damage in combat. A green strength bar indicates that a unit has more than two-thirds of its hit points remaining, a yellow strength bar means the unit has between one-third and two-thirds of its hit points, and a red strength bar shows that a unit has less than one-third of its total hit points remaining. Hit points can be restored by skipping turns, especially in cities with repair facilities.

Firepower indicates how much damage a unit can inflict in a round of combat. Units with a high firepower pack a powerful wallop.

A unit's status is important when you want to give it orders. Units can be on *active status*, which means they blink each time they become the active unit. Units on *sleep status* remain inactive until an enemy unit comes within one square of them. At this point, they "wake up" and become active. Units on *fortified status* are also inactive —their status is indicated by the letter "F" on the unit's shield, and by the brown "entrenchment" icon which appears around the base of the unit—in fact, they are entrenched in a defensive posture. They remain inactive even if rival units approach them. Clicking on either a sleeping or fortified unit allows you to change its status to active. When the unit becomes the active unit, you can give it new orders.

Every unit has an *observation factor*. Most units can only "see" units and objects on the edges of the terrain squares directly adjacent to their own. Early in the game, when most of the map is black, the limits of this observation area are obvious, as the blackness rolls back only so far with each move a unit makes. Even after you have explored a continent, barbarians and rival units can appear "out of nowhere" because they are lingering outside the limits of your units' observation.

Some advanced units have greater observation factors. They can "see" into a second square in all directions, which makes them useful for monitoring rival's movements and anticipating surprise attacks. Exceptional observation factors are noted in unit descriptions in the CIVILOPEDIA.

MILITARY UNITS

Through the years, the majority of your time is spent moving and positioning armies. A strong military is the best defense against rivals and barbarians. Military units are also the eyes of your civilization, exploring the world as they move. Finally, they can serve you offensively by defeating the armies of your rivals and capturing their cities.

Armies can be ground units (Legions, Cannons, and Armor, for example), naval units (Triremes, Ironclads, Battleships, etc.), or air units (Fighters, Bombers, and Nuclear missiles). Several non-combat units need further explanation, so they're discussed in detail a little later. All units, whether they are combat or non-combat oriented, are described in the MILITARY UNITS option of the CIVILOPEDIA.

GROUND UNITS

The majority of *Civilization II*'s units are ground units. These armies move over the map terrain square by terrain square. They spend movement points according to the type of terrain they are entering, observe movement restrictions like zones of control, and attack rival units when you move them into a square containing an enemy army. Most ground units have an observation of one square.

PILLAGE

Armies can strip the countryside through which they roam of any improvements any Settlers or Engineer units have built, tearing up roads, trampling crops, and collapsing mines. The occupying army destroys your choice of one improvement each time you press Shift P, or choose PILLAGE from the ORDERS menu. It takes one turn to pillage one improvement.

AIR UNITS

Air units operate under some special movement rules. These units can cross any terrain square at a cost of one movement point per square. Because they are airborne, they get no bonus for crossing squares improved by roads or railroads. All air units except missiles have an observation range of two squares in any terrain.

Most air units must end their movement in a friendly city with an airport, at an Airbase, or on a Carrier unit, as these are the only areas where they can safely land. Bombers and Stealth Bombers must land for refueling every second turn, giving them effective ranges of 16 (8 out and 8 back) and 24 (12 out and 12 back), respectively. Bombers and Stealth Bombers can only attack once, regardless of their remaining movement points. In addition, attacking uses all a unit's remaining movement points for the turn. Therefore, if you attack during a Bomber or Stealth Bomber's return flight, it does not have enough movement points to return home safely, and it crashes and disappears. Fighters and Stealth Fighters can attack targets as many times as they have movement points. However, be sure you save enough movement after the attack to return to a landing area, or your pilots kamikaze!

Both missile units are one-shot attackers; the icons represent missiles that are spent in the aggression. If you have miscounted the number of squares to your destination, or another unit's movement or position prevents a missile unit from reaching a target city or unit, you can attempt to return the missile to a friendly city or Airbase, or to a Submarine or Carrier unit. If your missile gets stranded—that is, there is no target unit or city within reach, and no safe landing area—the missile is a dud that falls to earth harmlessly. It disappears from the game.

If a city is the target of a Cruise missile attack, the strongest military unit defends against it (the unit in that city with the largest defense factor). There is no collateral damage to city improvements from Cruise missile attacks. If a city is the target of a Nuclear missile attack, half of the population is destroyed. All military units in and adjacent to the target square are destroyed as well, regardless of the civilization to which they belong. If a military unit or stack of units is the target, all units in the stack are destroyed. In addition to the loss of units, all land terrain squares adjacent to the impact square become polluted.

Helicopters are unique air units in that they don't need to return to a base for refueling, giving them an unlimited movement range similar to a ground unit. However, every turn a Helicopter starts in the field—not taking off from a friendly city, Airbase or Carrier—it suffers a small amount of damage. Eventually, it must return to a friendly city or Airbase for repairs. A Helicopter can only make one attack per turn; attacking uses all remaining movement points for that turn.

NAVAL UNITS

Naval units also adhere to some special rules. Some naval units have the capacity to carry passengers—ground units. These include Triremes, Caravels, Galleons, Frigates, and Transports. Carriers can only transport air units. Submarines can only transport missile units. When two ships occupy the same square, the one that leaves first takes up to its carrying capacity of passenger units with it.

Most naval units can conduct shore bombardments—that is, they can attack units standing on the coastal squares of continents and islands. Because of the high degree of inaccuracy, the firepower of both the ship and its target is reduced to one when a ship bombards a unit, city, or stack on shore. Submarine and Transport units cannot conduct shore bombardments at all.

Battleships, Carriers, Cruisers, Destroyers, and Submarines have enhanced observation ranges at sea. Each can "see" enemy ships and planes from two ocean squares away. Rival Submarine units are the only exception to this rule, as their ability to travel underwater camouflages them from most units' view (it likewise conceals your Subs from your enemies), unless the Submarine is attacking the observing unit. Destroyers, Cruisers, AEGIS Cruisers, and Helicopters can all spot Submarines if they are adjacent to them. Note that Submarines cannot spot rival Submarines!

COMBAT

Combat occurs when a unit attempts to enter a map square occupied by a unit or city of another civilization—unless the unit is a Diplomat or Spy, in which case it can offer bribes to units or conduct a variety of business in cities—or unless the unit is a Caravan or Freight unit, in which case it can establish a trade route when it enters a city. Everybody else just fights. Battles are resolved immediately.

Most battles result in the destruction of one army or the other. When more than one unit occupies the defender's square, the unit with the highest defensive strength (as determined by comparing the second digit in the units' ADM numbers, and making allowance for veteran status) defends. If it loses, then all other armies stacked with it are destroyed as well. However, stacked units taking advantage of Fortress improvements or taking cover in city squares are destroyed one at a time.

THE EFFECT OF DAMAGE

Successful attackers which have movement points remaining after combat can continue moving normally—and even continue attacking—if they choose. However, successful attackers often sustain damage in each battle. As a unit is damaged, its

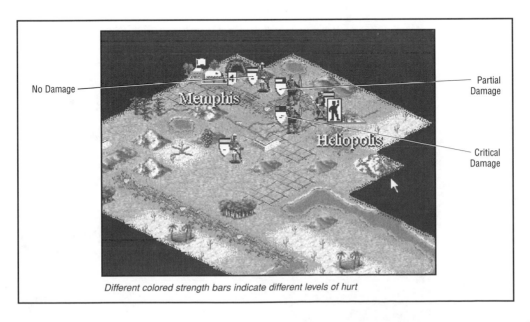

No Damage

Partial
Damage

Critical
Damage

Different colored strength bars indicate different levels of hurt

strength bar gets shorter and eventually changes color. Both the length of the strength bar and its color are significant. When a unit is reduced to approximately two-thirds of its full strength, the strength bar changes from green to yellow. When a unit's hit points are reduced to around one-third of its full strength, the bar changes from yellow to red.

In addition to losing strength, damaged units also lose mobility. A unit's damage is factored into its movement allowance, so a unit which has sustained damage of 30 percent only has 70 percent of its movement points. For example, if the damaged unit normally had three movement points, damage of 30 percent would reduce its movement to two (even though it would still have a green strength bar). There are two important exceptions to this rule: naval units are never reduced below two movement points per turn, and air units do not suffer reduced movement at all.

CALCULATING THE WINNER

Combat in *Civilization II* is essentially like a rapid-fire boxing match. Units fight one-on-one in rounds, with damage equal to the firepower of the winner being subtracted from the hit points of the loser of each round. When one unit loses all its hit points, it is destroyed. If the loser is defending a stack of units and they are not inside a Fortress or a city, the whole stack is destroyed.

The important factors in combat are the attack and defense strengths of the combatants, as well as their hit points and firepower, the presence of veteran units on either side, the terrain occupied by the defender, and any defensive improvements in the square. In addition to considering all of these factors, combat also includes an element of chance. Imagine that sometimes a unit just gets lucky. We don't want to drag you through lots of heavy arithmetic for each combination of factors, but the calculations for each round of combat can be boiled down to a simple comparison.

The total modified attack and defense factors are combined and the probability of either side winning is approximately the ratio of each side's factor compared to this total. For example, if an Elephant (attack factor 4) attacks a Phalanx (defense factor 2), the total of the factors is 6 (4 + 2). The Elephant has about a 66 percent chance of winning (4 out of 6) and the Phalanx about a 33 percent chance (2 out of 6).

Both the Elephant and the Phalanx have 10 hit points and a firepower of one, so the battle goes between 10 and 19 rounds, until one or the other unit is reduced to zero hit points. It is possible for one opponent to win every round and take no damage at all, and it is possible for the opponents to trade damage for damage until even the eventual winner is badly beaten up. Most combats fall somewhere in the middle.

ADDING IN ADJUSTMENTS

How do those adjustments for veteran status and terrain and so on work? They're added into each factor they affect before the total is determined. For instance, if both units are veterans, each gets a 50 percent bonus to attack and defense, giving the Elephant an attack factor of 6 (4 + 2) and the Phalanx a defense factor of 3 (2 + 1). Of course, modifying each unit's factors also changes the total: instead of 6, it is 9 (the total of each modified factor, 6 + 3). Now the odds are close to 6 out of 9 for the Elephant and about 3 out of 9 for the Phalanx.

If both are veterans and the Phalanx is behind City Walls (which triples a unit's defense factor, making the veteran Phalanx a 9), the odds are about 6 out of 15 for the Elephant and close to 9 out of 15 for the Phalanx. Though the adjustments change the odds of each unit winning a single round, they have no affect on the total number of rounds or on the amount of damage inflicted.

There are a number of special combat situations, which have special rules, detailed below.

AIR BATTLES

Only Fighters and Stealth Fighters can attack Bomber or Stealth Bomber units. In fact, Bombers and Stealth Bombers prevent enemy units (other than Fighters and Stealth Fighters) from even entering, much less attacking, the square they occupy.

When a Fighter or Stealth Fighter attacks a Helicopter unit, the Helicopter's disadvantage is represented by reducing its firepower to one and reducing its defense factor by 50 percent.

When a Fighter or Stealth Fighter is stationed in a city that is attacked by a Bomber or Stealth Bomber, the defending units scramble, gaining a defense factor four times their normal value. However, they gain no additional protection from SAM Missile Batteries (because the SAMs don't want to down their own planes).

AIR DEFENSE

When an AEGIS Cruiser is attacked by air units, it gains defense bonuses: its defense factor is tripled against plane or Helicopter attacks, and it is quintupled (x5) against missile attacks.

CITY ATTACKS

A successful ground attack on a city destroys only one defending unit at a time. However, each successful attack also reduces the population of the city by one point unless the city is protected by City Walls. Population loss does not result from naval or air attack, but is caused by a nuclear strike.

CITY DEFENSES

The City Walls improvement triples the defense strength of units within against all ground units except Howitzers, and it protects a city's population from reduction. The Coastal Fortress doubles the defense strength of all units within a city against shore bombardments by enemy ships. The SAM Missile Battery doubles the defense strength of all units within the city against all air units except Nuclear missiles. See **Nuclear Attacks** for the scoop on SDI Defense improvements.

FORTRESSES

Units within a Fortress gain significant advantages. A unit stationed within a Fortress doubles its defensive strength, and stacked units are destroyed one at a time. Settlers or Engineer units can build Fortresses on any terrain square (except a city square) once your civilization has discovered the Construction advance; see **Settlers & Engineers** for the complete scoop.

NUCLEAR ATTACKS

Nuclear attacks occur when a Nuclear unit attempts to enter a square occupied by enemy units or an enemy city. A Spy unit can make a suicide bomber attack by smuggling a Nuclear device into an enemy city, regardless of the presence of an SDI Defense city improvement. In any case, all units in the target square and adjacent squares are destroyed, regardless of their cultural allegiance (in other words, both theirs and yours). In addition, a bombed city loses half of its population. The defense against most nuclear attacks is the SDI Defense city improvement.

An SDI Defense improvement is like an umbrella that extends three squares from a city in any direction. The city and all units and improvements within this radius (including Airports, Fortresses, and other city squares) are protected from all effects of a direct Nuclear missile attack, other than the suicidal bomber Spy mentioned previously.

PEARL HARBOR

When air units or ground units attack ships in port (naval units defend a city against air units), the attackers' firepower is doubled against the defending units and the defender's firepower is reduced to one, to represent the defenders' vulnerability. Air units also pick off city defenders one at a time, except for Nuclear missiles (see **Nuclear Attacks**, above).

SHORE BOMBARDMENTS

Other than Submarines, any naval units with an attack factor greater than zero can attack enemy units on adjacent land squares (they are conducting shore bombardments). Cities along the coastline are vulnerable to shore bombardments, too. Naval units can defend the cities they occupy against attack, though their firepower is reduced to one because of their limited maneuverability.

CARAVANS & FREIGHT

Caravan units represent shipments of trade goods and materials. Though the icon remains a camel, as history progresses, your Caravan units are stand-ins for the continuum of trade vehicles from camel caravans to wagon trains. They can be used to establish trade routes between cities or to transfer resources for the construction of Wonders of the World. Caravans become available once you have achieved the advance of Trade.

Once your civilization has discovered The Corporation, the Freight unit replaces the Caravan unit on the PRODUCTION menu. Freight units have two movement points a turn. They represent the modern movement of goods and materials by truck convoys and cargo containers.

TRADE ROUTES

A Caravan or Freight unit can establish a trade route by entering any city, even a rival's city. Your treasury gains an immediate cash payment for delivery of the first load of goods, and your research scientists gain an immediate bonus for cultural exchange of an equal amount of science (beakers). The home city of the Caravan or Freight unit gains an increase in the trade generated each turn, which represents a continuing economic relationship. A listing in the GENERAL INFORMATION window shows the cities with which trade routes have been established and the amount of bonus trade generated every turn. The bonus is added to the total amount of trade your city produces, so that indirectly this boosts your research, tax, and luxury production in that city.

Each city can have up to three functioning trade routes, one for each commodity the city produces. As each route is established, the commodity traded on that route is enclosed in parentheses, to indicate a successful deal. Thereafter, when a Caravan is completed, loads of that commodity are no longer available. Food loads are always available.

The amount of trade generated by a trade route depends greatly on supply and demand, and partly on the size of the two cities. Bigger cities generate more trade. Trade with a city from another civilization is of greater value than trade with friendly cities. The farther apart the two cities are, the greater the bonus for trading between them. Trade bonuses also increase when the cities are on different continents. If you capture a rival city with whom you were previously trading, the trade route remains active. However, the amount of trade it generates is reduced, because items which were once exotic imports have become domestic commodities.

Caravans and Freight can enter any city they can reach. They are not hampered by movement restrictions like zones of control, but their ADM numbers are low enough that they might find it difficult to smuggle goods into an enemy city without being destroyed. Caravan and Freight units can take advantage of naval transport to trade overseas (you can load them aboard any ship that carries units), and they can disembark into a city directly from a ship.

SUPPLY & DEMAND

Each city in the game can supply three commodities because of their local abundance. Similarly, each demands three other commodities which are in short supply thereabouts. While a Caravan or Freight unit can deliver goods to any city, it gains the largest profits from delivering a commodity to a community that demands it. You can check the marketplace wisdom by clicking the SUPPLY & DEMAND button at the bottom of the TRADE ADVISOR's Report. A list of commodities appears. Choose the commodity in which you're interested, then click OK. A second list shows all known cities that supply the item and all known cities that demand it. The list is updated to reflect your exploration and contact with other cultures.

FOOD CARAVANS

A fourth and always available option for trade goods is food. You can transfer one food per turn to another city by sending a load of food from a city with a surplus to a city that needs help. A needy city can be on the receiving end of more than one food route. Once a food route is established, it cannot be countermanded. It is automatically canceled, however, if the sending city runs out of food for its own people.

BUILDING WONDERS

A Caravan or Freight unit can contribute shields equal to its construction cost to any Wonder of the World you are undertaking. Simply move your Caravan or Freight unit into the city in which construction of a Wonder is underway. A dialog box offers you the choice of contributing to the construction. If you decide to help build the Wonder, your Caravan or Freight unit disappears and its worth is added to the production of the Wonder, speeding its completion. If you divert goods to help build a Wonder, they are still available later to establish a trade route.

DIPLOMATS & SPIES

Diplomats are unique units that can act as ambassadors, envoys, secret agents, and saboteurs. They can open contacts with other civilizations and establish embassies to gather information about your rivals. They can steal information and otherwise disrupt your rivals. They can bribe enemy armies. Stationing Diplomat or Spy units in your own cities reduces the effectiveness of enemy Diplomats and Spies. When your civilization obtains the advance of Writing, you can build Diplomats.

Be aware that enemy Diplomats can use all the same techniques against your civilization as you use against theirs.

Once your civilization has developed the Espionage advance, the Spy unit replaces the Diplomat unit on the PRODUCTION menu. A Spy is superior to a Diplomat in several ways. Her greater sophistication and more elaborate training allow her to choose a specific technology or target improvement when entering a city intent on mischief. In addition, she can travel more rapidly, moving up to three squares a turn, regardless of the terrain. A Spy has an observation range of two squares in every direction. When a Spy successfully completes a mission, she has a chance of escaping and returning to the nearest friendly city. The easier the mission, the greater the chance that she will escape. For instance, stealing a random civilization advance is easier than stealing a specific one. Finally, Spies have the unique ability to plant nuclear devices in enemy cities, as we'll explain in **Entering Enemy Cities**.

BRIBING ENEMY UNITS

You might convince an enemy unit to defect and join your civilization. Only units of civilizations governed by Democracy are completely immune to bribery.

In game terms, simply move a Diplomat or Spy into a square occupied by a single enemy unit (neither Diplomats nor Spies can bribe units that are stacked together).

A dialog box appears, showing how much gold the unit demands to defect. If the unit is immune to bribery, a dialog box will remind you of this condition.

The farther a unit is from its capital, the less gold is required. If you accept, the gold is deducted from your treasury and the army switches sides (becomes your color). The Diplomat or Spy survives the discussion regardless of his or her success in negotiating; however, if you do not choose to pay the bribe, the enemy unit might attack your negotiator later. Diplomats and Spies can bribe naval and air units as long as these are not stacked with other units.

The nearest friendly city becomes the home city for a newly bribed unit (see **Unit Roster** for information on this point).

COUNTERESPIONAGE

Diplomats and Spies stationed in friendly cities have a chance to thwart "steal technology" attempts by enemy Diplomats and Spies. Each Diplomat has a 20 percent chance to do so per attempt. Spies have a 40 percent chance; veteran Spies have a 60 percent chance of catching their fellow envoys. Getting caught ends the interloper's turn.

ENTERING ENEMY CITIES

Diplomats and Spies can slip past enemy armies without pausing to observe zones of control, using superior powers of persuasion and/or diplomatic immunity as a shield. Diplomats and Spies are also subject to *deportation* (a special form of "attack") even from civilizations with which they are not at war. Any military unit can "attack" a Diplomat or Spy from a civilization with which it is at peace, provided that the envoy is nearer to a city of the military unit's culture than to one of its own cities. The offending envoy is returned to friendly territory. Diplomats and Spies can travel overseas in ships as do other ground units.

Diplomats and Spies are two of only four units that can enter defended enemy cities (Caravans and Freight are the other two). A menu listing the tasks a Diplomat or Spy can perform appears whenever you send your envoy on an urban mission. If, after you've looked over your choices, you decide not to take any action, click the CANCEL button to back out of the menu. Each task is fully explained below.

INTERNATIONAL INCIDENTS

Whenever a Diplomat or Spy *successfully* steals technology, sabotages a city improvement, poisons the water supply, or incites a revolt in a city of a civilization with whom you have signed a treaty, an international incident almost inevitably occurs. Your victim is likely to treat your treachery as an act of war, although a victim with whom you are allied may sometimes choose to disregard your act. In addition, if you are governing your civilization as a Republic or Democracy, there might be domestic repercussions as well. Your government may collapse into Anarchy when the scandal reaches the Senate floor.

Do not confuse international incidents with a Spy's ability to escape unharmed after a mission—the two events are completely independent. The only times when incidents do not occur are when you are already at war with your victim and when the Diplomat or Spy fails in its mission.

INVESTIGATE CITY

Your Diplomat or Spy unit gathers information about the rival city's production and development. In game terms, this option shows you the enemy's CITY DISPLAY. You can examine what armies are defending the city and what improvements have been built there. When you exit the CITY DISPLAY, you return to the MAP window. Your Diplomat has been eliminated, or your Spy has been charged one-third of a movement point for her efforts. There is no possibility that your envoy is detected. Until the end of the turn, you may click on the city again at any time to review the knowledge you have gained.

ESTABLISH EMBASSY

Your Diplomat or Spy unit establishes official contact with the rival civilization, setting up an office in the city to which you sent him or her. If you sent a Diplomat, he stays there to head the office, so the icon disappears; if you sent a Spy, she has been charged one-third of a movement point for her efforts. There is no possibility of international embarrassment. In game terms, you can access information about your rival's type of government, treasury, number of armies, the name of its capital city, treaties with other civilizations, diplomatic states, and technological advances whenever you look at your FOREIGN MINISTER's Report (see **Advisors** for the complete scoop). It is only necessary to establish an embassy once with any particular civilization.

STEAL ADVANCE

Your Diplomat or Spy attempts to steal one civilization advance from a rival civilization. In game terms, a Diplomat can only confiscate one advance per city. A Spy can make more than one attempt per city, although her chance of capture increases with every additional mission. If you send a Spy, she has the option to try the more difficult task of filching a specific advance from the list of unique technologies your rival has.

Even if he succeeds, a Diplomat disappears in the process (his cover is blown). If she evades capture, a Spy returns to the closest friendly city and is promoted to veteran status for her work. While veteran status cannot improve her ADM rating of zero defense, it does increase her chances of escaping detection on later missions.

If you have already stolen a civilization advance from this particular city, or if the enemy civilization has discovered no technology worth stealing, and your envoy is undetected, a Diplomat unit loses its turn but is not destroyed. If the enemy civilization has discovered no technology worth stealing, a Spy remains empty-handed. The only way a Spy can fail to steal an advance is if she has opted to confiscate a particular technology.

INDUSTRIAL SABOTAGE

Carefully maneuvering in the back streets, your envoy manages to infiltrate some critical city organization or defense. In game terms, your Diplomat or Spy destroys either whatever item the rival city currently has under production or one of the rival city's existing improvements—the item targeted is a matter of random chance. If you send a Spy, she has the option to try the more difficult task of destroying a specific target from the list of existing improvements that city has.

Regardless of his success, a Diplomat is lost in the effort (think mad, suicidal bombers if it helps). If your Spy is not captured, she returns to the closest friendly city and is promoted to veteran status for her work. While veteran status cannot improve her ADM rating of zero defense, it does increase her chances of escaping detection on later missions. The only way a Spy can fail to complete her sabotage is if you have opted to destroy a particular improvement.

If your envoy destroys a critical improvement, it might throw the city into unrest (Temple, Cathedral), weaken its defenses (City Walls, Coastal Fortress), or cut its production (Factory, Solar Plant). Diplomats and Spies never destroy Wonders of the World.

INCITE A REVOLT

Your Diplomat or Spy contacts dissidents within a city and provides the necessary means for them to overthrow their current regime. In game terms, for a suitable payment, the city revolts and joins your civilization. The amount needed to finance a revolt depends on the size of the city and its proximity to the enemy civilization's capital. If you wish to avoid an international incident, you must subvert the city by paying double the listed amount, as the dialog box warns.

Enemy capitals never agree to revolt, and neither do cities in a Democracy. Cities with Courthouses cost twice as much to bribe. Cities under Communism tend to remain expensive to bribe even when they are situated far from their capital. Also, it costs less to push a city already in civil disorder into open revolt than it does to undermine a contented city.

A Diplomat is lost in a successful revolt (he stays to organize the new government). A Spy returns to the closest friendly city if she is not captured, after appointing a new city government. A successful Spy is promoted to veteran status.

If you don't have enough cash to finance the project, your envoy doesn't even attempt to incite the natives. He or she escapes outside the city if you refuse to pay the cost.

If the overthrow is successful, all units within one square of the revolting city that belong to that rival civilization also revolt and join your regime. All other rival units who counted that city as home are disbanded. All existing city improvements except Temples and Cathedrals remain intact.

POISON THE WATER SUPPLY

Only Spies can attempt to weaken the resistance of a rival city by poisoning the water supply. In game terms, a successful attempt reduces the target city's population by one point. If your Spy is successful and undetected, she discards her environment suit and returns to the closest friendly city for promotion to veteran status.

PLANT NUCLEAR DEVICE

Only Spies can attempt to plant nuclear devices in rival cities. In game terms, this is the only way to nuke a city protected by the SDI Defense improvement. This is the most difficult mission to accomplish, and the likelihood of capture is high. Furthermore, there is the possibility that your Spy will be caught red-handed, causing a major international incident. If this happens, every civilization in the world will declare war on you, appalled by your atrocity (unless you have a Fundamentalist government).

SETTLERS & ENGINEERS

Settlers are groups of your most resourceful and adventurous citizens. As independent pioneers, they perform two critical functions for your civilization; they found new cities and they serve as civil engineers, improving the terrain for your empire's benefit. After your civilization develops the Explosives advance, the Engineer unit replaces the Settlers unit on the PRODUCTION menu. These industrial-era citizens have better training and better equipment than your basic Settlers unit. Engineers can accomplish all the same tasks as Settlers can, and they can perform them twice as quickly. In addition, Engineers have the unique ability to Transform formerly unimprovable terrain like Desert, Glacier, and Mountains squares.

Your civilization produces Settlers and Engineers in the same manner as it does any other unit, with one caveat. When one of these units is completed, the population of the city that produced it is reduced by one point (one citizen on the POPULATION ROSTER), representing the emigration of these pioneers. If a city has only one population point when it completes the task of building a Settlers or Engineer unit, the city disappears when its population is absorbed into the new unit. This is one of the only ways to eliminate a city that is in a poor or inconvenient location.

FOUNDING NEW CITIES & INCREASING EXISTING ONES

To found a new city, move a Settlers or Engineer unit to the desired location and press the BUILD B key, or choose BUILD NEW CITY from the ORDERS menu. The unit disappears as the people it represents become the first population point of the new city.

The ADD TO CITY order can be used to increase the size of an existing city with less than 10 population points. Move a Settlers or Engineer unit into an existing city and press the BUILD B key or choose ADD TO CITY from the ORDERS menu. The unit is absorbed into the city, adding one point to its population.

MAKING IMPROVEMENTS

Settlers, and later Engineers, can make a number of agricultural and industrial improvements to your civilization's topography. Each task takes a certain number of turns to complete, depending on the terrain being improved. Some improvements can only be undertaken after your civilization has acquired certain technologies. Engineers, being better trained and equipped, can accomplish tasks twice as fast as Settlers. Engineers are also the only units that can Transform terrain. Teamwork makes these units work faster. You can combine Settlers and/or Engineers to accomplish tasks more rapidly. For example, two Settlers units work twice as rapidly as one, and three can accomplish a task in one-third the standard time. One Settlers unit and an Engineer can also accomplish a task in one-third the standard time, since the Engineer naturally works faster than the Settlers.

There is no limit to the number of times your Settlers or Engineers can build new improvements on any given terrain square—if the changing needs of your civilization demand clearing, irrigation, reforestation, clearing, pollution clean-up (detoxification), and reforestation in succession, the land can take it. If an option is grayed out on the ORDERS menu, that task cannot be accomplished at this time. Perhaps undertaking another improvement will make the desired option available in the future. For instance, a Plains square surrounded by Forest has no access to water and cannot be irrigated. You'll need to clear at least one of the adjacent Forests (one that shares a side with the target square) and irrigate it, before irrigation becomes available to the target square.

We've extracted all the variations into a table which lists the task, the shortcut key, the required advance, if any, and the terrain types which benefit from this improvement. Full explanations of each activity appear after the table.

TASK	SHORTCUT KEY	REQUIRED ADVANCE	TERRAINS THAT BENEFIT
Irrigate	$\boxed{I}$	–	Desert, Grassland, Hills, Plains, River
Clear	$\boxed{I}$	–	Forest, Jungle, Swamp
Build Farm	$\boxed{I}$	Refrigeration	Any Irrigated Land Square
Build Fortress	$\boxed{F}$	Construction	Any Land Square
Mine	$\boxed{M}$	–	Desert, Hills, Mountains
Reforest	$\boxed{M}$	–	Grassland, Jungle, Plains, Swamp
Clean up	$\boxed{P}$	–	Any Polluted Land Square
Build Road	$\boxed{R}$	–	Any Land Square
Build Railroad	$\boxed{R}$	Railroad	Any Road Square
Transform	$\boxed{O}$	Explosives	Any Land Square
Build Airbase	$\boxed{E}$	Radio	Any Land Square

IRRIGATE

Depending on the form of government employed by your civilization, irrigation can improve the agricultural production of a city's relatively level terrain. A suitable square can be irrigated if it shares one side (diagonal doesn't count) with a source of water (Ocean square or terrain with a river running through it) or another irrigated square. Although your city square might be irrigated when the city is founded, it does not count as a source of water for further irrigation. Sometimes you might find it necessary to irrigate squares to which your city has no access in order to extend irrigation into squares the city uses. When your Settlers or Engineer unit is positioned in the appropriate terrain square, choose the BUILD IRRIGATION option on the ORDERS menu or press the $\boxed{I}$ key.

CLEAR

Clearing terrain improves the movement point cost of dense terrain (although it eliminates the defensive bonus), and provides land suitable to further improvement through irrigation or reforestation. Sometimes a terrain square might need to be cleared to allow for irrigation access, and later reforested to restore valuable resources. When your Settlers or Engineer unit is positioned in the appropriate terrain square, choose the CHANGE TO GRASSLAND (sometimes CHANGE TO PLAINS) option on the ORDERS menu or press the $\boxed{I}$ key.

BUILD FARM

Planting market gardens and other high-yield farmland is the post-industrial farmer's task. Once your civilization has discovered the Refrigeration advance, Settlers or Engineer units can intensify the food output of irrigated land by another 50 percent in cities that build the Supermarket improvement. When your Settlers or Engineer unit is positioned in the appropriate terrain square, choose the IMPROVE FARMLAND option on the ORDERS menu or press the $\boxed{I}$ key.

BUILD FORTRESS

Building Fortresses can be essential for defense of terrain that is not a city site. Fortresses provide a defensive bonus to rural or frontier units in the same way the City Walls improvement benefits urban defensive units (see **Combat** for the full details). In addition, representative governments can station troops in Fortresses that are within three squares of a friendly city without incurring a field service penalty (see **Happiness & Civil Disorder** for complete details). Once your tribe has discovered the Construction advance, this option becomes available in the ORDERS menu. When your Settlers or Engineer unit is positioned in the appropriate terrain square, choose the BUILD FORTRESS option or press the F key.

MINE

Mining terrain allows full utilization of the natural resources present. It is especially useful in special terrain like Coal and Gold. When your Settlers or Engineer unit is positioned in the appropriate terrain square, choose the BUILD MINE option on the ORDERS menu or press the M key.

REFOREST

Reforestation improves the shield production of most terrain (though it increases the movement point cost of open terrain if there is no road or railroad through the square). Reforesting Plains and Grassland squares also improves their defensive bonus. When your Settlers or Engineer unit is positioned in the appropriate terrain square, choose the CHANGE TO FOREST option on the ORDERS menu or press the M key.

CLEAN UP POLLUTION

Detoxifying squares by cleaning up the pollution there restores the full (pre-pollution) production capacity to the affected squares. A long-term benefit of cleanup is the reduced chance of global warming, which might otherwise occur (see **Terrain & Movement** for details). Both industrial pollution and nuclear contamination can be eliminated by cleanup efforts. When your Settlers or Engineer unit is positioned in the appropriate terrain square, choose the CLEAN UP POLLUTION option on the ORDERS menu or press the P key.

BUILD ROAD

Building roads across terrain reduces the movement point cost of that square by one-third, provided that the moving unit enters from an adjacent road square. Depending on the form of government under which you civilization operates, it can also improve the trade production of the square. Roads are the foundations for railroads. When your Settlers or Engineer unit is positioned in the appropriate terrain square, choose the BUILD ROAD option on the ORDERS menu or press the R key.

BUILD RAILROAD

Laying track across terrain eliminates the movement point cost of that square, providing the moving unit enters from an adjacent railroad square. Railroads also increase shield production by 50 percent, rounded down. You can only build railroads where you have already built roads. When your Settlers or Engineer unit is positioned in the appropriate terrain square, choose the BUILD RAILROAD option on the ORDERS menu or press the R key.

TRANSFORM

Modern equipment and engineering techniques allow workers to transform even the most inhospitable land into a productive terrain. Once your civilization has discovered the Explosives advance, this option becomes available to your Engineer units. When your Engineer unit is positioned in the appropriate terrain square, choose the TRANSFORM option on the ORDERS menu or press the ⓞ key.

BUILD AIRBASE

Building rural airbases allows your air units more flexibility in their flight plans and enables them to patrol a greater area. Once your civilization has discovered the Radio advance, this option becomes available on the ORDERS menu. When your Settlers or Engineer unit is positioned in the appropriate terrain square, choose the BUILD AIRBASE option or press the Ⓔ key.

AUTOMATED SETTLERS

If you tire of giving orders to your Settlers and Engineer units, you can turn control over to a subordinate—a friendly AI. Use the new AUTOMATE SETTLER Ⓚ order to put the unit "on automatic" for a while. Automated units improve the terrain around your cities, but will not establish any new cities. In some situations (the approach of an enemy unit, for instance), the unit might need instructions from you. At those time, the automated unit will revert to your control.

EXPLORERS

Explorers are non-combat units that treat all terrain as roads. Their bravery and resourcefulness makes them ideal for opening up new continents and discovering the far reaches of a landmass quickly. Explorers can ignore enemy units' zones of control; however, for diplomatic purposes (peace treaties and alliances) your rivals consider Explorers as dangerous as they do combat units.

BARBARIANS

Barbarians are small tribes of raiders that are not part of any opposing civilization. They always carry red shields. You can set the likelihood and frequency of barbarian attacks in the initial game choices you make. You might encounter them periodically as your civilization begins to expand and grow. They sometimes invade from the sea; other times they arise suddenly in unsettled parts of any continent. Barbarians might attempt to capture or destroy your cities and pillage your fields and mines. Most barbarian tribes are accompanied by a leader.

Because barbarians can appear along any coast or in any unsettled area, it is important to defend your cities with at least one military unit. Barbarians (and rival armies) can walk right into an undefended city, capturing it with only minor bloodshed (the captured city loses one population point, just as any city taken by force does—see **Capturing Cities** under **Cities** for the gory details).

Even if barbarians capture a city or several cities, they do not become a rival civilization—that is, they do not join the space race, or negotiate treaties, or earn rank in historians' reckonings. Sea raiders can be fought on land or engaged at sea in their ships. Land barbarians arise in areas that are outside the radius of a city. As time passes, they appear at even farther distances from civilization. Thus, expanding your network of cities over a continent eventually removes the threat of land barbarians, because the entire area has become more or less civilized by your urban presence.

RANSOMING BARBARIAN LEADERS

When you attack and destroy stacked barbarian units, the leader units fall with their troops and are also destroyed. However, if a barbarian leader stands alone in a square, and your army wins an attack against him, he is captured. His compatriots immediately give you gold to ransom him back—the amount they pay is based on the barbarian level you chose in game setup. Barbarian leaders who have lost their armies attempt to escape. If not captured in a few turns, they disappear.

DIPLOMACY

Other cultures share your world in ***Civilization II***. If your attitude is expansionist and your home continent is large, you might seek out—and find— your rivals early in the game. If you concentrate on perfecting your own cities or find yourself limited by a small continent, it might be centuries before you encounter other players. Whether you opt for peaceful communications or aggressive action depends on your style.

CONCEPTS OF DIPLOMACY

Eventually, no matter how isolated your location or how isolationist your policies, you will have contact with rival civilizations. Choosing to meet with a rival allows you to explore the intricacies of negotiation.

Every AI opponent has an *attitude* that he or she presents to negotiators. Your rivals' attitudes can range from friendly to inimical. You can tell what attitude a leader has by watching the body language of the emissary after he or she stops speaking and by observing the titles of the dialog boxes during negotiations. A ruler's personality affects his or her attitude. Your rivals' attitudes can change over time, depending on your rank in the game, the current balance of power, the gifts you offer them, and your *reputation* for keeping your word in negotiations: Every time you go back on your word, international observers notice and remember.

Diplomatic negotiations can result in five different states: *alliance, peace, cease-fire, neutrality* or *war*. A rival might demand money or civilization advances (the reverse is also true—you can demand money or civilization advances from rival rulers). In addition, negotiations can include requests to share maps and instructions to withdraw trespassing troops. A player might even ask you to declare war on a third party. All negotiations progress through a series of screens, each with a variety of pre-set options.

Establishing embassies in your rivals' cities allows you to increase your negotiating power. By checking your FOREIGN MINISTER's reports, you can see whether, for example, the bellicose Indians have the city base to back up their threats, or whether they are just bluffing. You'll have a better idea of when to back down and when to press for concessions.

YOUR RIVAL'S ANTECHAMBERS

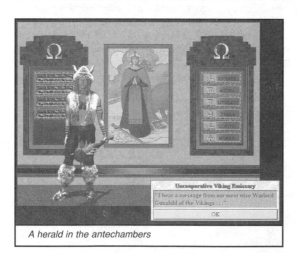

A herald in the antechambers

When you meet with an emissary of a rival ruler, the decor of his antechamber can tell you much about the relative size and type of government employed by the enemy civilization. One alcove displays icons relating to the military might of your rival, the other icons represent his or her knowledge and advancement. Decorative details indicate what type of government is in power.

CONDUCTING DIPLOMACY
WITH COMPUTER OPPONENTS

Diplomacy is conducted face to face with one rival emissary at a time. An opponent can contact you any time after units from each of your civilizations have met, and the reverse is also true. You can contact an opponent any time after your units have been adjacent to his or hers. Just select the SEND EMISSARY option from the FOREIGN MINISTER's report in the ADVISORS menu.

In game terms, once you choose the SEND EMISSARY option, a dialog box opens, offering you several responses from which to select your intent. The form of government under which your civilization currently operates can influence the choices you have; see **Governments** for the details.

Establishing embassies with other civilizations can be a very useful preparation for negotiations. Your FOREIGN MINISTER collects information from all of your embassies. From him you can learn important facts about your opponents, including the personalities of their leaders, their diplomatic states with respect to all civilizations with whom they have contact, the number and names of their cities, the extent of their technological advances, their current research project, and the amount in their treasury. This information is not available for civilizations with which you have not established an embassy.

MOOD AND PERSONALITY

The tone and result of any negotiations are greatly influenced by the mood of your rival. The opposing leader might be antagonistic, obsequious, or somewhere in between. This mood depends on the leader's personality and how your two civilizations compare to each other and to the rest of the world. You might pick up cues about a rival's mood from the body language of the emissary.

A rival leader's personality might be aggressive, rational, or neutral. Aggressive leaders are more likely to lean toward war or demand high payments for peace. Rational leaders are more likely to offer peace and might only be bluffing when asking for payment. If you have broken previous peace agreements with any civilization, your perfidy is remembered and influences all rivals' degree of antagonism.

If you are the largest, most powerful, and richest civilization in the world, all rivals are likely to be very demanding or antagonistic. However, if a particular opponent is puny in comparison to your might, his or her natural tendency to belligerence might be overridden. A civilization threatened with extinction is more interested in survival.

Leaders with whom you are allied tend to become jealous as your civilization grows larger and more powerful; they expect to be appeased with gifts of cash or knowledge. On the other hand, allies who leap ahead of you may be generous when asked to share their good fortune.

REPUTATION

Your reputation is based not on how peaceful or how warlike you are toward your neighbors, but on how often you keep your word. Breaking alliances or treaties can blacken your reputation in the international community. Savagely sacking the city of a treaty partner with Legions, or breaking a cease-fire to bombard your opponent's city by Stealth Bomber are acts likely to be deplored throughout the known world. The actions of your Diplomats and Spies can also damage your standing. Your computer opponents learn from your actions and adjust theirs to fit their expectations.

If you habitually break treaties, other leaders will have no qualms about doing the same to you. It is important to note that the most severe censure is reserved for the ringleaders in group actions. If you break your word because you were "incited" by another player, the diplomatic penalty is drastically reduced. For example, if you have signed a treaty with the Romans, and the Greek emissary asks you to declare war on your erstwhile friends, it is a chance for you to break your treaty with the Romans at a much-lessened penalty than if you had been the principle figure of treachery.

Julius Caesar

Over long periods of time, if you mend your ways by keeping your word to other rulers, the black marks on your reputation can be partially erased and your honor somewhat redeemed. If you build the Eiffel Tower Wonder, the process of character redemption is speeded by a "lump sum" 25 percent shift in your favor, followed by a more rapid recovery over time. Only through the effect of the Eiffel Tower can a player who has broken his word regain a spotless reputation.

Finally, your reputation matters on the domestic front, too. When you choose to govern your civilization as a Republic or Democracy, your Senate pays careful attention to your conduct in foreign affairs. They can, for instance, force you to sign a cease-fire or peace agreement. They are also vigilant in trying to force you to keep your agreements. If they catch you circumventing their oversight by intentionally provoking an enemy (by refusing to leave enemy territory during a peace treaty, for instance, or if a Diplomat or Spy causes an international incident), your government is likely to collapse into Anarchy because of the scandal.

THE FIVE DIPLOMATIC STATES

In *Civilization*, all negotiations ended with an offer of peace or a declaration of war. In *Civilization II*, however, there are finer gradations of posture, or diplomatic state, than just these two options. The relationship between two cultures can be expressed as one of five different states: alliance, peace, cease-fire, neutrality, or war. Each has repercussions in the movement and position of armies and other units, as well as on the international reputation of the participants. A short description of each state follows.

ALLIANCE

In an alliance, you and your ally agree to full (or almost full) cooperation against your common enemies. This shared purpose and trust manifests in a relaxation of restrictions. You can freely enter each others' territories, ignoring zones of control, although you cannot stack your units with those of your ally or actually enter each others' city spaces. If you have convinced a weaker power to ally with you, that ruler will expect occasional awards for his or her faithful service. Your ally also expects your military assistance if he or she is attacked.

Because an alliance involves a great deal of trust and cooperation, it is more difficult to cancel than other types of agreement. You cannot simply back-stab an ally by attacking him or her, but must first cancel your agreement during diplomatic negotiations. All units nearer to one of your former ally's cities than to one of your own are returned from the field to the closest friendly city. The reverse is also true: your former ally's armies are returned to his or her territory at the same time.

Breaking an alliance, for any reason, is remembered as a major transgression by all of the computer-controlled players. If you unilaterally cancel an alliance, your reputation suffers a "black mark" that is only very slowly erased by time. To cancel an alliance without receiving a black mark, you must maneuver your ally into terminating the agreement for you.

PEACE

A peace treaty is in theory a permanent arrangement, in which you and your rival agree not to attack each other or even enter the other's territory with military units. In *Civilization II* a ruler's territory encompasses any space within the radii of his or her cities. Units that violate this agreement may be asked to leave—and their failure to do so immediately can be considered a treaty violation, even if circumstances (like opposing units' zones of control) render the trespassing unit temporarily immobile.

Since it is a degree less cooperative than an alliance, there is no barrier that prevents you from breaking a peace treaty at any time—other than your concern for your reputation. Breaking a peace treaty is a serious matter, and your ruthlessness is long remembered by all other cultures, not merely the one you double-crossed. If you wish to avoid the black mark on your reputation, you can try taunting the other leader into declaring war on you. If he or she falls for the maneuver, your reputation remains spotless, though your military preparedness might suffer as your armies absorb his or her first strike.

Peace treaties are most useful when you want a long period of quiet on a particular border, since their recognition of territorial borders keeps enemy units from harassing you and fortifying near your cities. By the same token, they impede you from entrenching your units in your treaty-partner's territory.

CEASE-FIRE

A cease-fire is an agreement with a former enemy to end a war. Your enemy might agree to a cease-fire because he or she wants to make peace, is tired of fighting, or simply wants to get some breathing space before attacking you again. Once a cease-fire is signed, your former enemy ceases attacking your units and cities for approximately 16 turns.

Although a cease-fire enjoins you from attacking your former enemy, there are no territorial restrictions on where you may move your units—you can remain in your fortified positions, even adjacent to enemy cities. Of course, maintaining military units near enemy cities is considered a sign of bad faith and will lead to friction in the future.

Unlike a peace treaty, a cease-fire is only a temporary agreement whose effects dwindle with time. Once the cease-fire expires, your civilizations remain in a state of neutrality (described below) until some other negotiation or aggression takes place. A cease-fire is automatically extended for an additional 16 turns or so whenever tribute is paid by either side. A message informs you when a cease-fire you have signed expires. Violating a cease-fire is an act of treachery that is remembered internationally, and that blackens your reputation.

NEUTRALITY

This state represents not so much an agreement as a wary agreement to disagree—you are not openly at war with an enemy, but you have no formal connection, either. The lack of binding paperwork means that you can freely start a war at any time by simply attacking an enemy unit or city. On the other hand, you might also send an emissary to start negotiating a peace treaty or even an alliance with a neutral rival.

Territory is considered important while cultures maintain a neutral stance, and refusing to remove a unit that has entered the opponent's territory might be enough provocation for a declaration of war. The expulsion of your Diplomat or Spy from an opponent's territory is not in itself a contravention of neutrality.

WAR

This diplomatic state represents the likelihood of open hostilities at any point in which your units contact your opponent's units. However, there are times when you might enter or remain in a state of war without the exchange of gunfire, as when continents separate your main forces from the enemy's.

Wars can start for innumerable reasons, ranging from self defense to greed and conquest. War might be openly declared after a breakdown in negotiations or in return for offenses rendered by ill-placed troops, or it can start with a sudden sneak attack. Civilizations at war with yours might drag their neighbors into the conflict, too, by activating alliances (paying their allies to assist them in the attack).

Once you are at war with another civilization, that ruler considers you a hated enemy unless and until you sign a cease-fire or other, more permanent, agreement. You must make up separately with each opponent (even those allied with a civilization with whom you have already negotiated). If, for instance, the Vikings and the Sioux were allies in a war against you, you must negotiate one agreement to end hostilities with the Vikings and a separate one to placate the Sioux.

NEGOTIATIONS

To begin negotiations with another ruler, simply pull down the FOREIGN MINISTER's report from the ADVISORS menu, and click the SEND EMISSARY button. The options available to you depend on your current diplomatic state and the attitude of your rival. If you send too many emissaries, a leader can get annoyed and refuse to speak to you. Wait a few turns for his or her impatience to wear off, then try again.

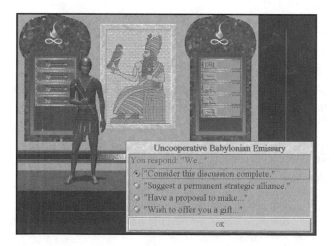

If you are at war with a rival, he or she might make a demand that you must satisfy if you wish to progress in your negotiations or might even refuse to meet with you. If you are in a state of neutrality or better and have not exhausted your welcome, you progress to the DIPLOMACY menu. Again, the options available to you depend on your current diplomatic state. We've prepared several tables to clarify your choices. The table below displays the gist of your emissary's polished phrases, the states in which he or she is allowed to offer such remarks, and the opponent's probable response. Most results are self explanatory; the two which direct you to other menus are expanded on below.

DIPLOMACY MENU

DIPLOMATIC OPTION	WHEN OFFERED	RESULT
"Consider this discussion complete."	always except war	end conversation
"Suggest a permanent strategic alliance."	peace	possibly sign alliance, might ask for concession
"Suggest a permanent peace treaty."	cease-fire/neutral	possibly sign peace treaty, might ask for concession
"Request a gift from you, our gracious allies."	allied	possibly receive gift, but possibly lower ally's esteem
"Demand tribute for our patience."	peace/cease-fire/neutral	possibly receive tribute, possibly declare war, possibly no reaction
"Insist that you withdraw your troops."	peace	possibly withdraw, possibly declare war
"Cancel this worthless alliance."	allied	end alliance, get black mark
"Have a proposal to make..."	always except war	go to PROPOSAL menu
"Wish to offer you a gift..."	always except war	go to GIFT menu

"HAVE A PROPOSAL TO MAKE..."

Once you have your rival's ear, you can make a variety of suggestions. Common sense tells you that the better an opponent likes you, the more likely he or she is to agree to your proposal. Opponents also take your relative standing in the game into account. They are more likely to be magnanimous if you are far behind than if you are the pre-eminent power in the world. The following table gives the gist of your emissary's remarks and the rival's likely response.

PROPOSAL MENU

COMMENT	RESULT
Never mind	Return to DIPLOMACY menu
Ask to exchange knowledge	Possibly exchange advance, possibly receive as a gift or for a fee
Ask to declare war against an enemy	Demand bribe of gold or knowledge to attack an enemy
Ask to share world maps	Possibly exchange maps

Exchanging Knowledge: Civilizations that are not extremely antagonistic might accept an offer to trade civilization advances. They negotiate by requesting a particular advance from you. Your options include accepting the deal as offered, vetoing the exchange, or offering an alternative advance instead of the one they requested. They, in turn, can accept or decline your revised offer. Sometimes an opponent thinks less of you for offering lesser alternatives. You may continue trading as many technologies as you possess, provided the other party is interested. Occasionally, you might be offered an advance as a gift or for a monetary fee.

Declaring War: Civilizations who see an advantage in changing the balance of power might be persuaded to declare war on a mutual enemy. They usually request a cash payment for their trouble, but might demand two advances in lieu of gold.

Exchanging Maps: Civilizations might agree to exchange knowledge of the world in the form of accurate maps of territory they have explored. If they accept, the darkness is rolled back in your Map window to represent their information.

"HAVE A GIFT TO OFFER..."

Sometimes rivals appreciate a tangible result more than mere flowery words. If you'd like to improve an opponent's attitude toward you, you have the option of offering a gift. Three categories of persuasion are available: knowledge, money, and troops.

GIFT MENU

COMMENT	RESULT
Never mind	Return to DIPLOMACY menu
Offer knowledge	Give knowledge, improve attitude
Offer money	The more money, the better the attitude
Offer military unit	Transfer military unit

Offer Knowledge: You can agree to offer knowledge to cement a better relationship. Your rival suggests an advance they are interested in. You can agree to that choice, change your mind about the exchange, or make a counter-offer. Your rival's opinion of you improves with each gift you make.

Offer Money: You can attempt to offer a gift of cash to placate your rival. A dialog box lists your three levels of generosity. If you change your mind, the NEVER MIND option is always available. Your rival's opinion of you always climbs if you give him or her gold.

Offer Military Unit: You can attempt to offer one of your existing military units to bolster a friend's army and encourage his or her good opinion. If the leader feels your technology is superior, a list of your cities appears. Choose one to see the roster of units stationed there. Click on a unit to send. That unit becomes part of the other civilization's army, and no longer draws support from your city.

WINNING THE GAME

As we explained in the Introduction, there are two ways to win *Civilization II*. You can either beat the other civilizations into space by being the first to successfully colonize a distant system or conquer all the other civilizations in the game.

THE SPACE RACE

The environmental pressures of growing populations in the modern world are forcing humans to look into space for resources and room to live. The question is not *whether* humans will travel to the stars, but *when*. The final act of stewardship you can perform for your civilization is to ensure that they lead this exodus.

The history of your civilization ends when either you or one of your rivals reaches a nearby star system with colonists. If your spaceship is the first to arrive, you receive a bonus to your civilization score in recognition of this final accomplishment. Regardless of how many colonists your spaceship is carrying or how fast it is, if a rival makes planetfall first, you receive no bonus.

No civilization can undertake spaceship component construction until one civilization has built the Apollo Program Wonder. Thereafter, the race is on and any civilization that has acquired the necessary advances can begin building the parts of a spaceship.

Spaceships are in many ways a one-shot deal. Each civilization, including yours, can build only one spaceship at a time. Restrictions prevent you from building a second, back-up ship once you launch the first. Once launched, ships cannot be recalled or turned around. You can construct a second spaceship only if your current ship explodes in space or if your capital city is captured while your spaceship is under construction (the conquerors burn it on the launch pad).

SPACESHIPS

The purpose of your spaceship is to carry as many colonists as possible to another star system. At a minimum, it must provide living space for colonists, life support, energy sources, propulsion power, and fuel for the engines. Spending more time constructing additional components can result in a faster voyage and a higher colonist survival rate.

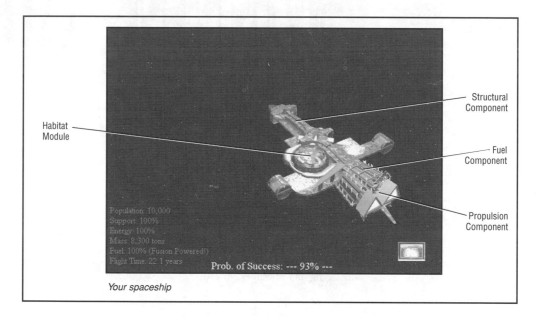

Your spaceship

As each new component is completed, the Spaceship display appears, showing where the component is positioned and updating the statistics and specifications. All spaceships have the same characteristics: population, food, energy, mass, fuel, flight time, and probability of success. We'll explain each in turn.

POPULATION

This figure represents the number of pioneers the spaceship is outfitted to carry. The more citizens it carries to the new planet, the higher your bonus.

SUPPORT

This figure shows what percentage of accommodations on the ship is currently serviced by life support: air, nutrient, and waste systems. Pioneers not provided with life support cannot survive the voyage.

ENERGY

This figure indicates what percentage of the energy required by habitation and life support modules is currently being provided. If sufficient energy is not available to power life support and habitation, the probability of success will be very low.

MASS

All of the components, modules, and structures add to the mass of your spaceship. The greater the mass, the more power is required from propulsion parts to move it.

FUEL

This figure indicates what percentage of the fuel your propulsion units require is currently aboard. If insufficient fuel is provided, the propulsion components cannot work to their maximum power and the ship cannot attain its best possible speed.

FLIGHT TIME

This calculation indicates the number of years required for your spaceship to reach the nearest star, based on the ship's current mass and engine power. Adding more engines and fuel reduces flight time.

PROBABILITY OF SUCCESS

This figure incorporates all the other data (including the amount of food and energy available and the estimated flight time) in an estimate of the approximate percentage of colonists who are expected to survive the voyage. The faster the flight, the higher the expected survival rate.

SPACESHIP LAUNCH

To send your spaceship on its voyage, click on the LAUNCH button. You cannot retrieve a spaceship once it has been launched.

CONSTRUCTION

Your spaceship is such a large undertaking that it cannot be built whole cloth the way improvements are built—it is, instead, constructed of parts. There are three types of spaceship parts: components, modules, and structures, each of which we describe in detail below. You must achieve a new civilization advance to make each type of part available for construction. However, the delivery of spaceship parts to your capital city is handled automatically as each part is completed.

Though you can construct parts in any order, and most likely will have multiple parts under production simultaneously, all modules and components must eventually be connected to structural parts if you want them to function. Unconnected modules or components are emphasized to signal that they are not working. Once sufficient structural parts have been added to provide supply and support lines, the problem disappears.

COMPONENTS

To build spaceship components, you must have achieved the technological advance of Plastics. You can then build components at a cost of 160 shields each. There are two kinds of components, propulsion and fuel. As each component is completed, you choose which type has been built.

Propulsion Components: These parts are the engines that provide the power for space flight. More engines mean the ship travels faster, reaches its destination sooner, and has a higher probability of a successful mission.

Fuel Components: These parts provide fuel for the propulsion units. In order for the propulsion units to perform at maximum levels, you must provide one fuel component for each propulsion component.

MODULES

Spaceship modules require the advance of Superconductor and cost 320 shields each to build. They exist in three types: habitation, life support, and solar panels. As each module is completed, you choose which type it is and add it to your ship.

Habitation Module: Each habitation module provides living space, community services, and recreational facilities for 10,000 colonists.

Life Support Module: Each life support module provides the food and other requirements for the 10,000 colonists carried in one habitation module. Colonists carried in a habitation module that doesn't receive life support have a very low probability of surviving.

Solar Panel Module: Each solar panel module provides enough energy to power two of the other types of module. Modules that don't receive power cannot function properly.

STRUCTURAL SUPPORT

Structural units require the advance of Space Flight and cost 80 shields each to build. You must build sufficient structural units to connect the components and modules together. Parts that are not connected do not work and provide no benefit to the ship.

CONQUERING THE WORLD

When striving to win this way, aggressiveness helps. Your object is to take over any and all rival civilizations. Note that if you vanquish other civilizations early enough in the game, some new tribe might develop a Settlers unit and found a civilization using the color originally assigned to the vanquished culture. In this way, some civilizations "re-start." Eventually, if you're lucky, you might be able to subjugate the entire world. If at any time you control the only settled civilization, you win, and the End Game sequence proclaims you the ruler of the world.

Bloodlust Option

If you prefer to eschew space exploration altogether, you can choose an optional rule during the initial setup of the game that disables the spaceship building sequences. Although you can still achieve, say, the Space Flight and Plastics advances, the spaceship parts remain grayed out on any menus on which they appear, and you remain planetbound. Thus, your only possible method of victory is total world domination.

SCORING

Completing a **Civilization II** game can take many hours, especially if you are playing at one of the tougher levels of competition. There are several ways to get a general idea of how you're doing along the way.

Throne Room

As your civilization achieves certain milestones, some of which are keyed to numbers and sizes of cities, attitude of population, and civilization advances, your citizens spontaneously show their approval—first by building and subsequently by offering to make additions to your Throne Room. Periodic reports notify you of these events.

A typical throne room

Do you have to take the time to direct the additions to your throne room? No. If you choose to, you can completely ignore it with no repercussions. Turn off Throne Room on the Graphics Options menu, and you won't even know it's there.

However if, like most of us, you enjoy making improvements to your seat of power, click once to see the schematic overlay. The colored elements of the overlay represent areas that you can change. Each element has four different looks, representing the increasing decorative sophistication of your people. Once you have indulged your tastes in interior decor to their fullest, your people update the various *objects d'art* scattered about your chamber. You can view the current state of your throne room at any time by selecting the View Throne Room option from the View menu.

DEMOGRAPHICS

This option, available on the WORLD menu, provides a number of real world statistics about your civilization's health, growth, economic, and military status. Each measure shows both an actual value and your rank among the world's civilizations. If you have established an embassy with the nation that is top-ranked in a particular measure, your rival's achievement is listed along with your own ranking. You can use the DEMOGRAPHICS report to compare your performance with that of your rivals and to determine what areas of your civilization need the most immediate attention.

CIVILIZATION SCORE

If you're the type who prefers the concreteness of numbers, choose the CIVILIZATION SCORE option from the WORLD menu for a numerical representation of your progress. *Civilization II* keeps a running total of the points you've earned for population size and various achievements. It also keeps track of penalties for pollution and other negatives. This chart covers basic scoring:

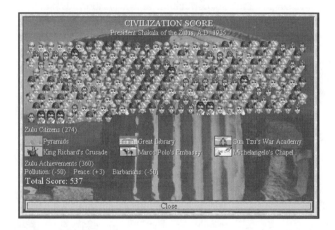

CONDITION	POINTS SCORED
Each happy citizen	2
Each content citizen	1
Each Wonder of the World that you possess	20
Each turn of world peace (no wars or combat)	3
Each futuristic advance	5
Each map square currently polluted	-10

When you reach the end of the game (in 2020 A.D.), this total becomes the basis of your score. However, the level of barbarian aggression you chose affects the final tally. The lowest level of activity (none) results in -50 points, the next higher level -25, and the normal level causes no change. Playing at the highest level of barbarian villainy adds 50 points to your final score.

The basic scoring goal—a challenging one—is to score 1,000 points or more. Of course, there are ways to score even higher, but they involve winning the game before time runs out.

If you conquer the world before the last year of the game (2020 A.D.), **Civilization II** calculates an alternate score, based on the number of rivals you've squelched and the speed with which you moved. You can earn up to 1,000 points for conquered cultures, and nearly as much for speed. **Civilization II** compares this alternate score to your running total and awards you the higher point value of the two.

If you successfully settle the stars, you earn a bonus based on the number of colonists to reach Alpha Centauri. This bonus is added to your running total score when you complete your mission.

PLAYING SCENARIOS

The original release of *Civilization II* included only two scenarios: **Rome** and **WWII**. Since then, we've put out quite a number of additional scenarios, and they're all included in the *Multiplayer Gold Edition*. Not only that, but you can play each and every scenario as a multiplayer game.

If you choose to play a scenario as a multiplayer game, pay close attention to the introductory text—especially the notes on which tribes are not fun to play with.

A QUICK REVIEW

The instructions regarding scenarios in **Setting Up a Game** are, well, light on detail. Here, we go through it in depth, including how you load scenarios for play and what it means to win one.

LOADING A SCENARIO

The first menu you see when the game starts up doesn't have a name. When it appears:

- Click the radio button next to BEGIN SCENARIO.
- Then click on the OK button.

Now you need to choose the scenario you want to play. The selection window works exactly like a typical Windows file selection window.

- First, double-click on the directory named **scenario**. (Unless you want to play the **Rome** or **WWII** scenario, that is; both of those are in the directory you see first.)
- Next, double-click on the directory of the scenario you want.
- Finally, double-click on the name of the scenario file itself.

The MicroProse scenarios are each in a separate directory:

SCENARIO	DIRECTORY	FILE
After the Apocalypse	Apocalyp	apocalyp.scn
Age of Discovery	Discover	discover.scn
The Age of Napoleon	Napoleon	napoleon.scn
The Age of Reptiles	Dinosaur	dinosaur.scn
Alexander the Great	Alexandr	alexandr.scn
Alien Invasion	Alien	alien.scn
American Civil War	CivilWar	civilwar.scn
Atlantis	Atlantis	atlantis.scn
The Crusades	Crusades	crusades.scn
The Great War	WW1	ww1.scn
Ice Planet	Iceplnet	iceplnet.scn
Jihad: The Rise of Islam	Jihad	jihad.scn
Mars Now!	Mars	mars.scn
Master of Magic, Jr.	Momjr	mom_jr.scn
Master of Orion, Jr.	Moojr	moo_jr.scn
The Mongol Horde	Mongol	mongol.scn
The Mythic History of Midgard	Midgard	midgard.scn
The New World	Newworld	newworld.scn
Samurai	Samurai	samurai.scn
The War for Independence	Independ	independ.scn
The World of Jules Verne	Verne	verne.scn
World War: 1979	WW79	ww79.scn
X-COM: Assault	Xcom	xcom.scn

The first set of Best of the Net scenarios are all in subdirectories of the directory named **BestoNet**:

SCENARIO	DIRECTORY	FILE
Atolon	Atolon	atolon.scn
The Cholera of Zeus	Zeus	zeus.scn
The Conquest of Britain	Brit1011	britain.scn
Cross and Crescent	Croscres	croscres.scn
The Fall of the Great Kesh	Kesh	kesh.scn
Persian Gulf War	Gulfwar	gulfwar.scn
Native Rebellion	Rebel	rebel.scn
East Wind, Rain	Eastwind	eastwind.scn

The Best of the Net II scenarios are all in subdirectories of the directory named **Best-Net2**:

SCENARIO	DIRECTORY	FILE
Battle of the Sexes	Battle	battle.scn
Civ-Life!	Bio	bio.scn
Hidden	Hidden	hidden.scn
Santa is Coming	Santa	santa.scn
Bears at Play	Bears	bears.scn
USA 2010	Usa2010	usa2010.scn
Mammoth	Mammoth	mammoth.scn
Paradise	Paradise	paradise.scn

Once you've chosen a scenario, you see the introductory text, which explains the situation you're getting yourself into. Click OK when you've finished reading it. Now, you go through the normal decisions for the beginning of a *Civilization II* game.

- Choose the civilization you want to lead. Every scenario includes empires that are interesting to play and those that are not. Some nations are only included for historical accuracy or to spice things up; they're not really fun to play.
- Select a DIFFICULTY LEVEL. The default is normally DEITY, since we assume scenario players are already somewhat experienced.
- Enter the name under which you rule.
- Choose the gender you want other civilizations' emissaries to use when referring to your ruler.

After that, the scenario begins in earnest.

Saving and Reloading

When you install the scenarios, the files for each are put into separate directories. *They absolutely must stay that way.* If you move files around, there's no telling what might happen, and Customer Support might not be able to fix it.

Do not move the scenario files.

The same goes for any scenario games you save. When you save a scenario game (even if you do so using the Autosave function), that save file goes into the directory with that scenario. When the time comes to load the file, look for it in the scenario directory, not in the normal *Civilization II* directory.

This brings up one more important rule. If you copy a scenario save file to use with *Civilization II* on another computer, make sure that you copy the file into the correct scenario directory.

Objectives and Winning

In some scenarios, scoring and winning are the same as in any normal game. However, most scenarios use the Objectives system instead. In this case, success and failure are measured in terms of who has how many objective cities (and sometimes wonders) under their control at the end of the game.

One civilization in each Objectives scenario is considered the *protagonist* nation. It's always the same nation (noted in the introductory text), regardless of which one you choose to play. The designer of the scenario has marked certain cities as objectives. (To tell which cities are objectives, select Find City from the Kingdom menu.) Some cities are Major Objectives; these count for three times as much as normal objectives.

The only object of the scenario is to capture and hold as many objectives as you can. This and this alone determines the outcome. If some of the Wonders of the World are also considered objectives, each objective wonder you capture also counts toward the total.

There are four possible results of any Objective scenario. The number of objectives required for each is a preset characteristic of the scenario. The protagonist nation can:

- win a Decisive Victory
- win a Marginal Victory
- suffer a Marginal Defeat
- suffer a Decisive Defeat

Whatever the outcome for the protagonist, every other civilization gets the corresponding, opposite result. Thus, for example, if you're the protagonist and you win a Marginal Victory, all your opponents get a Marginal Defeat.

WHEN YOU'RE DONE

When you quit or finish a scenario, you return to that unnamed first menu. You can begin another scenario (or a regular game) if you wish. If you prefer to leave *Civilization II*, click CANCEL.

WHAT'S NEW

For many of the scenarios, we weren't satisfied with just setting up situations using the existing *Civilization II* features. We took advantage of the fact that you can design new units, modify existing ones, rearrange the progress of advances, and pretty much change anything you want. In the MicroProse scenarios, we've even made some modifications to the way the game itself works.

UNITS

Some of the units you've come to know have had their characteristics changed. For the most part, you can assume that a familiar-looking unit is the same as (or at least very similar to) what you'd expect. However, use your MILITARY ADVISOR to check out your units. Compare the data in his report to the **Poster**; any changes will be fairly obvious.

Brand-new units have been included in several of the scenarios. In the MicroProse scenarios, all of the new units are represented by new icons. They're easy to spot. Again, you can get the details on the MILITARY ADVISOR's report. The new units are also described briefly in the section on each scenario.

> **Note:** In certain scenarios, some units are only available to selected civilizations, regardless of technological advances. (Only the Confederates, for example, could field a Robert E. Lee unit.) When this is the case, the entry for that unit in the text Civilopedia might mislead; it lists the required advance, but does not mention the fact that you might not be able to research that advance or be allowed to build that unit at all. Whenever possible, these types of unit are noted in the scenario descriptions.

ADVANCES

In certain scenarios, the progress of science takes a different track than it would in a normal game of *Civilization II*. Sometimes advances have simply been renamed or their effects modified, but there is at least one scenario (**Alien Invasion**) in which major sections of the research tree have been pruned or rearranged. Many scenarios also limit the availability of advances to protect the historical flavor of the situation.

One of the most common effects to look out for is a change in the TECH PARADIGM. This might make all research (yours and your opponents') take more or less effort, depending on the direction of the change.

A few of the MicroProse scenarios are designed in such a way that different civilizations must follow entirely separate lines of research. For example, advances available to the alien invaders are not available to human researchers, and vice versa.

The references you reach via the GOAL and HELP buttons have been updated in every case, so you can always find out what research is available to your civilization.

WONDERS

Coincident with changes to the advances are some modifications to the Wonders of the World. In some of the scenarios, existing wonders have been renamed to better fit the context. Their effects have not changed.

The wonder videos are not shown in a scenario, even if the wonder has not been renamed.

In those scenarios that are scored on the objectives system, capturing (and holding) a city with a wonder in it could count for more than conquering a wonderless city.

In every case, the renamed wonders are described in the CIVILOPEDIA.

THE CIVILOPEDIA

In each of the scenarios, the CIVILOPEDIA (new and improved especially for the *Civilization II Multiplayer Gold Edition*) has been updated to reflect the changes to units, advances, City Improvements, and Wonders of the World.

LIMITS ON PLAY

One of the things that the *Civilization II* scenario building tools allow a designer to do is place limits on the activities civilizations can engage in. This helps them bypass a few rules to add some realism to a situation. For example, a scenario in which aliens forcibly invade the Earth wouldn't ring true if the aliens offered you a peace treaty on the first turn, then settled down to slowly build their empire from scratch. Some of the common limitations you might run into are:

- You're unable to change your form of Government.
- There are no Minor Tribes to be found.
- Spaceship advances and parts are not in the game.
- Capturing a city never results in capturing an advance.
- Pollution never appears.
- A time limit is built into the scenario.
- Certain civilizations cannot communicate with others at all.

Note that, when you meet with the ruler of a scenario civilization, the leader's picture (and the heralds, if you have them active) might not seem to match the name or nation. This is a problem that's endemic to scenario building. When you create a new civilization, you can never be sure what representation *Civilization II* will choose for your leader. Those of you who regularly name your own civilization when playing are surely familiar with this minor inconsistency.

In addition to keeping the scenario running in the directions the designer intended, limits like these enhance the game by offering an extra challenge to experienced players.

EVENTS

As you play the MicroProse scenarios, you might notice some things happening that seem to defy the rules of *Civilization II* outright. Units appear out of thin air, empires declare war over trifles, and so on. Put down the phone; they're not bugs in the program. We've added something we call "events" to the game specifically for these scenarios. Every event is triggered by timing or a certain action, and all of them are designed to heighten the realism, historical or otherwise, of the scenario.

For technical-minded scenario builders, the details on inserting events into your own scenarios are in the **Appendix**.

AFTER THE APOCALYPSE

(Designed by Mick Uhl)

To play this scenario, load the file **apocalyp.scn**, which you can find in the directory named **Apocalyp**.

One of the most enduring themes in science fiction is the description of life in the aftermath of the fall of civilization as we know it. Whether the apocalypse comes though war, natural or man-made disaster, plague, or whatever, how humans respond makes for some interesting stories. Now it's your turn. The Earth has been ravaged by a war in which the use of radiation and other mutagens was commonplace. Humanity isn't what it used to be.

This scenario begins in 24 AD; in this case, "AD" stands for "After Doomsday." It goes on for about 250 turns.

After the Apocalypse is designed with the human player in mind. You should, therefore, play as one of the three "human" tribes: the Kamikazes, Serene Lights, or New Beetles. None of the other (mutant) civilizations has been play balanced, so if you choose to play one, it might not be fun.

This is not an Objectives scenario, so scoring is according to the normal *Civilization II* rules.

ADVANCES

For design reasons, some of the more futuristic advances aren't available for research in this post-apocalyptic scenario. Considering the time constraints, you might never notice.

UNITS

Practically every unit in this scenario is new, and many of them are specific to one civilization. It is far beyond the scope of this little section to cover them all. When you begin the scenario, regardless of which nation you play, examine your existing units on the DEFENSE MINISTER's report. Call up the PRODUCTION menu from any city screen, then use the HELP function liberally to see what you can build.

SPECIAL NOTES

Here are a few more things you ought to know:

- None of the nonhuman civilizations can negotiate with one another.
- This is a Bloodlust scenario, meaning that spacecraft are not a consideration. You can only win utterly before the timer runs out if you conquer the whole world.
- Each turn is one year.
- Scientific research progresses at a 7/10 rate, meaning that all advances take only 70% as long to discover as they would in a typical game.

THE AGE OF DISCOVERY

(Designed by Mick Uhl)

To play this scenario, load the file **discover.scn**, which you can find in the directory named **Discover**.

It's 1492, and the great royal families are restless. The resources of Europe have been exploited to their limit. Moribund economies require expanded horizons and exotic trading goods. Without some source of excitement and new products (and a place to exile political agitators and unwanted competitors), societal unrest threatens to upend the scales of power. Just in time, explorers discover unknown continents ripe for conquest and colonization. You have until 1741 to exploit them. Then, new political theories take up where the agitators left off.

We suggest that you play as any civilization but the Euro-Asians. They're really only in the scenario as a roadblock; they prevent expansion to the east.

There is no protagonist for this scenario, and objectives are not an issue. Your score is based on the usual *Civilization II* factors.

ADVANCES

In this scenario, only four of the usual advances are not available for researching: Conscription, Electricity, Plastics, and Steam Engine. These elisions, however, put a great number of the modern advances out of reach.

SPECIAL NOTES

Here are a few more things you ought to know:

- Changing governments is not possible in the Age of Discovery scenario.
- Pollution is not a factor.

- This is a Bloodlust scenario, meaning that spacecraft are not a consideration. You can only win utterly before the timer runs out if you conquer the whole world.
- Each turn is one year.
- Scientific research progresses at a 25/10 rate, meaning that all advances take roughly two and a half times as long to discover as they would in a typical game.
- To better reflect the times (and the great profit to be had from the spice trade), the **Gems** terrain special has been changed to **Spice 1**, and this provides an extraordinary amount of extra trade. To prevent confusion, the original **Spice** is now **Spice 2**.

THE AGE OF NAPOLEON

(Designed by Mick Uhl)

To play this scenario, load the file **napoleon.scn**, which you can find in the directory named **Napoleon**.

This scenario begins in 1798. Napoleon Bonaparte commands the armies of post-revolutionary France, and it is his intention to spread the benefits of liberty, equality, and brotherhood to as much as the world as possible—by force if necessary. In 1818, the people of France get tired of Napoleon and ship him off to Elba. Until then, you have a chance to be a part of what some call the "Napoleonic Era."

For this situation, any civilization is interesting to play, though the French or English perhaps more so than others. Napoleon and his French armies are the protagonists of the scenario, and their objective is to capture as many cities as possible. Everyone else intends to stop him.

ADVANCES

Several of the more advanced advances (and the units they lead to) are not available in this scenario, as they would detract from the historical accuracy of the situation. In any case, research is not likely to be a big factor in this particular situation. (The TECH PARADIGM is fairly high.)

UNITS

There are several new units in the Napoleon scenario. Among them:
- Each of the nations involved has its own specific infantry and cavalry units (**F Cavalry** for the French, and so on). The characteristics of these reflect the strengths and weaknesses of the armed forces of the time.
- **Imperial Guard** is a unique French unit that shows up as reinforcements late in the scenario.
- **Napoleon** represents one of the greatest military minds in French history.

- **Lord Nelson** is this scenario's version of the man generally recognized as the greatest admiral in history.
- **Wellington** shows up late in the scenario to reinforce the English.

The destruction of Napoleon or Wellington limits the corresponding nation to at best a Marginal Victory, no matter how successful its actual campaign might be.

In addition to these, a few of the usual units has been adjusted slightly. As always, you can examine the new units by calling up the DEFENSE MINISTER's report or using HELP.

SPECIAL NOTES

Here are a few more things you ought to know:

- Changing governments is not possible in the Napoleon scenario.
- No civilization can gain technological advances from the conquest of cities.
- Pollution is not a factor.
- This is a Bloodlust scenario, meaning that spacecraft are not a consideration. You can only win utterly before the timer runs out if you conquer the whole world.
- Each turn is two months.
- Scientific research progresses at a 40/10 rate, meaning that all advances take roughly four times as long to discover as they would in a typical game.

THE AGE OF REPTILES

(Designed by John Possidente)

To play this scenario, load the file **dinosaur.scn**, which you can find in the directory named **Dinosaur**.

Who among us has never wished to be the leader of a horde of gargantuan, rampaging dinosaurs? I don't see too many of you raising your hands. Good. You'll enjoy this scenario.

All of the dinosaur civilizations have a fair chance of prospering. Inexperienced players might want to play the Aalu, because they start out on an island (which provides a period of growth without major conflict). If you find you have resource troubles, try the Kore.

This scenario is not objective based, so there is no protagonist civilization. The only way to win is to wipe out everyone else—survival of the fittest.

ADVANCES

The entire technology tree has been uprooted and replaced.

Advances in the dinosaur scenario are based—quite loosely—on the progress of evolution from the Devonian period through the later part of the Cretaceous (or thereabouts). That means that you start out with few units available—fishes and one or two of the very early species of dinosaur. Research means taking part in an evolutionary arms race to discover new body parts and behaviors. Of course, not all of the "evolutionary advances" are biological or physical. For the sake of fun, we've departed from accepted paleological theory in a few instances.

That's all the detail we're giving away. After all, half the fun is in the discovery.

UNITS

Every unit has been changed.

What would be the point of a dinosaur scenario without dinosaur units? Here are the basics you'll need to know; the rest is up to you to discover:

- **Thecodontosaurus** is the Settler-type unit. This one can establish cities, stomp out roads, and so on. The faster version (the Engineer) is the **Maiasaurus** .

- There are *no* diplomatic or espionage units. (This was not a polite or subtle time.)

- Always check the Civilopedia before moving a sea unit around. Some of the larger ones are shallow water creatures, and sink rapidly when away from the coast. Many can carry other creatures, and some even carry flying creatures.

As always, you can examine units you've built by calling up the Defense Minister's report, and the text Civilopedia has listings for all possible units.

IMPROVEMENTS AND WONDERS

All the city improvements and Wonders of the World have been renamed and attached to different advances. Some have been removed from the scenario entirely. Those which are still available have not changed their functions, only the names and icons are new.

SPECIAL NOTES

Here are a few more things you ought to know:

- Changing governments is possible, but there is only one alternative to Despotism.

- This is a Bloodlust scenario, meaning that spacecraft are not a consideration. (Did you really think they would be?) You can only win if you conquer the whole world.

- Each turn is one million years, but you have nearly 400 of them. (After all, the dinosaurs were around for a lot longer than humans have been.)

- Scientific research progresses at an 8/10 rate, meaning that all advances take less research than they would in a typical game. This is offset, however, by the difficulty of getting a population of large-bodied, small-brained creatures interested in research.

- The special resources have been changed to better reflect the prehistoric reptilian situation. Also, the movement costs and resource production for some types of terrain have been modified.
- Watch out for the occasional volcano.

ALEXANDER THE GREAT

(Designed by Mick Uhl)

To play this scenario, load the file **alexandr.scn**, which you can find in the directory named **Alexandr**.

In this historical scenario, you play a part in the attempt by a teen-aged Alexander—heir to the throne recently vacated by his father, Philip of Macedon—to conquer the Greek, Egyptian, and Persian Empires and earn the moniker "Alexander the Great." It's a race against time, for the scenario begins in 335 B.C., and young Alexander is doomed to die of disease in 322 B.C. There are less than 13 years (150 turns) until his expiration date, so get moving!

We suggest that you play as either the Macedonians (Alexander intending conquest) or the Persians (Darius trying to stop Alexander). Ruling any of the other civilizations might prove to be an interesting challenge, except perhaps for the Thracians and Allies (Kotys), who are almost surely doomed to an early demise.

Alexander and his Macedonian Greeks are the protagonists of the scenario, and their objective is to capture as many cities as possible. Some cities are major objectives and are thus worth more than others.

UNITS

The only new units in this scenario are the two main emperors' personal guards. To exemplify his legendary bravery (some would say foolhardiness) at the front lines, Alexander is represented in battle by the Companion Cavalry. Darius is surrounded at all times by his hand-picked Immortals.

Nitpicker's Note: The Immortals replace Cavalry, and the Companions replace Armor. Thus, those two types of unit are never available in this scenario.

Both of these units are unique. You can neither build more nor replace them if they are destroyed, and no amount of research will change that. Since they're the personal bodyguards of the emperor in each case, if one of these units is overcome, the emperor himself is killed. Though successors are waiting to take over and continue the struggle, the death of the emperor limits that civilization to at best a Marginal Victory, no matter how successful the actual outcome may be.

As always, you can examine the new units by calling up the DEFENSE MINISTER's report or CIVILOPEDIA. None of the usual units has been tampered with significantly, with the exception of the Phalanx, which only the Greeks and Macedonian Greeks can build. A few others have been modified slightly to balance the scenario.

SPECIAL NOTES

Here are a few more things you ought to know:

- Changing governments is not possible in the Alexander scenario.
- No civilization can gain technological advances from the conquest of cities.
- Pollution is not a factor in the fourth century B.C.
- This is a Bloodlust scenario, meaning that spacecraft are not a consideration. You can only win utterly before the timer runs out if you conquer the whole world.
- Each turn is one month.
- Scientific research progresses at a 30/10 rate, meaning that all advances take roughly three times as long to discover as they would in a typical game.
- The Plastics advance has been removed.

ALIEN INVASION

(Designed by Mick Uhl)

To play this scenario, load the file **alien.scn**, which you can find in the directory named **Alien**.

It's a situation familiar to anyone who's played X-COM: hostile aliens have landed! Before they did so, however, they spread a plague that wiped out most of the human race, destroyed every satellite in orbit (completely disrupting global communications), and fried every bit of data on every computer in the world. Now, they're sending their ground troops in to mop up what's left while they settle in and build a new empire. As leader of one of the few remaining human nations, it's your job to stop the invaders.

For the most fun, we suggest that you play as any of the human nations. You can be Reismark I of the Hodad invaders, of course, but they have the advantage from the start, and it might not be very interesting to wipe out humankind so easily. This scenario takes place after a new calendar has been instituted. In this case, "AD" stands for "Alien Domination."

The Hodads are the protagonists of the scenario, and their objective is to capture as many cities as possible. The objective of the human civilizations is simply to survive and to take the fight to the invader—if they can.

ADVANCES

The human and Hodad forces follow completely separate research trees. The human-only tree begins at Steam Engine (which is totally off-limits to the Hodads) and it progresses normally except for these few changes.

- **Stealth** comes via Robotics and Labor Union, rather than Super Conductor.
- **The Laser** has Mass Production and Miniaturization as its prerequisites, rather than Nuclear Power.
- **Nuclear Power**, **Fusion Power**, and **Super Conductor** are completely unavailable.
- Genetic Engineering and Stealth together lead to **F.R.A.A.G.** (Final Response Against Alien aGgression). This in turn allows the T.I.G.U.R. unit.

The Hodad tree begins from **Nuclear Power**, which is completely off-limits to human civilizations.

- From there (with Electronics), they can get **Fusion Power** and **BioDome Research**.
- These two together lead to **Genetic Cloning**, which (with Computers) leads to **Organic Electronics**.
- Fusion Power and Genetic Cloning allow **Polymer Armor**.
- Polymer Armor and Organic Electronics allow **Magnetic Pulse Technology**.

Every one of these except Organic Electronics leads to at least one new unit.

UNITS

There is only one new unit available to the human nations. The **T.I.G.U.R.** (real name classified) promises to be the salvation of the human planet, the ultimate in anti-Hodad weaponry.

The Hodad units are, of course, totally alien.

WONDERS

The Apollo Program wonder is not available for building. Otherwise, things are as usual.

SPECIAL NOTES

Here are a few more things you ought to know:

- The Hodads do not negotiate—ever.
- No civilization can gain technological advances from the conquest of cities.
- This is a Bloodlust scenario, meaning that spacecraft are not a consideration. You can only win utterly before the timer runs out if you conquer the whole world.
- Each turn is one year.
- Scientific research progresses at a 30/10 rate, meaning that all advances take roughly three times as long to discover as they would in a typical game.

THE AMERICAN CIVIL WAR

(Designed by Mick Uhl)

> To play this scenario, load the file **civilwar.scn**, which you can find in the directory named **CivilWar**.

By the time 1861 rolled around, the Confederate States of America had declared themselves independent of the United States of America. The nation from which they seceded, however, refused to accept the secession, and things got ugly.

Incidentally, a small group of states (represented by the Kentuckians) declared themselves neutral, but also warned that they would join the enemy of whichever side attacked them first.

We strongly suggest that you play as either the Federals or the Confederates. The Kentuckians might be fun if you're interested in a real challenge, but the other civilizations are included only as trading partners and have no chance at all of winning.

Abe Lincoln and the Federals are the protagonists of the scenario, and their objective is to recapture as many of the seceding cities as possible. Jefferson Davis means to protect his new nation, no matter what it takes.

ADVANCES

Very few advances are available for research in this scenario. They are:

Repeating Weaponry requires Physics and Invention. This advance allows you to build the new Adv. Infantry unit, an improved version of the normal Infantry unit.

Submarine Tech requires Magnetism and Invention. It allows you to build Civil War Submarines.

Entrenchments requires Masonry and Physics. This makes Ent. Infantry (Entrenched) possible. Ent. Infantry have a stronger defense than normal Infantry, but cost the same to build.

WONDERS

Forget about the usual list of wonders. In this scenario, there are only a handful available.

King Cotton is the new name for the Hanging Gardens. The Confederates have this at the beginning of the scenario.

Secession! takes the place of the Oracle. The Confederates start the scenario in possession of this one, too.

Emancipation Proclamation is Bach's Cathedral renamed. Only the Federals can build this wonder.

Note that, though they've been renamed, these wonders have the same effects as usual.

Units

The Civil War scenario is up to its ears in new units. Many of these represent important military leaders, including **Geo. Custer**, **Benj. Grierson**, **J.E.B. Stuart**, **N.B. Forrest**, **Ston. Jackson**, **U.S. Grant**, **W.T. Sherman**, and **R.E. Lee**.

Otherwise, the most important ones to know are:

- **River Fort** is a unit that cannot move. It is a defensive installation, not a place, and thus cannot be captured like a city might. River Forts obstruct the movement of enemy units on waterways.

- **Monitor** is the Federal version of an Ironclad unit. The normal Ironclad represents the Confederate version—the *Merrimac*.

The destruction of U.S. Grant or R.E. Lee limits the corresponding nation to at best a Marginal Victory, no matter how successful its actual campaign.

In addition to all these, the **Submarine** unit is not the typical *Civilization II* sub. Reflecting the reality of the time, the Civil War Submarine is substantially weaker than the unit you've come to know.

As always, you can examine the new units by calling up the Defense Minister's report or Help.

Special Notes

Here are a few more things you ought to know:

- The Confederates and Federals cannot negotiate with each other.
- No one can negotiate with the Europeans.
- Changing governments is not possible in the Civil War scenario.
- No civilization can gain technological advances from the conquest of cities.
- Pollution is not a factor.
- This is a Bloodlust scenario, meaning that spacecraft are not a consideration. You can only win utterly before the timer runs out if you conquer the whole world.
- Each turn is one month.
- Scientific research progresses at a 40/10 rate, meaning that all advances take roughly four times as long to discover as they would in a typical game.
- The trade item **Cotton** replaces **Dye**.

Those of you interested in historical accuracy should know that the railroad systems that played such an important part in the actual war are represented by Roads. During testing, Roads proved to represent the travel advantage of early rail travel better than Railroads, which made the scenario far too easy to win. You can, of course, still build your own railroads.

ATLANTIS

(Designed by Mick Uhl)

To play this scenario, load the file **atlantis.scn**, which you can find in the directory named **Atlantis**.

Around 345 B.C., in the dialogues *Critias* and the shorter *Timaeus*, Plato wrote of the fate of a highly advanced civilization far from his Greek home. He claimed to have retrieved the story of this "Atlantis" from the notes of his ancestor Solon. Solon, in turn, had heard the tale from some priests while studying ancient history during a visit to Egypt in 570 B.C.

Set on two islands, this bronze age monarchy supposedly boasted (among other advances) hot and cold running water, equality of the sexes, and a written code of laws that was revised every five years. Atlantis was so secure in its power that its rulers were considering the conquest of Athens and Egypt (then at the height of its power). Unfortunately for the inhabitants, however, someone in Atlantis managed to tick off Poseidon, the god of the seas. Not much later, the entire civilization was destroyed by a "natural" cataclysm.

In recent years, historians and archaeologists have concluded that Atlantis was probably Minoan Crete. The Minoans did have hot and cold running water, a code of laws revised every five years, and so on, and their civilization abruptly disappeared following a major eruption of the volcano Thera. (It helps to keep in mind that Egyptian historians of that long ago time were primarily interested in the activities of their rulers. They are notorious for omitting or distorting facts about the rest of the world.) Regardless of whether the story of Atlantis is taken as historical truth or a simple moralistic fable, it has inspired innumerable works of fiction and fantasy. This scenario is one more of those.

Who should you lead? Well, naturally, playing as the Atlanteans is a special challenge. The Greeks, Sumerians, and Egyptians also have a role to play in this history. You can play the Lemurians, but they're weak and cannot complete any quests; it's not much fun. The Europeans and Africans are not meant to be played.

This scenario is not objective based. That means that to win, you must either conquer the entire world or be the first to settle Alpha Centauri.

Advances

For the most part, research in this scenario progresses as in the typical classical world of *Civilization II*. After all, except for those extra land masses out in the ocean, this *is* the classical world. However, certain technologically superior civilizations can acquire special advances. In addition, there is a slightly unusual (and secret) method for discovering particular advances.

Units

A few of the units that are normally available have been removed to make room for monsters and super new units. For the most part, though, the units you know and love are still in there. In addition, some of those special advances we mentioned earlier lead to special new units.

As always, you can (and should) examine units you've built by calling up the Defense Minister's report, and the text Civilopedia has listings for all possible units. (There are some surprise units in this scenario. If you don't want to ruin the surprise, don't peek in the Civilopedia.)

Improvements and Wonders

A few of the City Improvements have been renamed to better fit the Atlantean milieu. Otherwise, things are as usual.

All the Wonders of the World have been renamed. None of them have changed their functions, however; only the names and icons are new.

Special Notes

The only significant other thing you ought to know is that each turn in Atlantis is 30 years, and you have about 400 turns.

THE CRUSADES

(Designed by Mick Uhl)

To play this scenario, load the file **crusades.scn**, which you can find in the directory named **Crusades**.

Toward the end of the 11th century A.D., political, religious, and economic pressures resulted in a call from the European Christian hierarchy to drive the "infidel" Turks from the Middle East. Those same pressures encouraged the leaders of the time to acquiesce. The resulting decades of rapine, torture, and other senseless violence are collectively called the Crusades. In this scenario, you have from 1096 until 1220 A.D. to take part in this wanton bloodshed—or try to change the course of things for the better.

From the start, the forces of the European powers are set against the Seljuk Turks, though they do tend to squabble among themselves. The poor Byzantines are caught in the middle, and the Fatimid Egyptians aren't allowed to remain neutral for long.

Barkiyarok and the Seljuk Turks are the protagonists of the scenario. Their goal is to protect their cities, lands, and peoples from the armies sweeping down on them with the blessing of the European churches. The Crusading armies' goal, conversely, is to liberate as many cities as possible from the infidel Turks, in the name of Christianity.

ADVANCES

In part because of the emphasis on religion and warfare throughout the Crusades, civilization in Europe had not quite yet escaped the Dark Ages. To reflect that in the scenario, the research possibilities are severely curtailed. If you look at the **Advances Chart** that came with your original copy of ***Civilization II Multiplayer Gold Edition***, you can pretty much forget anything in the purple and pink boxes—and about half the blue ones, too.

One important result of this is that quite a number of units, improvements, and wonders are not available in this scenario.

There are two new advances, each of which has been granted to a particular civilization at the beginning of the scenario and neither of which any civilization can research.

- The **Holy Lance** makes it possible to build the new Knights Templar unit.
- The **True Cross** similarly allows the Knights Hospitaler unit.

You must capture at least one of these advances if you expect to do well in the Crusades.

UNITS

This scenario has more new units than you can shake a piece of the True Cross at. In addition, the stricture of the advances tree makes quite a number of units totally unavailable. There are two new units worth special mention:

- **Knights Templar** are built only by civilizations that hold the secret of The Holy Lance.
- **Knights Hospitaler** units form only for a leader who has knowledge of The True Cross.

> **Nitpicker's Note:** Both Knights units are in User Defined slots. Thus, no types of unit are made unavailable by their existence.

As always, you can examine the new units by calling up the DEFENSE MINISTER's report. None of the other units has been tampered with significantly.

WONDERS

On top of the fact that many wonders are simply not available because of the limited research opportunities, a few of those you can get have been modified.

- **Marco Polo's Embassy** has been renamed **Roman Embassy**.
- The effects of the **Great Library**, **Great Wall**, and **Sun Tzu's War Academy** have all expired already when the scenario begins.

Here are a few more things you ought to know:

- The Seljuk Turks cannot negotiate with anyone.
- Changing governments is not possible in the Crusades scenario.
- Pollution is not a factor.
- This is a Bloodlust scenario, meaning that spacecraft are not a consideration. You can only win utterly before the timer runs out if you conquer the whole world.
- Each turn is one year.
- Scientific research progresses at the normal 10/10 rate.

THE GREAT WAR

(Designed by Mick Uhl)

To play this scenario, load the file **ww1.scn**, which you can find in the directory named **WW1**.

World War I has been called by many names, but "The Great War" was one of the most popular while the fighting was still going on. In the beginning, some felt that this would be a gentlemen's war, but that fantasy evaporated quickly when truthful reports from the front lines began filtering back home. When chemical warfare entered the field, Europe got its first taste of what modern warfare was to be like. They didn't like it a bit.

We suggest that you play the Central Powers, French, or Russians. Most of the combatants have some chance, but the Americans, Neutrals, and Italians have such limited resources at the start that you might find them less than fun to play.

Wilhelm II and his Central Powers are the protagonists of the scenario, and their objective (as always) is to capture as many cities as possible.

ADVANCES

Three new advances appear in this scenario, reflecting areas of concern at the time.

Aeronautics requires Flight and Machine Tools. This advance makes Zeppelins possible.

Chemical Warfare requires Chemistry and Mass Production. Once you've researched this, you can start building Poison Gas units.

Special Training requires Chemical Warfare and Mobile Warfare. This allows the building of Storm Troops.

WONDERS

Two wonders have been renamed, and some are not available due to missing advances.

- **Orthodox Church** replaces and has the same effects as Michelangelo's Chapel.
- **The Gaussian School** replaces and has the same effects as Copernicus' Observatory.

Otherwise, things are as normal.

UNITS

The new units in this scenario are few, but interesting.

- Some of the nations involved have their own specific infantry and cavalry units (**F Cavalry** for the French, and so on). The characteristics of these reflect the strengths and weaknesses of the armed forces of the time.
- **Adv. Fighter** is a more powerful version of the early fighter planes developed during the war.
- **Storm Troops** are an elite infantry unit.
- **Zeppelin** is a long-range bomber. Though slow and not quite as powerful, these have a longer range than the Bomber unit.
- **Poison Gas** is an assassin-style unit (single attack, like the Cruise Missile). Perhaps more than any other single weapon, gas attacks symbolize the brutality of this war.

As always, you can examine the new units by calling up the DEFENSE MINISTER's report. Many of the usual units have been tempered to match their historical counterparts.

SPECIAL NOTES

Here are a few more things you ought to know:

- The French and the Central Powers cannot negotiate with each other.
- Changing governments is not possible in the Great War scenario.
- Pollution is not a factor.
- This is a Bloodlust scenario, meaning that spacecraft are not a consideration. You can only win utterly before the timer runs out if you conquer the whole world.
- Each turn is one month.
- Scientific research progresses at a 20/10 rate, meaning that all advances take roughly twice as long to discover as they would in a typical game.

ICE PLANET

(Designed by Matt Bittman and Brandon Martin)

To play this scenario, load the file **iceplnet.scn**, which you can find in the directory named **Iceplnet**.

The Ventry are the native inhabitants of Jharlei, an icy world far from Earth. Their civilization is neither primitive nor backward, but the lack of resources on their continents has kept production slow and prevented them from leaving their home world. The Ventry were unaware that there are other intelligences in the universe—until recently, that is.

The Kydextrians are community organisms, like termites and bees. Their ancestors flew, but as their bodies grew in size, they lost this ability. They have depleted the natural resources of their home world, and now send out scout ships to comb the nearby solar systems in search of Tronadium, a rare mineral necessary for their reproduction. Unfortunately for the Ventry, Jharlei has rich deposits of Tronadium. The Kydextrians have landed an invasion force with the intention of destroying all other living things and taking the planet for their own. The invaders are industrious producers, but they have no regard for the effects of pollution on their environment. Even if the invasion is not successful, they will leave a dirty legacy on Jharlei.

In the midst of this growing violence, a group of human Galaxial Troops have crash-landed on the planet. They have not taken sides in the local war (yet), but are merely fighting to survive and return home. These elite soldiers field more powerful units than either of the other civilizations.

All three of the civilizations can be interesting and challenging to rule, and each has its pros and cons. As ruler of the Ventry, your goal is to eliminate both sets of invaders before the scenario ends. If you are the commander of the Galaxial Troops, all you really want is to build another spacecraft and leave this worthless planet. The Kydextrian queen has a single-minded determination to destroy every living thing that is not of her brood.

ADVANCES

There are substantial changes to the technology tree. (What else would you expect on a distant planet in the far future?) Each of the three civilizations has its own, private research branch, and the branches do not intersect. This means that each civilization has its own individual units, city improvements, and Wonders of the World.

UNITS

Every unit has been changed (or at least renamed).

Obviously, alien species have different units than the ancient humans of the normal game. In this scenario, the units are civilization-specific. That is, the Kydextrians can build one set of units, the Ventry another, and the human Galaxial Troops a third. Here are some vital details:

- The units that can act as Settlers are the **Nomads** 🐪, **Builder** 🛠, **Drone** 🛸, and **Slave** 🧍.

- The only diplomatic units are the **Diplomat** 🧍 and the **SNEAK** 🛫.

- The trade units (Caravan replacements) are called **Trader** 🚚 and **Air Freight** ✈.

As always, you can (and should) examine units you've built by calling up the Defense Minister's report, and the text Civilopedia has listings for all possible units.

IMPROVEMENTS AND WONDERS

Almost all of the city improvements and Wonders of the World have been renamed, and some have been attached to different advances. One or two have been removed from the scenario entirely. Those which are still available have not changed their functions, only the names and icons are new.

SPECIAL NOTES

Here are a couple more things you ought to know:

- Each turn is five years, and there are only 200 turns.

- There is no chance of technological gain when taking over a city.

JIHAD: THE RISE OF ISLAM

(Designed by Mick Uhl)

To play this scenario, load the file **jihad.scn**, which you can find in the directory named **Jihad**.

Beginning in 624 A.D., Islam spread through the Middle East like a forest fire. Many historians have given the credit for this to the able and inspiring leadership of Mohammed. In the Jihad scenario, you have the chance to see if you can live up to his example—or prevent him from becoming an example. The scenario ends in 756, so don't dawdle.

Any of the civilizations in this situation can be interesting to play, though the Arabs (under Mohammed) might be the most fun. Heraclius and his Byzantines are the protagonists of the scenario, which means they'll be aggressive about capturing cities.

ADVANCES

Before introducing the new units, let's go over what you must do to gain access to them. The designers have inserted three new advances early on and changed things around just a little. Here's the lowdown:

- **Chivalry** no longer has Horseback Riding and Feudalism as prerequisites. Rather, you reach Chivalry through two of the new advances: Military Science and Stirrups.

- **Stirrups** becomes available when you've researched Horseback Riding and Iron Working.

- **Military Science** is a consequence of University and Engineering.

- You can research the third, **Greek Fire**, once you've finished Military Science and Chemistry.

Otherwise, the research tree is not significantly different. A few advances are more easily accessible (to more closely reflect the historical situation), but most have not been modified at all. Invention is not available, which puts most of the modern advances out of reach.

UNITS

The new advances lead to two new units.

- The **Cataphract** is one result of researching Military Science. The Romans used this name for their version of armored cavalry—clothing both horse and rider in scale armor. (A certain type of heavily armored Greek war galley is also a Cataphract, but not in this scenario.)

- The **Dromon** comes with the invention of Greek Fire. This swift, fire-spouting ship was once the height of floating weaponry, though it certainly had its drawbacks—among them the tendency to burn itself up when firing against the wind.

Nitpicker's Note: The Cataphract and Dromon are in two of the User Defined slots. Thus, no types of unit are made unavailable by their existence.

As always, you can examine the new units by calling up the DEFENSE MINISTER's report (once you've built at least one). Many of the usual units have been altered slightly to balance the scenario, but none significantly. Note that Crusaders units are not available at all in this scenario.

SPECIAL NOTES

Here are a few more things you ought to know:

- Changing governments is not possible in the Jihad scenario.

- This is a Bloodlust scenario, meaning that spacecraft are not a consideration. You can only win utterly before the timer runs out if you conquer the whole world.

- Each turn is one year.
- Scientific research progresses at a 20/10 rate, meaning that all advances take roughly twice as long to discover as they would in a typical game.

MARS NOW!

(Designed by John Possidente)

To play this scenario, load the file **mars.scn**, which you can find in the directory named **Mars**.

The situation has been evolving for some time. Seven governments established bases on Mars. Working together, they managed to convert large portions of the Martian polar ice caps into a useable water supply. Just as this international cooperative effort was poised to begin the next step, warming the atmosphere to begin the overall terraforming of Mars, something went wrong back home. Communications ceased without warning; even the navigational telemetry from the Mars orbiters stopped. Assuming the worst—either a major war, the end of civilization, or both—the normally sanguine research and engineering staffs succumbed to irrationality. Contact between the seven bases was cut off, and attitudes grew cold.

As leader of one of the national bases, you have a choice. You can seek to conquer your neighbors and unify Mars by force, or you can strive to regain contact with Earth and find out what happened.

All of the civilizations in this scenario are meant to be playable. That is, every one has a fighting chance. However, if you're not particularly good at getting the best out of the land around your cities (resource management), you might not enjoy leading the landlocked Martian or Ukrainian colonies.

TERRAIN

As you'll no doubt notice as soon as you begin, the terrain on Mars is a wee bit different from Earth's. (The special resources are all new, too.) Here's a quick introduction:

Cratered: The thin atmosphere of Mars allows more meteorite impacts than does the thick protective blanket around the Earth. Volcanic and seismic activity on Mars is relatively rare as well, so that old craters are not erased as quickly as on more active planets. There is no liquid water to erode Martian craters, and though the wind there is fast, it cannot do the job that rivers do on Earth. What all this adds up to is that most of Mars is covered with craters of all sizes and shapes.

Volcanic Plains: In the past, the deep regions of Mars were warmer and more active. When a volcano erupts on a planet with Mars' low gravity, the hot mud and molten rock that spew forth spread over a wide (and sometimes oddly shaped) area. The relatively flat plains formed when these materials solidify are called, aptly enough, volcanic plains.

Channel Deposits: There is strong evidence that liquid water once ran on Mars as it does today on Earth. One of the visible clues is the existence of areas that resemble channels dug by rivers and floods. If water is truly to blame for these features, the soil in these areas should have a different composition than that in other places. There might even be water not far beneath the surface.

Canyon: Mars is home to some of the most dramatic and breathtaking canyons in the solar system. They're just like the canyons on Earth, except that many are much deeper and wider. Some are so deep, in fact, that you might look down from the rim on a cold morning and see the tops of clouds below.

Dark Dust: Like Earth's moon, most of the surface of Mars is covered with a layer of dust. However, not all Martian dust is created equal. Some of it is significantly darker than the rest (and no one knows exactly why, though there are respectable theories). This dark dust is often moved about by dust storms, which is one of the reasons two photos of Mars taken a few months apart can show entirely different color patterns.

Volcanic: All mountains on Mars are volcanic (crater rims don't count), though they're all also long extinct. In Mars' low gravity, eruptions can build incredibly high peaks, but the makeup of Martian rock is such that these mountains are also generally not very steep. Thus, the highest mountain in the solar system, Mons Olympus, is so broad that if you were walking on it you might not even notice that you were headed uphill! It wasn't only normal seismic activity that created the volcanic mountains on Mars; massive meteorites sometimes strike with enough violence to spark eruptions.

Permafrost: It's very cold on Mars. Much of what looks like ordinary soil is in fact laced with frozen carbon dioxide and (perhaps) water ice. In all recorded history, Mars has never been warm enough to thaw this soil. Nevertheless, some scientists believe that Martian permafrost holds most of the water on the dry planet. Despite this, mining permafrost produces only craters, not more water.

Icecap: The north and south polar regions of Mars, like those of Earth, are covered by thick layers of ice. Spectroscopic analysis shows these icecaps to be mixtures of frozen water and frozen carbon dioxide. Smart colonists would set up their base near the edge of a polar ice region, to ensure a reliable supply of water.

Terraformed: This land is much like that of Earth—moist, nutrient rich, and fertile. There is no naturally existing terrain of this type on Mars. Civilizations create it by terraforming other types of terrain (any *except* Canyon, Watershed, Icecap, or Volcanic). Important: terraformed ecosystems are terribly fragile; irrigation or mining will destroy it.

Watershed: Any open body of water on Mars is a resource bonanza—and the only way to irrigate other terrain. Until the icecaps began to melt, there were are no naturally existing watersheds; civilizations can create more by mining Icecap terrain. (This can cause problems for the unit doing the mining.)

ADVANCES

The entire technology tree has been uprooted and replaced.

Advances in this scenario are not all based on gaining new knowledge via research. Quite a few of the technologies represent the use of ingenuity—finding ways to do things that are already understood (and sometimes even common) on Earth, but doing them with only local Martian resources. In fact, all but a few of these technologies already exist! For the most part, the science is realistic, but for the sake of fun we've departed from accepted theory in a few minor instances (like positing a working pantisocracy).

That's all the detail we're giving away. After all, half the fun is in the discovery.

UNITS

Every unit has been changed.

The sort of military units that work well on Earth would, with minor modifications, probably function on Mars. However, a tiny colony, cut off from its homeland, must make do with the resources at hand. The types of unit that become possible are dictated by available materials, rather than knowledge. Scavenging parts from other machinery works for a while, but eventually any self-reliant colony must build up its own industrial base.

Here are the basics you'll need to know; the rest is up to you to discover:

- **Field Scientist** 🧍 is the Settler-type unit. This one can establish cities, build roads, and so on. The faster version (the Engineer) is the **Terraformer** 🧍.

- Naval units are few. Without large bodies of water, they aren't particularly useful.

As always, you can examine units you've built by calling up the Defense Minister's report, and the text Civilopedia has listings for all possible units.

IMPROVEMENTS AND WONDERS

All the city improvements and Wonders of the World have been renamed and attached to different advances. A few have been removed from the scenario entirely. Those which are still available have not changed their functions, only the names and icons are new.

SPECIAL NOTES

Here are a few more things you ought to know:

- Changing governments is possible, but they all have new names.

- This is a Bloodlust scenario, but that only means that spacecraft *bound for other stars* are not a consideration. There are two ways to win this scenario: regain contact with the Earth or conquer all of Mars. (Some would argue that, if you manage to terraform most of Mars, you will have won a more significant victory. We don't disagree.)

- There are no villages on Mars, but there might be Barbarians. After all, not all colonists remain sane.

- Each turn is one year, and you have quite a lot of them.

- Scientific research progresses at the normal rate.

MASTER OF MAGIC (JR.)

(Designed by Ken Burd)

To play this scenario, load the file **mom_jr.scn**, which you can find in the directory named **Momjr**.

Arcanus is a land similar in many ways to the medieval Earth. The primary difference, other than its location in another dimension, is the power of magic and the presence of fantastic creatures created using that magic. Magical knowledge is composed of many forces, but in Arcanus they are grouped into five specialties. Life magicians study and use the positive forces of protection and purity. Nature magi work respectfully with natural forces and the element Earth. Sorcerers weave the subtle fabric of the mind and command the elements Air and Water. Chaos wizards toy recklessly with destructive forces and the element Fire. Finally, the necromancers—Death Magicians—risk the very cores of their beings to draw on the negative powers of undeath and decay.

In this world, you have emerged as the champion of one of the elemental categories of magic. You begin with a single Wizard unit (representing yourself) and a small band of Peasants. Your goal is to create a mighty empire from these humble beginnings and prove the superiority of your magical abilities over those of the other wizards.

Each type of magic has its own benefits and drawbacks, but none is essentially better than any other. Your choice of which civilization to play is thus entirely up to you. This is not an objective based scenario, so scoring goes according to the normal rules.

ADVANCES

The entire technology tree has been uprooted and replaced.

A few of the civilization advances in this scenario are the same as those you're familiar with—Alphabet, Bronze Working, and so on. Don't let that fool you. These advances are the exceptions, not the rule. Most of the research in this scenario is territory that is completely new—and magical. The advances reflect Arcanus' dependence on magic rather than technology. Those of you who have played the original *Master of Magic* will find most of the names and concepts familiar.

The civilization you choose to lead determines what knowledge you begin with; each one has mastery of one category of magic. Any civilization can do limited research in the other fields, but none can progress to the more advanced spells that begin with Eldritch Lore, except within their chosen category.

That's all the detail we're giving away. After all, half the fun is in the discovery.

UNITS

Every unit has been changed.

The use of magic in place of technology has led the development of Arcanian military units in slightly different directions than that of Earth. The evocation of fantastic beings from other dimensions and realms has proved to be more popular than training and arming the local talent.

Here are a couple of clues that you'll need to know; the rest is up to you to discover:

- **Peasants** 🛉 is the Settler-type unit. This one can establish cities, build roads, and so on. The tougher version (the Engineer) is the **Zombies** 🍴.

- **Minion** 🍴 has the function of a Diplomat.

As always, you can examine units you've built by calling up the Defense Minister's report, and the text Civilopedia has listings for all possible units.

IMPROVEMENTS AND WONDERS

All the city improvements and Wonders of the World have been renamed and attached to different advances. A few have been removed from the scenario entirely. Those which are still available have not changed their functions, only the names and icons are new.

SPECIAL NOTES

Here are a few more things you ought to know:

- Knowledge of magic (of any category) can be traded, demanded, or stolen.

- This is a Bloodlust scenario, meaning that spacecraft are not a consideration. You can only win utterly before the timer runs out if you conquer the whole world.

- Each turn is one month.

- Magical research progresses at a 12/10 rate (120%), meaning that all advances take roughly one fifth longer to discover as they would in a typical game.

MASTER OF ORION (JR.)

(Designed by Ken Burd)

To play this scenario, load the file **moo_jr.scn**, which you can find in the directory named **Moojr**.

Several races of intelligent beings have their home in this volume of the galaxy. As they research new technology and expand the borders of their empires, it is inevitable that they come into conflict over the limited resources of this region.

There are many legends interwoven with the history of this region. They speak of an era of peace and prosperity brought about by the mighty Orion empire. Little is known about the fall of this empire, but there are hints and dark whispers that mention an ancient enemy called Antares. The past has had little affect on the races that inhabit this quadrant, except for the occasional new technology found in a derelict ship floating in space. There are rumors, though, of powerful warships that appear from nowhere, bent on destruction. Some think that the ancient enemy of the Orions may have returned. If this is so, only the fantastic technologies known only to the Orions will save the galaxy. Unfortunately, the location of Orion is unknown, except perhaps to a few Elerian mystics, and the legends speak of a terrible Guardian that watches over Orion.

ADVANCES

The entire technology tree has been uprooted and replaced.

Civilization advances in this scenario are the sort of futuristic technologies that would be useful to a spacefaring civilization. Those of you who have played the original **Master of Orion** or **Master of Orion II** will find some of the names and concepts familiar.

That's all the detail we're giving away. After all, half the fun is in the discovery.

UNITS

Every unit has been changed.

Interstellar exploration and combat requires a different sort of unit than is typically found on Earth. For the most, part, the units in this scenario are spaceships capable of traveling between the stars.

Here are the basics you'll need to know; the rest is up to you to discover:

- There is no Settler-type unit. The **Terraformer** 🦋 can improve your planets, but it takes time.

- Many units come in several levels of technological sophistication (for example, **Destroyer I**, **Destroyer II**, **Destroyer III**). Later versions of a unit are always more powerful, and they replace the earlier versions.

As always, you can (and should) examine units you've built by calling up the Defense Minister's report, and the text Civilopedia has listings for all possible units.

IMPROVEMENTS AND WONDERS

The city improvements and Wonders of the World have not been modified—not even renamed. However, at the start of this scenario, a few of them are already in existence. These are meant to simulate the Racial Attributes of each species in the original **Master of Orion** games:

Darloks: The species with great espionage abilities begins the game with the Great Library.

Klakons: The hive mind species enjoy all the benefits of a Fundamentalist government, but without the research penalty.

Elerians: The mystical warrior species starts the scenario with complete knowledge of the map *and* with Sun Tzu's War Academy.

Humans: The most charismatic species owns both the Eiffel Tower and United Nations.

Gnolams: The mercenary species has Adam Smith's Trading Company *and* a per-turn income that is 10 gold more than it would normally be.

Sakkra: The species with an incredible reproductive rate starts the scenario with the Pyramids.

SPECIAL NOTES

Here are a few more things you ought to know:

- Changing governments is not possible in the Master of Orion scenario.
- This is a Bloodlust scenario. You can only win before the timer runs out if you conquer all of the other civilizations in the game.
- Irrigation is not possible in this scenario. The Terraformer unit can, however, transform any planet into a more hospitable form. Keep in mind that terraforming takes a long, long time.

THE MONGOL HORDE

(Designed by Mick Uhl)

To play this scenario, load the file **mongol.scn**, which you can find in the directory named **Mongol**.

There was a time when the steppes of Asia were overrun with wild horsemen. In this case, that time is 1209 to 1328 A.D. The real Mongols swept southwest through the heart of the Chinese empire, then westward and north in an arc that brought them into violent contact with the Turks and other eastern European nations. Under Temujin, these warriors lost not one battle.

We suggest that you play as the Mongols, Chinese, or Turks. The other nations could be interesting, but these three are involved in the action earliest.

Temujin and his Mongol hordes are the protagonists of the scenario, and their objective is conquest, pure and simple. All the other civilizations would prefer to survive and, if possible, contain the spread of the hairy horsemen from the plains.

ADVANCES

Many of the usual advances (and thus all those things that rely on them) are not available for research in the Mongol scenario. Keep in mind that this does not necessarily mean that no civilizations have these. Some might begin the scenario with one or more of these advances.

Rampaging hordes aren't supposed to be interested in science, anyway.

UNITS

The new units in this scenario are legion. (Many of them are the same units as in the Crusades scenario.) Of course, the limits on advances also make several types of unit unavailable. In addition, a few have been cut out intentionally. A few of the new units deserve special mention.

- The Mongols are best represented by their **Elite Cavalry** (Elephant) and **Light Cavalry** (Mechanized Infantry) units. These bands of horsemen are not to be trifled with.

- The Chinese have their own special **C. Infantry** (Warriors) and **C. Cavalry** (Paratroopers), as well as one more powerful, elite unit, the **Sheng-ch'uan** (Partisans).

- The strength of the fledgling Japanese empire rests in the **S. Cavalry** (Cavalry), **Samurai** (Archers), and the new, assassin-style **Ninja** unit.

For those of you who keep track of the details, the Trireme is never made obsolete in this scenario. Musketeers are not available at all, and Cannon is a result of Gunpowder, not Metallurgy.

As always, you can examine the new units by calling up the DEFENSE MINISTER's report. None of the few leftover usual units has been tampered with too seriously.

WONDERS

Only three of the normal wonders have been modified:

- The Lighthouse and Great Wall are obsolete from the beginning.

- The Apollo Program is not available.

Otherwise, everything is as usual, wonder-wise.

SPECIAL NOTES

Here are a few more things you ought to know:

- Changing governments is not possible in the Mongol scenario.

- Pollution is not a factor.

- This is a Bloodlust scenario, meaning that spacecraft are not a consideration. You can only win utterly before the timer runs out if you conquer the whole world.

- Each turn is one year.

Scientific research progresses at the normal 10/10 rate.

THE MYTHIC HISTORY OF MIDGARD

(Designed by Mick Uhl)

To play this scenario, load the file **midgard.scn**, which you can find in the directory named **Midgard**.

Midgard is one of the names for this special land in which elves, humans, and other intelligent races have lived peacefully for quite some time. All that is changing, though, for the civilizations of Midgard have entered the Years of Encroaching Darkness, a period of restlessness and turmoil foretold by the sages and legends. A new and violent race, the Goblins, has appeared in Midgard. They breed uncontrollably and attack anyone or anything they meet. Ferocious attacks by marauding monsters have occurred, too. There is no evidence connecting this to the rise of the Goblins, but no one really knows.

Perhaps worse, sinister powers seem to be flexing and stretching long-unused muscles. The dead have begun to rise and harry the living; dark armies have launched savage attacks on peaceful settlements, then vanished with the dawn; legendary nightmare creatures, absent so long that they had been dismissed by most as fables, have reawakened to spread terror.

The civilized races of Midgard have been battered nearly to the brink of extinction. Your duty is obvious. Return your people to their former glory and beat back the encroaching darkness.

This is not an objective-based scenario. Space flight is unavailable. Therefore, conquest of the entire world would seem to be your goal. However, the designer says there are "other roads to winning" out there. You can play any of the civilizations, but two of them aren't designed to be played. Ruling the Stygians (and thus all the nasty monsters) wouldn't really be much fun. Leading the Goblins would be a little better, but still no challenge for a good player.

ADVANCES

The technology tree in this scenario has been modified pretty significantly, but not as drastically as it might seem at first glance. Many of the advances have been renamed to fit the fantasy milieu, but they haven't been changed in any other way. Some sections of the tree *have* been rearranged a bit, but the changes are fairly minor.

UNITS

There are just oodles of new units in this scenario, and most of the usual units are not available. That's to be expected, though. After all, when's the last time you heard of Elves in tanks? Many of the new units are specific to a certain civilization. (That means that you will *not* be able to build all of the units listed for advances you get; some are reserved for other tribes.) There are also some really outlandish creatures out there.

As always, you can (and should) examine units you've built by calling up the Defense Minister's report, and the text Civilopedia has listings for all possible units.

IMPROVEMENTS AND WONDERS

Many of the city improvements and most (if not all) Wonders of the World have been renamed to fit the milieu. As always, none have changed function.

SPECIAL NOTES

Here are a few more things you ought to know:

- Some of the terrain types do not produce exactly what they normally would. Specifically, the amount of trade (arrows) has been modified.
- This is a Bloodlust scenario, meaning that spacecraft are not a consideration.
- Each turn is one year, and there are only 400 turns.
- There are a few surprises lurking in this scenario. Enjoy them.

THE NEW WORLD

(Designed by Mick Uhl)

To play this scenario, load the file **newworld.scn**, which you can find in the directory named **Newworld**.

Take the continent of North America, with its early inhabitants, and prevent the exploration and colonization by the European powers. What do you get? In this case, that's for you to decide.

As leader of one of the major North American tribes, you can run your empire without fear of *conquistadores* or epidemics. Your lands will not be overrun by people from across the ocean. You do, however, have to watch out for those pesky *other* tribes...

This is not an objective-based scenario, so the victory conditions are those of standard ***Civilization II***: conquer the world or reach the stars. Any of the tribes should be fun to play. Steer clear of leading the Africans, however; they weren't designed to be played and probably wouldn't be any fun.

ADVANCES

Naturally, the progress of science is a bit different. For the most part, the early advances are new, and there are a few more than usual. Once your research gets beyond the Iron Age (or thereabouts), all the new strings weave into the old cloth— the advances become exactly what you're used to.

UNITS

The changes to the units you can build and use in this scenario follow a similar pattern as do the modifications to the advances. There are new ones early on, but they gradually shade into the usual progression. Some of the new units are special and unusual, but you'll find out for yourself.

As always, you can (and should) examine units you've built by calling up the Defense Minister's report, and the text Civilopedia has listings for all possible units.

IMPROVEMENTS AND WONDERS

Just about all of the city improvements and Wonders of the World have been renamed. None have changed function, however; only the names and icons are new.

SAMURAI

(Designed by Mick Uhl)

To play this scenario, load the file **samurai.scn**, which you can find in the directory named **Samurai**.

At roughly the same time as Europe was experiencing its "medieval" period, the Japanese were going through a major transition of their own. The nation was split under the control of several warring clans, feudal dynasties each run by a warlord— the *daimyo*. This era was every bit as chaotic, underhanded, and filled with palace intrigues as any in Western history. Peace and security came only after reunification had established one dominant daimyo clan as the rulers of the country.

In this scenario, you assume the role of daimyo of one the four major warring clans. Your goal is straightforward—defeat the other families and reunify Japan under your control. Your samurai, ninjas, and the crews of your warships are loyal and strong, but that is true of every clan. Leadership will be the deciding factor in this conflict. Be also watchful against the influence of outsiders. Their advanced weapons can be a critical aid, but there is no guarantee that they will deal solely with your clan.

You should play only as leader of one of the four feuding families—the Hojo, Taira, Shimaru, or Minamoto. The other civilizations (Europeans, Koreans, and Fujiwara) are not designed for play and won't be much fun.

ADVANCES

The technological advances in this scenario are not significantly different from those in the usual game. However, progress stops at a certain point; Future Tech comes much earlier than you would expect. Also, different civilizations might have access to advances not available to others—except through trade, of course.

UNITS

The samurai scenario contains a number of units specific to the setting (Ninja, for example). In addition, a few of the units are only available to certain civilizations. (After all, a Samurai would seem out of place as a European unit.) Other than these few, however, the units are essentially what you're accustomed to.

As always, you can (and should) examine units you've built by calling up the Defense Minister's report, and the text Civilopedia has listings for all possible units.

IMPROVEMENTS AND WONDERS

Pretty much all of the city improvements and Wonders of the World have been renamed. None have changed function, however; only the names and icons are new.

SPECIAL NOTES

Here are a few more things you ought to know:

- This is a Bloodlust scenario, meaning that spacecraft are not a consideration. You can only win utterly before the timer runs out if you conquer the whole world.

- Each turn is 2 years, and there are only 225 turns.

- Scientific research progresses at a 12/10 rate, meaning that all advances take roughly 120% as long to discover as they would in a typical game.

THE WAR FOR INDEPENDENCE

(Designed by Mick Uhl)

To play this scenario, load the file **independ.scn**, which you can find in the directory named **Independ**.

In 1776, the English colonies along the eastern coast of North America decided to break with the British Empire and go it on their own. Of course, mother England was not about to allow *that*.

We suggest that you play as either the Americans (Continental Congress) or the British (George III). Ruling the Iroquois or the French could be interesting, but not very.

King George III and the British are the protagonists of the scenario, and their objective is to recapture as many American cities as possible. Sounds easy enough. They have until 1783.

ADVANCES AND WONDERS

In the interest of historical accuracy, quite a number of advances are not available for research in this scenario. Considering the high price for research, you might not even notice.

Similarly, many of the Wonders of the World are either already obsolete or already built at the beginning of the scenario, or they simply are not available for building. This is a war, and you should be too busy to build them, anyway.

UNITS

There are too many new units in this scenario to even begin to describe here. You'll see Hessians, Tories, Continentals, Royal Infantry, and many more. As the Alexander the Great scenario does, this scenario includes two unique, irreplaceable units.

- **Geo. Washington** represents the top general of the rebel forces.

- **C. Cornwallis** stands in for the leader of the British empire's North American forces.

Though successors are waiting to take over and continue the struggle, the death of either general limits that side to at best a Marginal Victory, no matter how successful the actual outcome may be.

As always, you can examine any unfamiliar units using the HELP system and the DEFENSE MINISTER's report.

SPECIAL NOTES

Here are a few more things you ought to know:

- The British and Americans cannot negotiate with one another.
- If you are playing neither the British or French (both are computer-controlled), those two nations cannot negotiate with each other.
- Changing governments is not possible in the War for Independence scenario.
- No civilization can gain technological advances from the conquest of cities.
- Pollution is not a factor.
- This is a Bloodlust scenario, meaning that spacecraft are not a consideration. You can only win utterly before the timer runs out if you conquer the whole world.
- Each turn is one month.
- Scientific research progresses at a 40/10 rate, meaning that all advances take roughly four times as long to discover as they would in a typical game. (In other words, don't bother.)

THE WORLD OF JULES VERNE

(Designed by Mick Uhl)

To play this scenario, load the file **verne.scn**, which you can find in the directory named **Verne**.

Adventures in exotic lands, weird discoveries made by men with odd philosophies, travels and experiences beyond the imagination of the average person—these are the foundation on which Jules Verne built his world. These are the things you can expect in this scenario.

In the Victorian era (of which Monsieur Verne was a part) the romance of exploration was upon the world. Africa was still called "the Dark Continent" and had not yet been fully mapped by European explorers. Asia was "the Mysterious East" the inhabitants of which were "inscrutable" to the average gentleman and lady. "The South Seas" remained an unexplored enigma in which anything—*anything at all*—might be discovered. Despite growing awareness of the horrors of industrialization, the population of "the civilized world" had faith that a grand new universe was being built on the twin pillars of Science and Invention.

It is into this world that you step. There are two ways to succeed in this situation. One may, of course, attempt to conquer the world. The other option is to make the voyage *From the Earth to the Moon* before any other civilization does so. Generally speaking, a gentleman or lady would not consider world conquest a victory; that is the province of madmen. To succeed honorably, without deceit or unnecessary violence, is the mark of a truly superior intellect.

We strongly recommend that you chose to lead either the Anglo Alliance or the Continental Alliance. The scenario really revolves around them. It can be interesting to play the ruler of the Muslims, the Asians, or the Secret Evil Society, but it's not really as much fun. Do not expect to enjoy it if you play as the Aborigines; at the start of the scenario, they are extremely far behind technologically, and their chances of winning are almost nil. The Exotics are not meant to be played at all; their existence serves the purposes of the scenario, but that's all.

Get out and explore!

ADVANCES

Though Exploration (with a capital 'E') was the primary motivating force in Verne's stories, the imagery of his worlds epitomizes for many the concept of Science (with a capital 'S'). It's a reminder that there was once a time when it was possible to believe that Science could fix just about anything. It's only natural, then, that the progress of science is important to this scenario.

Generally speaking, the early advances have not been monkeyed with. Once your research gets past a certain point, however, all bets are off. You've entered the Verne Zone, and there's no telling what you might discover.

UNITS

The list of units you can build has been modified pretty substantially. Many of the units are civilization-specific; they can only be built by a certain civilization. A few are special, individual units that no civilization can build. The key in this situation is to use what you have and *explore, explore, explore!*

As always, you can (and should) examine units you've built by calling up the Defense Minister's report, and the text Civilopedia has listings for all possible units.

IMPROVEMENTS AND WONDERS

A few of the city improvements and Wonders of the World have been renamed, but not many. Most are exactly what you're used to. As always, none have changed function.

SPECIAL NOTES

There are a couple more things you ought to know:

- This is a Bloodlust scenario, meaning that spacecraft *destined for other star systems* are not a consideration. The Moon is not in another star system.
- Each turn is two months, and there are roughly 320 turns.

WORLD WAR: 1979

(Designed by Mick Uhl)

To play this scenario, load the file **ww79.scn**, which you can find in the directory named **WW79**.

In 1979, when Iranian religious fanatics invaded a U.S. Embassy and took a number of hostages, then-President Jimmy Carter took the sane and intelligent route out of the situation—but what if he hadn't? Considering the state of nuclear readiness at that time, the result might have been something like this scenario.

We suggest that you play as one of the four big nuclear powers—North America, the Soviet Bloc, China, or the West Europeans. The other nations are small (and the Middle East has no nukes), but could present a challenge for the experienced player.

Brezhnev and the Soviet Bloc are the protagonists of the scenario. Their objective is the usual: capture as many cities (or what's left of them) as possible before 1990 rolls around and ends the scenario.

UNITS

There are no new units in this scenario. Only one of the existing units has been modified significantly; **Paratroopers**' range for paradrops is much shorter than normal. Otherwise, everything is pretty much unchanged, except for minor tweaks to keep things fun.

SPECIAL NOTES

Here are a few more things you ought to know:

- No civilization can gain technological advances from the conquest of cities.
- This is a Bloodlust scenario, meaning that spacecraft are not a consideration. You can only win utterly before the timer runs out if you conquer the whole world.
- Each turn is two months.
- Scientific research progresses at an 80/10 rate, meaning that all advances take roughly eight times as long to discover as they would in a typical game. Don't even try.

X-COM: ASSAULT

(Designed by Bob Abe)

> To play this scenario, load the file **xcom.scn**, which you can find in the directory named **Xcom**.

The year is 2008. In the years since the First Alien War, manned exploration and salvage missions to Cydonia have been common. Recently, however, X-COM has discovered eight previously undetected alien bases on Mars' moon Phobos. X-COM has built three new assault ships capable of crossing the vast interplanetary void and sent them to wipe out this last vestige of alien activity.

You are the Commander of X-COM's Alpha Assault Team. Your objective is to use the limited manpower at your disposal to wipe out all eight of the known alien bases. A great deal of effort went into organizing this attack, and the entire human race is counting on you. You have only the units that could fit into three ships, plus their weapons, so don't concern yourself with the upkeep or improvement of your landing sites. You might, however, want to post sentries at each one; the aliens saw you land, and they will more than likely attempt to destroy your means of returning to Earth.

We strongly recommend that you play this scenario only as the Commander of the X-COM forces; the scenario is not designed to be played from the alien point of view. Your three landing sites are in close proximity to one another, and your units have already begun to set up a perimeter around each ship. To secure a victory, you must find and destroy all eight of your objectives *and* prevent the aliens from capturing all of your ships.

TERRAIN

You'll notice right away that the terrain (and everything on it) looks different. Many of the terrain types have been renamed, as well. Though this may seem like a significant change, in terms of city resources it is actually not important, because you will not be building any cities or improving terrain.

Where the new terrain types do affect the game is in the defense modifier. As would be the case on any alien planet, however, you must find out for yourself what type of terrain is most defensible.

ADVANCES

This scenario is an all-out battle, and all of the X-COM personnel are soldiers; therefore, researching anything is virtually impossible. Even if you were to acquire some new technology, it wouldn't provide any assistance in your war against the aliens. You have what you need to win at the start of the scenario, it's whether or not you use your units wisely that matters.

UNITS

There are a few new units in this scenario. Those on the X-COM side of things are:

Alpha Squads are elite squads equipped with heavy, yet flexible armor. They're armed with modified machine guns that fire unconventional ammo.

M.O.U.T. Team soldiers specialize in close-quarters combat (MOUT stands for Military Operations in Urban Terrain). Their light armor and medium force weapons—Heavy Plasma Rifles—allow them take the fight to the enemy in a fast and furious attack style.

Scout Platoons are the best at quick intelligence gathering in alien-controlled areas. Their long-range sighting and radio communications help provide you with the big picture. Armed only with machine guns and light armor, they're best kept out of battles.

Heavy Sections provide the knockout punch in any major assault. Protected by heavy armor and packing the ever-so-powerful Blaster Launcher, these soldiers like nothing better than authorization to cut loose on the aliens.

B.A.U. (Base Assault Units) are one to a ship. These powerful attack vehicles can destroy even the most heavily defended units, but they aren't much on defense; you must protect them from attack. The B.A.U. project was still in the prototype stage when your mission was launched, and their armor has not been optimized against heavy plasma weaponry.

The alien units are completely unknown to you. Don't worry, you'll find out about them soon enough.

IMPROVEMENTS AND WONDERS

There is no point in building improvements and Wonders of the World in this scenario. This is an invasion, not a colony.

SPECIAL NOTES

Here are a few more things you should know:

- Neither side can obtain technological advances from the conquest of a base.
- Changing governments is not possible in the X-COM scenario.
- This is a Bloodlust scenario, meaning that the only way you can win is to completely eliminate the aliens.
- You have just over 300 turns to defeat the alien menace. Each turn is one month.
- The total lack of scientists in the invasion force hampers research efforts a bit. You're not in this to putter around in a lab coat; you're here to kick alien butt!

THE BEST OF THE NET

These are the scenarios we chose from among the hundreds available on the Internet. We hope you enjoy them as much as we did.

ATOLON

by Antonio Leal

To play this scenario, load the file **atolon.scn**, which you can find in the directory **Bestonet\Atolon**.

THE CHOLERA OF ZEUS

by Antonio Leal

To play this scenario, load the file **zeus.scn**, which you can find in the directory **Bestonet\zeus**.

THE CONQUEST OF BRITAIN

by Jeppe Grue and Jan Dimon Bendtsen

To play this scenario, load the file **britain.scn**, which you can find in the directory **Bestonet\Brit1011**.

CROSS AND CRESCENT

by Eric Hartzell

To play this scenario, load the file **croscres.scn**, which you can find in the directory **Bestonet\Croscres**.

THE FALL OF THE GREAT KESH

by Tim McBride

To play this scenario, load the file **kesh.scn**, which you can find in the directory **Bestonet\Kesh**.

EAST WIND, RAIN

by Don Melsom

To play this scenario, load the file **eastwind.scn**, which you can find in the directory **Bestonet\EastWind**.

PERSIAN GULF WAR

by Kevin Bromer

To play this scenario, load the file **gulfwar.scn**, which you can find in the directory **Bestonet\GulfWar**.

NATIVE REBELLION

by Mike Regan

To play this scenario, load the file **rebel.scn**, which you can find in the directory **Bestonet\Rebel**.

THE BEST OF THE NET II

These are some more scenarios we chose from among the hundreds available on the Internet. We hope you enjoy them as much as we did.

BATTLE OF THE SEXES

by Brian D. Wassom

To play this scenario, load the file **battle.scn**, which you can find in the directory **BestNet2\Battle**.

CIV-LIFE

by Charles Magee

To play this scenario, load the file **bio.scn**, which you can find in the directory **BestNet2\Bio**.

HIDDEN

by Antonio Leal

To play this scenario, load the file **hidden.scn**, which you can find in the directory **BestNet2\Hidden**.

SANTA IS COMING

by Mike McCart

To play this scenario, load the file **santa.scn**, which you can find in the directory **BestNet2\Santa**.

BEARS AT PLAY

by Mike McCart

To play this scenario, load the file **bears.scn**, which you can find in the directory **BestNet2\Bears**.

USA 2010

by Jeff Head

To play this scenario, load the file **usa2010.scn**, which you can find in the directory **BestNet2\Usa2010**.

MAMMOTH

by Jeff Head

To play this scenario, load the file **mammoth.scn**, which you can find in the directory **BestNet2\Mammoth**.

PARADISE

by Jeff Head

To play this scenario, load the file **paradise.scn**, which you can find in the directory **BestNet2\Paradise**.

MULTIPLAYER GAMES

Like most things in life, *Civilization II* is more fun when it involves other people. That's what the multiplayer aspect of *Civilization II Multiplayer Gold Edition* is all about—sharing the fun. You can play with others in the same room or with a group of people on a network or over the Internet.

The differences in how the game plays are relatively minor. There are some new diplomatic functions, and the method of taking turns has a few new twists. Otherwise, multiplayer *Civ II* is the same game you already know. It's just more fun.

GETTING CONNECTED

Before you attempt to start a multiplayer game of *Civilization II*, make sure that you are connected to at least one other computer via the type of communications you expect to use—an Internet service provider (ISP) or a network. (If you're planning on playing a *Hot Seat* game, naturally this is a moot point.) The hardware connection is your responsibility; we cannot instruct you in this.

If you're the technically oriented sort, it might help to know that you can modify the time-out (latency) for each of the various types of connection. The default values are stored in a text file in the Windows directory; this file is named **civ.ini.** Note that this file does not exist until you have started up the game at least once, and the value for each type of connection is not established (and written into the file) until you have used that type of connection at least once. Each of the values is on a line by itself, and they're all in seconds.

Do not edit anything else in this file, or you risk causing problems with the game.

STARTING THE GAME

Getting a multiplayer game started is a relatively simple process. For the most part, it's just like setting up any other game of *Civilization II*—there are just a few additional steps. The first difference is that you must select MULTIPLAYER GAME from the first menu. Once you've done so, you go directly to the MULTIPLAYER GAME menu. The options on this menu represent the different ways you can play a multiplayer game of *Civilization II*.

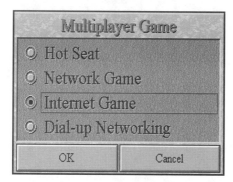

Hot Seat: Everyone plays on the same computer; you just take turns at the keyboard. (You might be surprised how much fun this can be.) When it's not your turn, the AI handles diplomacy for your empire.

Network Game: The game takes place over a Local Area Network (LAN). Each player plays at his or her own computer. Diplomacy between human players takes place in the NEGOTIATION window.

Internet Game: This is just like a network game, except that you're playing over a really big network called the Internet.

Dial-up Networking: This is also just like a network game, except for the method you use to contact the network.

Choose the type of multiplayer game you plan to play, then click the OK button to confirm your choice or CANCEL to return to the previous menu.

After you've chosen the type of game, you end up at a menu that's remarkably similar to the first menu in *Civilization II Multiplayer Gold Edition*. The list of options includes many that you are already familiar with, and also one or two that are specific to multiplayer games. Here are all of the options that might appear on this menu.

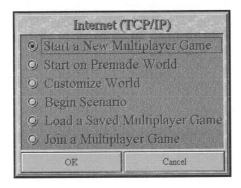

Start a New Multiplayer Game: Begin an entirely new multiplayer game of the type you chose. Choosing this option means going through the usual game setup steps, plus a few additional ones, as we explain below. The person starting a multiplayer game is considered the *host* for that game.

Start on Premade World: Play a multiplayer game on a custom map created with the MAP EDITOR utility or a map extracted from a saved game. Choosing this option is no different from starting a new game (as above), except that you choose a particular map.

Customize World: Specify the general characteristics of the world on which to start your new game. Choosing this option is no different from starting a new game (as above), except that you go through the world design setup, too.

Begin Scenario: Choose this option to load a scenario and play it as a multiplayer game. *Civilization II Multiplayer Gold Edition* doesn't discriminate between scenarios and other games; you can play any scenario as a multiplayer game. There's one minor caveat. When you load a scenario as a multiplayer game, each player chooses an empire to rule from among the civilizations already existing in the selected scenario—no one can start a new civilization.

Note: If you're playing a scenario as a multiplayer game, every player involved must have that scenario installed. Keep in mind that the scenarios were not designed for multiplayer games, and they might not function exactly as you expect.

Be especially wary of advances designed to prevent tribes from building each other's "private" units. If you gain the wrong advance, you might find all your units are obsolete!

Load a Saved Multiplayer Game: Load and continue a previously saved game. You can load *any* valid saved game (see the sidebar for a list of the possible types) and play it as the type of multiplayer game you chose, regardless of whether the saved game started life as that type—or even as a multiplayer game. Even though you're loading a saved game, you are still considered the *host* for the game.

Join a Multiplayer Game: Add your name to the list of potential rulers for the type of game you chose—one that someone else is hosting. To join a *Network* game, you select from the GAMES ON THE NETWORK list. Click on any game in the list to get the scoop about it, then click OK to ask to join. If a game is not available, it is either closed or already full. To join an *Internet* game, you must enter the IP Address of the game you want to join. If you don't know the IP Address, you can't ask to join the game.

Use the OK button to confirm your choice or CANCEL to quit **Civilization II**.

TYPES OF SAVED GAMES

There are several different types of saved game files, one for each type of game that you might save. So that you (and the game) can recognize each kind of saved game at a glance, every type has an distinct file extension. They are:

- **.SAV** for normal, single player games
- **.NET** for scenarios saved during a multiplayer game
- **.HOT** for *Hot Seat* games
- **.NET** for *Network* and *Internet* games

Remember that scenario saved games are stored in the scenario directory.

The following small sections describe the few unusual setup procedures required for multiplayer games in general and those for each type of multiplayer game. Outside of these exceptions, the rest of the setup is not significantly different from the way you begin any other game of **Civilization II**. There are also a few features, menu options, and other items of interest peculiar to multiplayer games; we cover all of those in **Special Features**.

GENERAL SETUP

If you're setting up a multiplayer game, you are the *host*. As host, you have control over how the game will behave. (You have no control over how the other players will behave.) The MULTIPLAYER FEATURES menu gives you the opportunity to decide on several important issues.

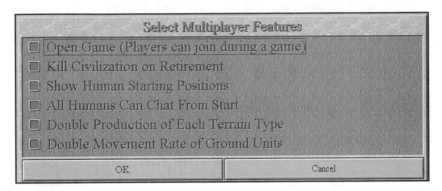

Select Multiplayer Features

☐ Open Game (Players can join during a game)
☐ Kill Civilization on Retirement
☐ Show Human Starting Positions
☐ All Humans Can Chat From Start
☐ Double Production of Each Terrain Type
☐ Double Movement Rate of Ground Units

OK	Cancel

Open Game: A *closed* game is one in which no new players can join once the action has started. In an *open* game, you allow new human players to jump in and take over any civilizations not already controlled by someone, provided that there are any. For example, in a seven-civilization Open multiplayer game with only two human players, two more players could join during the game. Enable this option to make your game an open game.

Kill Civilization on Retirement: When this option is enabled, all of the cities and units of any player who retires or quits are immediately destroyed. If you leave this disabled, the game takes over instead and rules the civilization. Note that, in an open game, this would allow another player to join and take over that civilization.

Show Human Starting Positions: In some games, you'd prefer that all of the players know each others' starting positions. (It makes finding one another much easier if you're planning to cooperate.) When this option is enabled, the starting positions of *all* human-led civilizations in the game are visible on *everyone's* WORLD MAP from the beginning of the game. When this option is disabled, starting positions are hidden, just as they are in a single-player game.

All Humans Can Chat From Start: You cannot normally speak with other kings until you have encountered one of their ground units or cities. This option is a partial way around that; when it's enabled, you can use the CHAT WITH KINGS option (described in **Special Features**) to contact any other human ruler in the game. You still cannot negotiate, however, until you've met face to face. Leave this disabled, and the original rules apply.

Double Production of Each Terrain Type: Sometimes, multiplayer games progress more slowly than you'd prefer. If you want to speed up the rate at which things get done (city growth, research, income, and production), use this option to double the output of every terrain type—food, trade, and production shields.

Double Movement Rate of Ground Units: Another way to speed up the pace of a multiplayer contest is to allow units to move faster. If you check this option, every ground unit in the game (but not sea or air units) has its movement allowance doubled. Note that this does not affect the movement cost of terrain.

When you've got those options as you want them, the next step is to decide on the GAME TIMER. This clock determines the length of time each player has to take a single turn. After all, you might be waiting while three other people take their turns, and you don't want them dawdling. You can use the GAME TIMER to keep games moving at a reasonable pace. Choose one of the preset time limits or set this to any turn length between 10 seconds and 3600 (one hour). If you don't want to limit the length of turns, select *Unlimited*. The turn timer countdown is displayed in the title bar of the MAP window.

During the game, the Host can propose to change the time limit and the status of either (or both) of the doubling options. If all of the players agree (the vote must be unanimous), the change goes into effect.

HOT SEAT

There is only one extra choice to make when setting up a *Hot Seat* game. After you have already decided how many civilizations there will be, you're prompted to choose the number of human rulers participating in the game. Select any of the number from two players up to four. Any civilizations left over are controlled by the game, as usual.

NETWORK GAME

When you choose to play over a network, there are two extra steps you must take.

- Step One is to select the network protocol that you are using. **Civilization II Multiplayer Gold Edition** supports both the TCP/IP and IPX/SPX protocols.

- Step Two is entering your NET NAME. This is simply the name by which you want to be known on the network. You can enter any name you want, but you cannot leave your NET NAME blank.

If you're *joining* someone else's game, that's all the extra setup you need to do. If, on the other hand, you are *hosting* your own game, there are two more steps to take.

1. *Name the game.* You must give your game a name. This is the name that appears on the GAMES ON THE NETWORK list, from which other players select a game to join. The name can be whatever you want, but you cannot leave it blank.

2. *Choose the players.* Once you've named your game, you see the PLAYERS ON THE NETWORK list. On it are the names of all the players who want to join your game. When you click on the START GAME button, the game begins with *all* of the listed players included. (You *can* start a game by yourself, and if it's open, others can join later.) If there are players in the list you don't want included, select each in turn and click the REJECT PLAYER button to remove the highlighted name from the list. (Rejected players are notified.) Use CANCEL if you change your mind about the game entirely.

Once you've clicked the START GAME button, the game begins.

INTERNET GAME

When you choose to play over the Internet, there is one extra step you must take.

The one step is to enter your NET NAME. This is simply the name by which you want to be known online. You can enter any name you want, but you cannot leave your NET NAME blank.

If you're *joining* someone else's game, that's all the extra setup you need to do. If, on the other hand, you are *hosting* your own game, there are a few more steps to take.

1. *Name the game.* You must give your game a name. This is the name that appears on the GAMES ON THE NETWORK list, from which other players select a game to join. The name can be whatever you want, but you cannot leave it blank.

2. *Choose the players.* Once you've named your game, you see the PLAYERS ON THE NETWORK list. On it are the names of all the players who want to join your game. When you click on the START GAME button, the game begins with *all* of the listed players included. (You *can* start a game by yourself, and if it's open, others can join later.) If there are players in the list you don't want included, select each in turn and click the REJECT PLAYER button to remove the highlighted name from the list. (Rejected players are notified.) Use CANCEL if you change your mind about the game entirely.

3. *Verify the IP Address.* Before the game can begin, you must verify the IP Address of your computer (the *host machine*). If the displayed IP Address is incorrect, type in the correct address before proceeding.

Once you've clicked the START GAME button and verified the IP Address, the game begins.

A Note on Choosing Tribes

After all the setup is complete and the game begins, every player makes the usual choices—a tribe, a name, titles, a city style, and so forth. At this point, you'll notice one of the only differences in the game setup procedure for multiplayer games.

As players select tribes to rule, the choices become more and more limited. That's because the civilizations selected by players who have already passed this point are no longer available. In addition, all the tribes that normally use the same color as a civilization already spoken for (the ones in the same row) are also unavailable. That's because there can only be one tribe of each color in the game, and the colors are preset. For example, if Player 1 chose the Egyptians as his tribe, Player 2 would not be able to select the Egyptians, the Aztecs, or the Spanish, because all three civilizations share a single color (Yellow).

If you dawdle, you might see tribes disappear as other people make their choices. Also, in the rare instance when you and another player pick a tribe of the same color at the same time, only one of you gets that tribe; the other player must pick again.

SPECIAL FEATURES

There are a few features in **Civilization II Multiplayer Gold Edition** that are applicable only to multiplayer games. (These features are not even available during single player games.) This section introduces them all.

Note that during multiplayer games, all of the pop-up boxes and notices have time limits. Be sure to deal with them in a timely manner, or you might lose your chance.

On the Game Menu

The GAME menu includes a few multiplayer-only options.

Join Game: This option is available only during *Hot Seat* games. Use it to add a new player to a game already in progress.

Set Password: Allows you to protect your civilization from poachers by setting a password lock on it. Whenever you load a saved multiplayer game or join a game loaded by someone else, each player reselects their civilization from those included in that saved game. Unless you have assigned a password to your civilization, an unscrupulous player could select *your* civilization as their own.

Change Timer: Allows the host player to reset the GAME TIMER. This clock determines the length of time each player has to take a single turn. Choose one of the preset time limits or set this to any turn length between 10 seconds and 3600 (one hour). If you don't want to limit the length of turns, select *Unlimited*. The turn timer countdown is displayed in the title bar of the MAP window. If the Host proposes to change the time limit during the game, all of the players must agree (the vote must be unanimous) before the change goes into effect.

Multiplayer Options: This option calls up a checklist of other options. Each of these is a toggle; those with checked boxes are currently "on," and those with empty boxes are "off." Click on an option to toggle it on or off. When you have these options set as you want them, click OK to return to the game. If you change your mind and wish to discard your changes, click on CANCEL instead. The MULTIPLAYER OPTIONS are:

- *Clear chat buffer at the start of a new game*: When you enable this, old messages are cleared out of the CHAT window whenever you start a new game or load a saved game.

- *Clear chat buffer each time we boot up*: Turn this on to have old CHAT messages cleared every time you start **Civilization II Multiplayer Gold Edition**.

- *Double production of each terrain type*: If you're the Host, use this to propose a change in the doubling status for terrain output. If you propose to change this during the game, all of the players must agree (the vote must be unanimous) before the change goes into effect.

- *Double movement rate of ground units*: If you're the Host, use this to propose a change in the doubling status for the movement allowance of ground units. If you propose to change this during the game, all of the players must agree (the vote must be unanimous) before the change goes into effect.

In addition, one of the normal game options is not available. The TUTORIAL HELP option under GAME OPTIONS does not function during multiplayer games.

ON THE ADVISORS MENU

The ADVISORS menu contains one new option, CHAT WITH KINGS. This opens the CHAT window, in which you can exchange messages with other players. For the detailed description of how chatting works, please read the **Chat with Kings** section in **Playing a Multiplayer Game**. Chat features are not available in *Hot Seat* games.

ON THE CHEAT MENU

If you're playing a multiplayer game, no one has access to the CHEAT menu. The CHEAT menu features are not available in multiplayer games.

ON THE EDITORS MENU

If you're playing a multiplayer game, no one has access to the EDITORS menu. The EDITORS menu features are not available in multiplayer games.

NEGOTIATION WINDOW

Whenever you enter into negotiations with another human player, the bargaining process takes place in the NEGOTIATION window. This window includes all sorts of options, so that you have the flexibility when dealing with humans that is certainly necessary during multiplayer games. For the detailed description of how the window works, please read the **Initiating Negotiations** section in **Playing a Multiplayer Game**. The NEGOTIATION window is irrelevant in *Hot Seat* games, and thus it does not appear.

PLAYING A MULTIPLAYER GAME

Once the setup is done and everyone has connected to the game and taken over a civilization, play begins in earnest. Multiplayer *Civilization II* is turn-based, just like single-player games.

Remember, if the host player has activated the GAME TIMER, you have a limited amount of time to complete your turn.

This basic truth applies to every multiplayer method of playing, but not all of them works in exactly the same way. There are some features and differences intrinsic to each method. We'll take them one at a time.

HOT SEAT

In a *Hot Seat* game, all the players take their turns at the same computer, one after the other. (Those players who are not currently taking their turns should probably avert their eyes.) The computer-controlled civilizations (if there are any) make their moves in turn, just as in any other game of *Civilization II*.

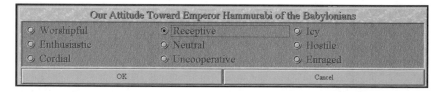

If it's not your turn and someone wants to negotiate with your civilization, the negotiations are handled by the computer as if it were ruling your empire. Obviously, this could leave you vulnerable to another player's ethical lapses—even if you are standing nearby. The negotiating tactics of the AI are somewhat predictable, and almost certainly won't match your intentions. To compensate for this loss of control, you can set your civilization's attitude toward each of the other empires in the world:

- Call up your **Foreign Minister** and select a civilization to set your attitude toward.

- Click the **Set Attitude** button.

- Choose an attitude by checking the appropriate box.

- Click **OK** to put the new attitude into effect or **Cancel** to leave without changing your attitude.

Thus, for example, you could set your attitude to *Hostile* or *Icy* to prevent the computer from giving anything away (particularly money and advances) while you're not watching.

If additional players want to join a *Hot Seat* game already in progress, each can take over one of the computer-controlled civilizations using the JOIN GAME option on the GAME menu—but only if there is at least one civilization in the game which is not already controlled by a human player.

ALL OTHER TYPES

The games you play over a network or the Internet are likely to be among the most challenging and exciting *Civilization II* games you'll ever play. You'll be facing at least one and as many as six human opponents—possibly from all over the world—each one an experienced emperor.

These games play in the same order as any other. There's one big difference, however. During your turn, all you should do is move your units. All of the other tasks a leader is responsible for—city management, negotiation, production planning, changing the tax rates, consulting advisors, and so on—is possible *between* your turns, while everyone else is moving their units. Why use up valuable unit-moving time when there's no need to?

TOAST THE HOST

If the Host player is eliminated during a network or Internet game, the game does not end. The "Host" status is automatically transferred to another player, so that the game can continue. If the Host is wiped out in a two-player game, the other player can continue against any remaining AI civilizations.

This is a new concept in *Civilization II*, so let's take a closer look at how it works.

BETWEEN TURNS

In *Civilization II Multiplayer Gold Edition*, the GAME TIMER limits the length of each player's turn (unless, of course, the host player sets the timer to *Unlimited*). The idea behind this is to help keep multiplayer games from becoming tedious and slow in the online environment (among other reasons, because you're usually paying for the time you're online). However, one negative side effect of this timer is that it might prevent you from completing all of the things you want to do during your turn—especially late in the game, when management tasks come to take up more and more time.

To alleviate this problem, during network and Internet games of *Civilization II*, you can perform most of your management while you are waiting for other players to complete their turns. Between turns, you can:

- **Manage cities.** You can do anything you need to inside your cities, including changing production orders, reassigning citizens working in the City Radius, creating specialists, and selling improvements.

- **Consult your advisors.** You have access to all of the advisors' reports.

- **Change your tax rates.** You can also change your map view and modify any of the options that don't affect other players (most of them are on the Game menu). If you're the host player, you can also fiddle with a few options that *do* affect others.

- **Chat.** You can trade chat messages with the other human players. See **Chat with Kings** for the details.

- **Send and respond to emissaries.** If you want to engage in negotiations, you can. The details are in **Initiating Negotiations** and **Responding to Negotiations**.

Any changes you make between turns to your cities, production, tax rates, and so on take effect at the start of your next turn. If something happens to prevent or moot a change you made between turns, that change does not take effect. For example, if you chose to sell off the Barracks in one of your cities, but that city is captured before your next turn begins, the Barracks remains in the city and you don't get the cash.

There is only one game function that you *cannot* access between turns: moving and giving orders to your units; this is reserved for use during your turn.

CHAT WITH KINGS

Whenever you wish to send a message to another player or read one that someone has sent to you, you can do so using the Chat with Kings feature. Select the **Chat with Kings** option from the Advisors menu to open the Chat with Kings window.

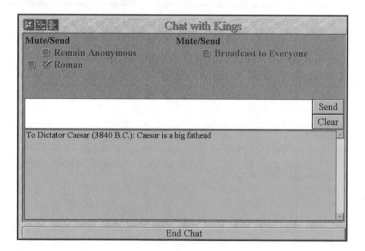

In this window, you can send and receive text messages and thereby conduct conversations with other human players. (The AI players cannot chat.)

The top section of this window contains all of your chat controls.

Remain Anonymous enables you to send messages without the source of the message being identified.

Broadcast to Everyone transmits your chat messages to *all* the human players.

Civilization Names below the other two check-boxes list all the civilizations ruled by human players with which you can communicate. If the host player selected the **All Humans Can Chat From Start** option during setup, everyone is listed; otherwise, only those players with whom you have made contact are shown. Click on the check-box next to the name to select a civilization. Any message you send is transmitted to *all* of the selected civilizations. The other column of check-boxes, Mute, is what you use to refuse to receive chat messages from a civilization.

If you have muted chat from a player, you can still negotiate with that player, and the chat window in negotiation works as normal. You've only stifled this one type of communication.

In the center portion of the screen—where your cursor is—you create your messages. Simply type your missive here (or use the shortcut keys—see the sidebar). When you're satisfied with it, click the **Send** button.

The scrolling section at the bottom of the window displays both the messages you receive from other players and every message you send. If you get tired of seeing old messages, you can wipe them away (permanently) by clicking the **Clear** button. (Note that there is no way to retrieve erased chat messages.)

When you're through chatting, click the **End Chat** button.

CHAT SHORTCUTS AND FILES

There are four chat-related files stored in the game directory. Three of these—**Chat-Mac1.txt**, **ChatMac2.txt**, and **ChatMac3.txt**—contain text that you can add to a chat message at the press of a single key. To add these "chat macros" to a message, you must be in the process of creating a message. At that time, press:

Ctrl F3 to add text from ChatMac1; press this repeatedly to cycle through the messages in that file.

Ctrl F4 to add text from ChatMac2; press this repeatedly to cycle through the messages in that file.

Ctrl F5 to add text from ChatMac3; press this repeatedly to cycle through the messages in that file.

Note that you can edit these text files (using any text editing program) to contain whatever text you want to appear when you press these keys—messages you send often, for example.

In addition to these, there are two more chat shortcut keys that add text to your chat messages.

Ctrl F1 adds the name of a civilization (i.e., Roman); press this repeatedly to cycle through all the civilizations in the current game.

Ctrl F2 adds the title and name of a civilization's leader (i.e., Imperator Caesar); press this repeatedly to cycle through all the civilizations in the current game.

Lastly, all of the text that appears in the scrolling section of the CHAT WITH KINGS window is stored in a file called **ChatLog.txt**. Unless you change the settings in the MULTIPLAYER OPTIONS (see **Special Features** for the scoop), this data is saved from one game to the next. You can clear it manually using the **Clear** button in the CHAT WITH KINGS window.

INITIATING NEGOTIATIONS

During a multiplayer game played over a network or the Internet, negotiations with other human rulers are *not* handled by the AI; they're face to face (well, face to screen, anyway) bargaining sessions with a real person on the other end. (When you're dealing with computer-controlled civilizations, negotiations proceed exactly as they would in the single-player game; for the details, please read the **Diplomacy** section.) At any time you choose, you can initiate negotiations with any other civilization using the FOREIGN MINISTER, just as you would in a single-player game. If you send an emissary to an empire ruled by a human player, the NEGOTIATION window opens.

Pick an Action:

○ Offer Treaty

◉ Offer Proposal

○ Offer Gift

○ Barter

○ Make Threat

Check Intelligence	Continue	Never Mind

Send

Clear

From Dictator Caesar (3800 B.C.): How are ya?
To Dictator Caesar (3800 B.C.): Small and weak. How are you?

End Negotiations

The name of the civilization on the other end is listed in the title bar of the window.

The bottom half of the NEGOTIATION window is the PRIVATE CHAT area. This works exactly like the CHAT WITH KINGS window, except that there's only one ruler you can trade messages with. This makes some of the usual chat controls (like **Remain Anonymous**) superfluous, so they're not here. Note that even these private chats might be intercepted and repeated to a third party—if there's a listening post in your capital. (Read **Diplomats and Spies** for the details.)

ATTITUDE

The other ruler's attitude toward your civilization—displayed during communications in the NEGOTIATIONS window—is determined by that player. By the same token, your attitude toward the other empire is under your control:

- Call up your **Foreign Minister** and select a civilization to set your attitude toward.

- Click the **Set Attitude** button.

- Choose an attitude by checking the appropriate box.

- Click **OK** to put the new attitude into effect or **Cancel** to leave without changing your attitude.

All of the negotiation options are provided in the upper section of the window. To choose one, simply select it and click the **Continue** button. The upper portion of the window then fills with the relevant options for the activity you chose. If you decide to, you can back out of any negotiation option you've chosen using the **Never Mind** button. You can also cut off the negotiating session entirely by clicking the **End Negotiations** button. The five negotiation options are:

175

Offer Treaty: This is your method for making and breaking treaties with human opponents. Your present treaty status with the other ruler is noted, and the types of treaties you can propose—plus the option to cancel the current treaty—are available for selection. Pick an option and click the **Transmit Offer** button to send the proposal (or notice of cancellation) to the other ruler.

Make Proposal: There are two types of proposal you can send to another human ruler.

1. *Ask to Declare War* is just like the **Ask to declare war against an enemy** option available when negotiating with computer-controlled civilizations; you're asking the other leader to immediately declare war on one of your enemies. You can choose from all of the empires with which you have no treaty. Select one or more, then click the **Transmit Offer** button to send the proposal to the other ruler.

2. *Ask to Share Maps* is exactly like the single-player option **Ask to share world maps**; you're asking the other leader to give you his map of the world in trade for yours. Click the **Transmit Offer** button to send this proposal.

Offer Gift: This is the method you use to give things away and demand nothing in return. In a multiplayer game, you might sometimes trade a "gift" for some less tangible return, but be wary. There are five types of gift you can offer:

1. *Knowledge* means a Civilization Advance. Select one of the advances listed in the scrolling box, then click the **Transmit Offer** button to send your offer. Note that this offer will probably be rejected if the other ruler already has that advance.

2. *Money* means gold from your treasury. Enter the amount you wish to offer, then click the **Transmit Offer** button. It's rare that gifts of cash are rejected.

3. *Military Unit* means exactly what it says. A scrolling box lists all of your military units and their home cities. (You can sort this list by unit type or by home city.) Click on a unit to select it, then click the **Transmit Offer** button to send the offer. If the offer is accepted, the unit's new owner takes control of it.

4. *Cede Territory* is how you give away cities.

5. *Offer Maps* is a one-sided version of **Ask to share world maps**; you gave away your map without getting anything in return.

Barter: This option is strictly for human to human negotiations; you can't barter with computer-controlled civilizations. Essentially, the **Barter** option allows you to offer almost anything to another ruler in exchange for nearly anything (including the same thing). Use the column on the left to choose the type of thing you want to offer, then choose the type of thing you want to get in return from the column on the right. When you click **Continue**, you'll be prompted to pick exactly what you want to send and receive—the exact amount of gold, for example, or the specific advance.

Make Threat: This is how you make demands of other human rulers. When you send a threat, the other ruler receives a message like this: *"We agree not to attack you if you give us:"* followed by what you've chosen to extort. You can demand a specified amount of gold, a specific advance, a military unit, or a copy of that ruler's world map, among other things.

Sooner or later, you might be called upon by an emissary from one of the other human rulers. Should you grant that ruler an audience, you'll find that responding to negotiations is a bit different from initiating them. (You might also be approached by emissaries from computer-controlled civilizations, but those situations are handled in the usual way, described back in the **Diplomacy** section.)

The audience takes place in the usual way, and all of the information you're accustomed to having is available. (Remember that attitudes are under player control; see **Initiating Negotiations** for the scoop.) The PRIVATE CHAT sub-window (described in **Initiating Negotiations**) is functional as well.

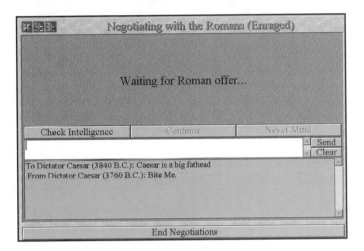

The player who requested the audience opens the negotiations—composes and sends the first message. There's nothing you need to do but await the offer, threat, proposal, or invitation to barter. You can, of course, send chat messages, and that's often how much of the real negotiations take place. When the "official" communiqué arrives, you have three response options. To use one, select it and then click the OK button.

No Thanks: Sends a negative response appropriate to the other ruler's proposal. You do not propose a counter-offer, but simply wait for another proposal (or an end to the negotiations).

Accept Offer: Sends the positive response appropriate to the proposal—you accept the offer, proposal, or invitation, or you accede to the threat. Lieutenants *immediately* put the agreement into practice. Note that if it is not possible for you to hold up your end of the proposed bargain (for example, you have not discovered the advance someone asks you for), this option is not available. After this, the other ruler can make another proposal or end the negotiations.

Make Counter-offer: Does not accept the other ruler's proposal. Rather than a negative response, however, you send a proposal of your own as an alternative. When you choose this option, you use a modified version of the NEGOTIATIONS screen (the full version is described in **Initiating Negotiations**) to determine the terms of your offer. When the other ruler receives your counter-proposal, he or she has the same three response options.

At the bottom of the window is the **End Negotiations** button. This cuts off the communication immediately and closes the window. Use this to leave a concluded negotiating session—or as an alternative, and less than polite, way of responding to a proposal.

DIPLOMATS AND SPIES

During a multiplayer game played over a network or the Internet, Diplomats and Spies have one new mission. If you move a diplomatic unit into the *capital* city of a civilization ruled by a human player, the usual menu of missions has one extra option—**Spy on Chat**.

When you assign this mission, the unit taps into the opposing leader's communications lines and installs itself in a listening post inside the city. As long as the tap remains active, copies of all of that player's incoming and outgoing chat messages are sent into your chat window.

This continues until the tap is noticed and traced to the listening post. The number of turns a unit can successfully continue to intercept messages varies with the type of unit (Spies last longer than Diplomats), the unit's status (Veteran units last longer), and the game difficulty. Once the leak is discovered, your unit is destroyed.

CREATING YOUR OWN WORLDS

Civilization II offers a number of options to keep the worlds you civilize fresh. Undoubtedly, the most powerful of these is the MAP EDITOR. With this tool, you can create your own worlds: determine the size and shape of the continents, the type and extent of the terrain, and the starting locations of all the civilizations in the game.

You can literally create any world you like. However, it is possible for a custom-drawn map to violate the map conventions that *Civilization II* needs to run a successful game. Therefore, it is important that you, as map designer, include a sufficient combination of Plains and Grassland squares for every civilization to have at least one potential city site. The world also must have at least one ocean and preferably more than one continent. An "illegal" map will lower the quality of your game by forcing your computer opponents to play at a significant disadvantage—and hence pose a much less interesting challenge.

To begin using the MAP EDITOR, double-click the MAP EDITOR icon in the Windows program group to which you assigned *Civilization II*. Once you're in the program, you have a couple of screens, a tool box, and a few menus that let you create your own worlds. Each of these components is described below.

YOUR TOOLS

The main features of the MAP EDITOR are the TOOLBAR and three display areas: the MAP, WORLD, and STATUS windows. In brief, the TOOLBAR holds your terrain type "brushes," the tools you use to place squares into the MAP window. The WORLD window allows you to quickly center the MAP window around any place on the planet you're creating. The STATUS window shows you the brush you are currently using, its position in the MAP window, and the dimensions of the map.

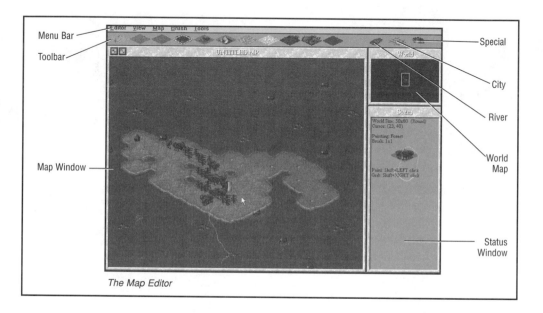

The Map Editor

THE TOOLBAR

The TOOLBAR contains all the basic types of terrain available in **Civilization II**, plus three special icons: RIVER, CITY, and SPECIAL. When you select one of these icons, it becomes your brush, and you can then use the brush cursor to place that terrain (or river or city) onto the world. When you use the CITY icon, you can set the starting locations for some or all of the game civilizations.

Placing Terrain: Click on the terrain type you want to "load" your brush. Then, hold down the (Shift) key and click anywhere on the map (even atop existing terrain) to place that type of terrain square there. To place larger areas, you can choose a larger brush size (see below) or drag the cursor while you hold down both the (Shift) key and the left mouse button.

Placing Rivers: To place rivers onto the map, first click the RIVER icon. Once your brush is "loaded," you can lay rivers in the same way as you do terrain. Note that you can also *remove* rivers by holding down the (Shift) key and right-clicking on a location. You can (Shift)-right-click-and-drag to remove a long length of river.

Placing Starting Locations: To place a city square on the map, click the CITY icon. When your brush has thus been loaded, you can place cities in the same way as you do terrain or rivers. As soon as you place a city, you are prompted to choose which civilization will start at that location when the game begins. Civilizations that already have starting locations are noted in parentheses. Note that you can *remove* a city by holding down the [Shift] key and right-clicking on a location, or simply by placing that civilization in a different location. If you place starting locations for some civilizations but not others, **Civilization II** will decide where to place the unassigned ones. When you load a map you have created (to use in a game), you will always have the option to ignore the preset city locations and use random locations instead.

Multi-terrain Brushes: You might find it convenient to paint your map with a brush that contains more than one type of terrain. To do so, you use the SPECIAL brush, which operates like the cut-and-paste functions of many applications. First, lay down an area of terrain squares on the map that is exactly the size and the types that you wish to have fill your brush. Next, select a multi-square brush of the same size as this area (multi-square brushes are described below). Click the SPECIAL icon on the TOOLBAR. Finally, hold down the [Shift] key and right-click on the terrain area (you can use any existing map section). This "grabs" that terrain and uses it to fill your brush. Now use the brush as usual to place an area of terrain that is an exact copy of the area you "grabbed."

MAP WINDOW

The MAP window is the one you'll use the most, the one in which you actually place terrain squares. This is where you build your world. Clicking anywhere in this window centers the map at the location you clicked (the cursor location). The MAP window can also be sized, like most windows; click-and-drag a side or corner of the frame to the dimensions you like. A large MAP window is most useful for creating detailed continents.

To paint using the current brush, hold down the [Shift] key while you click or click-and-drag.

To remove rivers or cities from squares, hold down the [Shift] key and right-click.

If the current cursor location is a basic terrain, without a city or river, you can select that type of terrain as your brush without recourse to the TOOLBAR. Hold the [Shift] key and right-click on the spot.

WORLD WINDOW

This window shows the entire map of your world in miniature. Click anywhere in the WORLD window to center the MAP window on the spot you clicked.

STATUS WINDOW

The STATUS window is a convenient quick reference. It shows the dimensions of your map, the current cursor location, and the current brush.

THE MENUS

The MENU BAR (along the top of the screen) provides access to the following menus. Each option on each menu is described briefly.

EDITOR MENU

This menu contains options for loading and saving maps.

New Map: This option creates a new, blank map into which you can place terrain.

Load Map: This option allows you to load a previously created map. This can be a map you have made or one from a saved game.

Save Map: This option allows you save the map you are currently editing. If you have not already named it, you will be prompted for a name.

Save Map As: This option allows you to save the current map under a new name.

Quit: Choose this option to stop using the MAP EDITOR and return to Windows.

VIEW MENU

This menu contains options that let you adjust the amount of detail you see and the location of your windows.

Zoom In [Z]**:** This option enlarges the view by one level, lessening the amount of the world you can see.

Zoom Out [X]**:** This option constricts the view one level, increasing the amount of area you see.

Max Zoom In ([Ctrl][Z]**):** This option zooms the view in to maximum magnification.

Standard Zoom ([Shift][Z]**):** This option resets the zoom to the default level.

Medium Zoom Out ([Shift][X]**):** This option sets the zoom at a level roughly midway between the default and the maximum.

Max Zoom Out ([Ctrl][X]**):** This option zooms the view out to see the maximum area.

Arrange Windows: This option cleans up the desktop, returning the windows to their starting configuration.

Center View [C]**:** This option centers the MAP window on the current cursor location.

MAP MENU

This menu contains options to get your map started, to check your map when it's done, and to help you recover from mistakes.

Generate Random Map [R]**:** This option creates a world in the same way as the map generator does when you start a new game. You will be asked all the world customization questions that *Civilization II* normally asks.

Generate Blank Map [B]**:** Choose this option to generate an ocean world, a map filled with water, as your blank canvas.

Set World Shape [H]**:** This option allows you to select a flat or round world, which determines whether or not units will be able to cross from the western edge of the map to the eastern (think of it as the International Date Line, if you will), and back.

Analyze Map [N]**:** This option searches for potential problem areas in your map. This is especially useful for avoiding "illegal" maps.

Undo Last Change [U]**:** This option cancels the last edit you made to your world.

Brush Menu

The items in this menu allow you to change the characteristics of the brush you use to insert terrain on your map. The brush can be various sizes and shapes, giving you the flexibility to quickly and easily create the worlds you want.

1x1 [F1]: This option sets the size of the brush to a single terrain square.

3x3 [F2]: This option gives you a brush that is 3 squares by 3 squares (it looks like a 3x3 diamond). Selecting a terrain type from the TOOLBAR to use with this brush allows you to create 3x3 blocks of that terrain type.

5x5 [F3]: This option sets the brush size to 5 squares by 5 squares.

Cross [F4]: This option gives you a cross-shaped brush to work with. This brush is the same as the 3x3 brush, but with the top, bottom, and side squares (all four corners) lopped off.

City Radius [F5]: This option allows you to paint with a brush the same shape as a CITY RADIUS.

Tools Menu

The tools in this menu add some special controls to fine-tune your map building.

Coastline Protect [P]: This option locks all ocean squares into place, allowing no changes to oceans until you toggle the option off again. This makes it easy to fill in terrain without worrying about overwriting oceans and changing your coastline by mistake.

Warning: If you start a new map (containing only ocean) and you have COASTLINE PROTECT turned on, you will not be able to paint any terrain onto your world. Be sure this option is turned off when you start a new map.

Autoscroll During Paint [A]: When turned on, this option causes the MAP window to automatically scroll in an attempt to follow your brush (the cursor) as you paint. This might slow the program significantly on some computer systems.

Set Resource Seed [S]: The pattern of Special Resources that is scattered over the map is determined (in a manner too complex to describe here) by a number generated when the game creates a map. The MAP EDITOR allows you to set this number and see its effects immediately. You do this by simply entering any number you choose into this option's dialog box. Click OK to see the effects of your number. Note that if you set the value to "1," the pattern of resources will be random. (Even if you set a number other than "1," when you load this map to use in a game, you are still given the option of using a random pattern.)

SCENARIO BUILDING TOOLS

There is a menu stuffed in between CHEAT and CIVILOPEDIA. When we released *Fantastic Worlds*, we added the EDITORS menu, which includes several keen new tools that make it easier for you to create your own scenarios. Note that these editors are *not* covered in any detail in the **Reference: Screen by Screen** section. The details are right here.

Before we begin, you should be made aware of the one drawback: using the new editors automatically enables the **Cheat Mode**, which has the usual effect on your score.

SCENARIO BUILDERS' NOTE

When we released *Fantastic Worlds*, we modified the formats of some of the files you might have worked with previously when creating scenarios. (**Rules.txt** includes more 'slots' for units and advances, for example.) In most cases, your old scenarios should still work just fine. However, you might sometimes get unexpected text when using old scenarios. We suggest you update your scenarios to take advantage of the improved files.

The topmost option on the new menu is **Toggle Scenario Flag**. This is the overall activation switch that tells the game you want to begin building a scenario. It makes all the other editors available. Select this to begin. If you have not already activated the **Cheat Mode**, you must verify that you really want to do so.

Once you do, the game you are playing is marked down as a scenario, and you must create a scenario directory in which to store it. When you're prompted, enter any name (8 letters or less, please). Note that you cannot accidentally (or intentionally) overwrite an existing scenario directory; if you pick a name that's already in use, you must try again.

When you name a directory, you actually create *two* directories:

1. The one you just named is the *scenario directory*; it's created as a subdirectory of the **Scenario** directory.

2. Inside your new directory is a subdirectory called **Sound**; this is where all your new sound files will be stored.

As you use these editors, each one of them modifies an existing file, but no changes are made to your normal *Civilization II* game; the editors make copies of the files they change (except for the Events editor, which creates a file) and saves those files in the scenario directory you named.

ADVANCES EDITOR

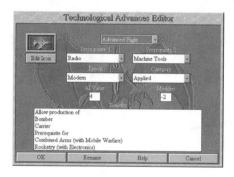

Messing with what *Civ* aficionados call the "Tech Tree" is one of the most powerful tools you have for scenario building. It's also one of the most likely to cause problems. One glance at the *Civilization II Advances Chart* (the poster) tells you how complex the progress of advances can be. If you choose to edit the advances in your scenario, keep close track of your changes.

When you select **Advances Editor** from the menu, the Technological Advances Editor window opens. You can change almost everything about an advance. To avoid trouble, you should know what you're messing with:

Name: The name of the advance is listed in the top box. Use this box to select the advance you want to edit. Once you've chosen an advance, you can rename it using the Rename button at the bottom of the window. Keep in mind that the name of an advance is only text; it doesn't have ramifications. However, names longer than 15 characters do not fit well in all of the onscreen boxes, and special characters (anything that's not a letter or a space) can cause problems.

Icon: The icon associated with an advance is determined by the **Epoch** and **Category** you assign to it. To change the icon, click on the Edit Icon button. (For the scoop on using the Icon Editor, see the **Icon Editor** section.) Note that when you edit an advance icon, that icon changes for *every advance* in the same Epoch and Category. Your changes to these icons are saved in the directory in which you are building the scenario. The file they're in is named **icons.bmp**.

Prerequisites: Every advance can have one or two prerequisites—other advances which must be successfully discovered to make this advance available for researching. (To have no prerequisite, use ***nil***.) Be very careful when choosing these precursor advances. If you choose imprudently, you could eliminate the advance from the scenario entirely. For example, if you set as a prerequisite an advance that had the advance you're editing as a prerequisite, you'd create a closed loop, and neither advance would ever appear in the research selection list. If you *want* to remove an advance from the scenario, don't do that; instead, use the prerequisite ***no***.

Epoch: There are four **Epochs** in *Civ* (*Ancient, Renaissance, Industrial,* and *Modern*). Which one you assign to an advance helps to determine what **Icon** is associated with the advance. It can also help you keep track of when things are supposed to show up

Category: There are five **Categories** of knowledge in ***Civilization II*** (*Military, Economic, Social, Academic,* and *Applied*). Which one you assign to an advance helps to determine what icon is associated with the advance.

AI Value: The research efforts of computer-controlled civilizations are led to a great extent by the value you place on each advance. A high value makes a civilization more likely to research and more willing to steal or trade for an advance. The advances are valued from a low of 1 (Future Technology) to a high of 8 (Mobile Warfare, Gunpowder).

Civ Modifier: The personality of the leader also influences a civilization's research efforts. Thus, the value of an advance to a particular leader is modified by how "civilized" the leader and the advance are. Set a positive value (up to 2) to make this advance more enticing to civilized leaders and less so to militaristic ones. A negative value (as low as -2) makes the advance more appealing to warriors and more distasteful to scholars. Mark balanced advances with a modifier of zero.

You cannot edit the text in the Benefits box. This information is culled from other sources, and serves to alert you to other things this advance affects. You should always consider the potential ramifications before making any change.

When you're finished, click OK to save your changes or Cancel to undo them.

CITIES EDITOR

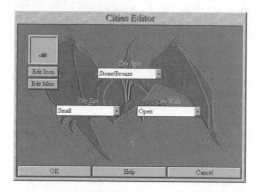

No, this is not a replacement for the **Edit City** option on the CHEAT menu. Instead, the Cities Editor allows you to change the way all cities look. When you select this editor from the menu, the CITIES EDITOR window opens.

Your first step should be to select the type of city you want to modify. There are three characteristics that define any city in *Civilization II*:

City Style: This includes the four city styles from which you can choose at the beginning of the game (*Bronze Age, Classical, Far Eastern,* and *Medieval*). There are also two further styles. *Industrial* is the style used for every city in a civilization that has discovered Industrialization (or the scenario equivalent) but not yet researched Automobile. *Modern* is the style used for cities in a civilization that has discovered Automobile (or the scenario equivalent).

City Size: Cities come in four sizes: *Small* (1–3), *Medium* (4–5), *Large* (6–7), and *Extra Large* (8+). Choose one. (Note that a civilization's capital city is never displayed as *Small*.)

City Walls: This one's simple; a city either has walls or it doesn't. To work with the icon for a walled city, select **Walled**. For the other kind, select **Open**.

When you have decided on the characteristics, the corresponding city icon is displayed in the icon box. Click on the EDIT ICON button to start making changes. (For the scoop on using the Icon Editor, see the **Icon Editor** section.) Your changes to the city icons are saved in the directory in which you are building the scenario. The file they're in is named **cities.bmp**.

That's it for editing cities, but there's one more button we haven't covered: EDIT MISC. When you click on this one, you get a list of miscellaneous icons you can edit. These are icons associated with the structures each civilization can build. You can change the look of Airbases, Fortresses, unit fortifications, and the flags carried over each city. Selecting one of the icons and clicking on the OK button takes you to the Icon Editor.

When you're finished, click OK to save your changes or CANCEL to undo them.

EFFECTS EDITOR

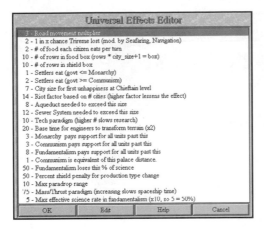

Universal Effects Editor

3 - Road movement multiplier
2 - 1 in x chance Trireme lost (mod. by Seafaring, Navigation)
2 - # of food each citizen eats per turn
10 - # of rows in food box (rows * city_size+1 = box)
10 - # of rows in shield box
1 - Settlers eat (govt <= Monarchy)
2 - Settlers eat (govt >= Communism)
7 - City size for first unhappiness at Chieftain level
14 - Riot factor based on # cities (higher factor lessens the effect)
8 - Aqueduct needed to exceed this size
12 - Sewer System needed to exceed this size
10 - Tech paradigm (higher # slows research)
20 - Base time for engineers to transform terrain (x2)
3 - Monarchy pays support for all units past this
3 - Communism pays support for all units past this
8 - Fundamentalism pays support for all units past this
1 - Communism is equivalent of this palace distance.
50 - Fundamentalism loses this % of science
50 - Percent shield penalty for production type change
10 - Max paradrop range
75 - Mass/Thrust paradigm (increasing slows spaceship time)
5 - Max effective science rate in fundamentalism (x10, so 5 = 50%)

| OK | Edit | Help | Cancel |

Note: This one is dangerous. There are a number of basic, universal numbers in the game. This editor lets you change most of them. Some of these have straightforward effects, but others have consequences that can be difficult to foresee. Be careful when messing with the universal effects.

If you modify the universal effects numbers and have problems with the game afterward, the solution is to use this editor to change the numbers back. Do not call Customer Support unless you have undone your changes and the problem still persists.

Select **Effects Editor** from the menu to call up the UNIVERSAL EFFECTS EDITOR window. It's fairly simple. Select one of the universal effect numbers to change, then click the EDIT button. At the prompt, enter the new number you want for this effect, then click OK. Your changes to the universal numbers are saved in the directory in which you are building the scenario. The file they're in is named **rules.txt**.

When you're finished, click OK to save your changes or CANCEL to undo them.

CITY IMPROVEMENTS EDITOR

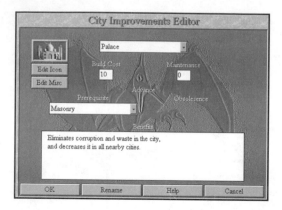

Infrastructure is what holds an empire together, and it's sloppy design work if the city improvements and Wonders of the World in your scenario don't match up with the rest of it. Select **Improvements Editor** from the menu, and the CITY IMPROVEMENTS EDITOR window opens.

Note that, for scenario building purposes, the term 'improvements' includes both city improvements and Wonders of the World.

As with the advances, you should be careful when modifying the city improvements. Small errors can have large consequences.

Name: The name of the improvement is listed in the top box. Use this box to select the one you want to edit. Once you've chosen an improvement, you can rename it using the RENAME button at the bottom of the window. Keep in mind that the name is only text; it doesn't have any other effects. However, names longer than 15 characters do not fit well in all of the onscreen boxes, and special characters (anything that's not a letter or a space) can cause problems.

Icon: Click on the EDIT ICON button to modify the graphic associated with this improvement. Changing the icon around has no far-reaching effects; it just changes the little picture. (For the scoop on using the Icon Editor, see the **Icon Editor** section.) Your changes to improvement icons are saved in the directory in which you are building the scenario. The file they're in is named **icons.bmp**.

Build Cost: The cost to build the improvement (in shields) is 10 times the number you enter. For example, the cost of a Library is 8, so a city must amass 80 shields to complete a Library. The cost should be proportional to the effect of the improvement. (Wonders should be expensive!)

Maintenance: Every turn, a civilization must pay this amount of gold in upkeep on each improvement of this type. As with **Build Cost**, **Maintenance** should be proportional to the effects of the improvement. Once built, Wonders of the World cannot be sold off, so the maintenance cost for them should always be zero—unless you want to punish the builders.

Prerequisite: Every improvement can have one prerequisite—an advance that must be successfully discovered before a civilization can build the improvement. Make sure that this advance is one that is included in your tech tree. Otherwise, no civilization will ever be able to build the improvement.

Obsolescence: Technological progress makes some Wonders of the World obsolete. Whenever any civilization discovers the advance you select, it cancels the effects of the wonder. Keep in mind that it's not *necessary* to have wonders become obsolete, but it is often wise. Also, make sure that you leave enough time between the availability of a wonder and its becoming obsolete for the wonder to be built and have its effect for a while; otherwise, there will be no point in building it, and players discover that sort of thing quickly.

Note that Barracks or whatever improvement replaces it becomes obsolete with the discovery of Gunpowder (or whatever advance replaces it). You cannot change this.

You cannot edit the text in the BENEFITS box. This information just lets you know the effects of this improvement (or wonder). You cannot change these effects.

That's it for editing improvements, but there's a button we haven't covered: EDIT MISC. When you click on this one, you get a list of miscellaneous icons you can edit. These are icons associated with combat and viewing the map. You can change the look of the cursor (the little white diamond), and you can modify the eight frames of the combat damage animation (Explosion 1 through 8). Selecting one of the icons and clicking on the OK button takes you to the Icon Editor.

When you're finished, click OK to save your changes or CANCEL to undo them.

TERRAIN EDITOR

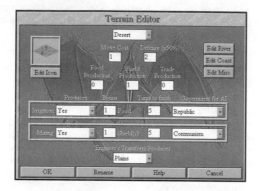

The terrain underfoot is one of the most basic elements in any scenario, and it's one that many designers never think to modify. Select this editor from the menu to open the TERRAIN EDITOR window. Here's what you can do:

Name: The name of the terrain type is listed in the top box. Use this box to select the one you want to edit. Once you've chosen a type, you can rename it using the RENAME button at the bottom of the window. Keep in mind that the name is only text; it doesn't have any hidden effects. However, names longer than 15 characters do not fit well in all of the onscreen boxes, and special characters (anything that's not a letter or a space) can cause problems.

Icon: Click on the EDIT ICON button to modify the look of this type of terrain. (For the scoop on using the Icon Editor, see the **Icon Editor** section.) Be careful! Changing the way the terrain looks can have all kinds of consequences. (For example, units, special resources, or even cities might become partially invisible.) Your changes are saved in the directory in which you are building the scenario. The files they're in are named **terrain1.bmp** and **terrain2.bmp**.

Move Cost: Each type of terrain costs each unit a certain number of movement points to cross. In this box, you set that cost for the selected type of terrain. (Remember that, no matter what the cost of the terrain, any unit can always move at least one square per turn.)

Defense: Some types of terrain are more defensible than others. In this box, you set how easy (or hard) this type is to defend, in units of 50%. So, for example, if the **Defense** factor is 1, a unit on that terrain defends at 50% of its usual defense power. A factor of 2 is normal—100%. Any factor of 3 (150%) or more *adds* to the defensive strength of units on that type of terrain.

Food: This is simply how much food the terrain produces in its natural state. Be careful with this, as players can add to this in many ways, and production has far reaching effects on the game.

Shields: This is how many production shields the terrain produces in its natural state. Be careful with this, too, because players can enhance the number in many ways, and production has far reaching effects on the game.

Trade: This determines how many trade arrows (science, luxuries, and income) the terrain produces in its natural state. Players can enhance this in many ways, and production has far reaching effects on the game, so be wary.

Irrigation: What happens when you irrigate a particular type of terrain? It's up to you.

Produces: Irrigation can act as a transformation, changing the terrain to another type. Other options are **No**, which means the terrain cannot be irrigated at all, and **Yes**, which determines that irrigating does not transform the terrain, but has the **Bonus** effect.

Bonus: This determines how much *more* food the terrain will produce once it has irrigation on it.

Turns to Finish: Here, you set how many turns it take a Settler unit to irrigate this type of terrain. Note that an Engineer will take only half this time.

Government for AI: The computer-controlled civilizations will not bother to irrigate this type of terrain until they reach a certain level of government. In this box, you can determine what that level of government is. Of course, if you choose **Despotism**, they are able to irrigate this terrain from the start of the game. There is also the **Never** option; this tells the AI not to ever bother irrigating this type of terrain (useful for those types that cannot be irrigated).

What are the "levels" of government? Glad you asked. Oddly enough, they don't necessarily conform to the order in which they become available in the game.

Level 1 = Despotism

Level 2 = Monarchy

Level 3 = Communism

Level 4 = Fundamentalism

Level 5 = Republic

Level 6 = Democracy

For the purposes of AI irrigation and mining, reaching any level beyond the required level is just as good as reaching the specified level.

Mining: How about mining? You can edit that, as well.

Produces: Like irrigation, mining can act as a transformation, changing the terrain to another type. Other options are **No**, which means the terrain cannot be mined, and **Yes**, which determines that mining does not transform the terrain, but has the **Bonus** effect.

Bonus: This determines how many *more* shields the terrain will produce once it has been mined.

Turns to Finish: Here, you set how many turns it take a Settler unit to mine this type of terrain. Note that an Engineer will take only half this time.

Government for AI: The computer-controlled civilizations will not attempt to mine this type of terrain until they reach a certain level of government. In this box, you determine what that level of government is. Of course, if you choose **Despotism**, they are willing to mine this terrain from the start of the game. There is also the **Never** option; this tells the AI not to ever bother mining this type of terrain (useful for those types that cannot be mined).

Transform: In this box, you can set what terrain type will result when an engineer transforms a square of this type.

That's the whole scoop on editing the basic terrain types, but there's more. The two buttons at the top right can be extremely handy.

Edit River: This lets you edit the river pictures. There are two things you should keep in mind when messing with these. One is that rivers are *overlaid* on the icons of the basic terrain types, and any type of terrain except Ocean can have a river running through it. Second is that the many river pictures are designed to fit together according to a predefined pattern that you cannot change. If you change the rivers around, you take the chance that the edges might not match up, and your rivers (or whatever) will look sloppy. Select one of the icons and click OK to go to the Icon Editor.

Edit Coast: Every ocean has a coastline. You can edit the look of the coast with this editor. As with the rivers, the many coastline icons are designed to fit together according to a predefined pattern that you cannot change. If you change the coastline icons, you take the chance that the edges won't not match up, and your coasts will look sloppy. Select one of the icons and click OK to go to the Icon Editor.

When you're finished, click OK to save your changes or CANCEL to undo them.

TRIBE EDITOR

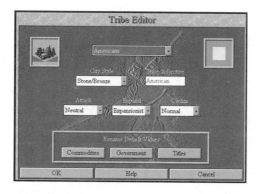

A "tribe" is what *Civ* scenario designers call a potential civilization. Even though there can be only seven civilizations in play at any one time, there are 28 tribes defined in the rules. Any tribe can be placed into a scenario as a civilization. The Tribe Editor allows you to defined each of these 28 tribes and their salient characteristics.

Name: The name of the tribe you're working with is listed in the top box. Use this box to select the one you want to edit.

City Style: You can select the default city style for each tribe. The styles include the four city styles available at the beginning of the game: *Bronze Age, Classical, Far Eastern,* and *Medieval.* The other two styles (*Industrial* and *Modern*) are not available.

Adjective: Each tribe has an adjective associated with it. Other leaders use this adjective when referring to your civilization. (For example, cities held by the Mongols would be *Mongolian* cities.) Type in whatever adjective you think is appropriate. Remember, though, that anything longer than 15 characters might not fit well in all of the onscreen boxes, and special characters (anything that's not a letter or a space) can cause problems.

Attack: How likely is this tribe to mount an unprovoked attack or break a cease-fire? There are three possibilities: **Rational** (as trustworthy as anybody), **Neutral**, and **Aggressive** (watch your back).

Expand: How quickly and how recklessly does this tribe try to expand its territory? There are three possibilities: **Expansionist** (more is better), **Neutral**, and **Perfectionist** (a few developed cities are better than several lame ones).

Civilize: What is the basic personality of this tribe? There are three possibilities: **Civilized** (world peace and the conquest of space are humanity's brightest goals), **Neutral**, and **Militaristic** (might makes right). Note that this is used in relation with the Civilization Modifier for advances.

Rename: In the rename box, you can change most of the important text associated with a tribe. Note that all of these fields are only text; they have no hidden effects. However, names longer than 15 characters do not fit well in all of the onscreen boxes, and special characters (anything that's not a letter or a space) can cause problems. Note also that city names longer than 15 characters are not allowed, and they *will* cause problems.

Tribe: This is the name of the tribe (Romans, for example).

Leader: This allows you to specify the default names of both the male and female leaders of the tribe. Of course, a human player has the option of entering a personalized name when playing.

City: Every tribe comes with 20 to 25 predefined city names. Using this editor, you can specify those names.

Commodities: When a city builds a trade unit (Caravan or Freight, for example), that unit is assigned a commodity to trade. This allows you to rename all of the possible trade commodities. The new names will show up in the supply and demand listings, as well, but will not affect the special natural resources of terrain.

Government: This simply lets you rename all of the basic government types. Note that this has no effect on the way each government works or on the "levels" of government noted in the **Terrain Editor** section.

Titles: Just as you can customize the titles of yourself as leader when you begin a new game, this option allows you to customize the default titles for a tribe.

When you're finished, click OK to save your changes or CANCEL to undo them.

UNITS EDITOR

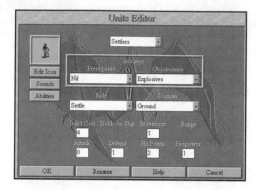

One of the things almost every scenario designer wants to do is to modify the military and non-military units civilizations can build. Let's get started. Select **Units Editor** from the menu to open the UNITS EDITOR window.

Name: The name of the unit is listed in the top box. Use this box to select the one you want to edit. Once you've chosen a unit, you can rename it using the RENAME button at the bottom of the window. Keep in mind that the name is just text; it doesn't have any hidden effects. However, names longer than 15 characters do not fit well in all of the onscreen boxes, and special characters (anything that's not a letter or a space) can cause problems.

Icon: Click on the EDIT ICON button to modify the look of this type of unit. Be careful! Changing the way a unit looks can sometimes make it blend in with certain types of terrain and become partially invisible. (For the scoop on using the Icon Editor, see the **Icon Editor** section.) Your changes are saved in the directory in which you are building the scenario. The file they're in is named **units.bmp**.

Sounds: Click on this button to determine what sounds (.wav files) are associated with this unit. There are six possible sounds, but very few units use all six. To listen to the current sound, double-click on the listed .wav file. To replace it with a different .wav file, click the button below the file listing. You can explore all of your directories to find the sound you want to use. When you have selected a file, listen to it (again, by double-clicking the file name) before you accept it. You can use the CANCEL button to change your mind now, but once you have made the switch, it cannot be undone. (Of course, you can always replace the new file with another .wav file.)

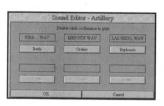

The name of the sound listed does not change, but the new sound is copied into the original file. Listen to it to make sure.

Abilities: This button allows you to select which of the special abilities this unit will have. As with many other things, you must be careful when choosing abilities. Some have far-reaching effects, and other might be nonsensical (naval units with settler abilities, for example). Unusual or paradoxical combinations can cause problems.

196

Prerequisite: Every unit has one prerequisite—an advance that must be successfully discovered before a civilization can build the unit. Make sure that this advance is one that is included in your tech tree. Otherwise, no civilization will ever be able to build the unit. A prerequisite of *nil* means that the unit is available from the beginning. A prerequisite of *no* means that the unit does not appear in the scenario at all.

Obsolescence: Technological progress makes many units obsolete. Whenever a civilization discovers the advance you select, it becomes unable to build the unit any longer. Keep in mind that it's not *necessary* to have units become obsolete, but it is often wise. Also, make sure that you leave enough time between the availability of a unit and its obsolescence for the unit to be built and have some effect; otherwise, there will be no point in building it, and players discover that sort of thing quickly.

Role: A unit's **Role** is the part it is meant to play. This affects the way the computer-controlled civilizations use the unit. In addition, certain roles (**Settle**, **Diplomacy**, and **Trade**) change the possible actions of the unit.

Make sure that the **Role** you assign to a unit corresponds with its **Domain**. For example, an Air unit assigned to Settle would be pointless, as would a Naval unit assigned to Air Superiority.

Domain: Every unit travels on or in one environment. A unit is either Ground, Air, or Naval.

Build Cost: The cost to build the unit (in shields) is 10 times the number you enter. For example, the cost of a Settler is 4, so a city must amass 40 shields to complete a Settler. The cost should be proportional to the overall utility of the unit.

Holds: Only naval units that can carry other units have holds. This is the number of other units that the unit can carry at one time.

Movement: This is the number of movement points with which the unit begins each turn *if it is undamaged*.

Range: Only air units have a range. This is the number of turns that the unit can be out of a city or airfield. Note that the **Movement** of the unit is divided by the **Range** to determine the number of moves the unit can make each turn. A **Range** of zero makes the unit like the Helicopter; it can travel for any number of turns, but it loses hit points every time it begins a turn away from a city or airfield.

Attack: This determines the attack power of the unit. An attack power of 99 converts the unit into a nuclear device.

Defend: This sets the defensive power of the unit.

Hit Points: Use this to determine the hit points (the amount of damage) the unit can take before being destroyed.

Firepower: This is the amount of damage the unit does each time it hits another unit.

When you're finished, click OK to save your changes or CANCEL to undo them.

ICON EDITOR

Half the fun of a new scenario is seeing all of the new art for the first time. If you enjoy creating scenarios, you'll certainly want to customize the look of many of the existing icons. Here's how.

Icon: The area in which the icon image is displayed is also your working space—where you actually draw with the cursor. At first, it shows the icon as it is. As you make edits, it shows the icon as it will be once you save it.

Note: Behind every icon, there is a diamond-shaped background. This represents the terrain square on which every unit icon must be placed. Your icons must not spread beyond the lower borders of this diamond, or there will be graphics problems when anyone plays the scenario. An icon may extend past the upper borders somewhat (be reasonable) without causing problems.

Colors: Below the icon box is every color you are allowed to use in your scenario. Left-click on one of the colors to make it the selected "left paint" color (the one you'll "paint" with by holding down the left mouse button). Right-click on any color to make that the "right paint" color.

Tools: When drawing, there are a number of common jobs that can be automated for your convenience. The buttons to the right of the icon box do just that. There are a number of tool buttons:

 Select an icon from the icon library to replace the current image.

 Undo whatever you just did and revert to the image as it was before that change.

Select the size of the "paintbrush" you want to use.

 Draw a solid line with your paintbrush.

 Draw a dotted line with your paintbrush.

 Choose a color directly from the icon, rather than from the color spots.

 Completely erase the icon and start with a blank image.

This finds every pixel in the icon that is the background color you selected and changes it to be the current foreground color.

Exchange the selected background and foreground colors.

 This one is only useful when you're editing a unit icon. All units carry shields, and you must determine where the shield will appear. Click on this to get the shield placement cursor, then click anywhere in the icon square to place the upper left-hand corner of the shield. If you don't like the look, click somewhere else to re-place it. When you're satisfied, click OK or any of the other buttons (except CANCEL) to save the change.

When you're finished, click OK to save your changes or CANCEL to undo them.

EVENTS EDITOR

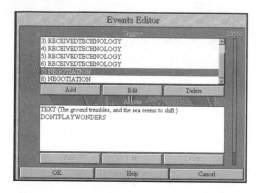

As mentioned in **What's New**, it is possible to add *events* to any scenario. Until now, doing so could be a bit daunting; you had to learn to make event files using the scenario macro "language" our programmers had created. With the new **Events** Editor, you still create a file and you still use the macro language, but the process is much simpler.

Warning: The *events* are a supplementary design tool. They have not been tested as well as the game itself and could cause problems if used incorrectly. If you experience difficulties in the game after creating events, do not immediately call Customer Support. The best solution is to delete (or at least rename) the **events.txt** file in the directory where you store your scenario. If you do so and the problems still persist, *then* call Customer Support.

TERMINOLOGY

Before we start explaining how to use the **Events** Editor, we should define a few terms.

- An *Event* is the combination of a *Trigger* and an *Action*. Each event is a simple cause-and-effect sequence. Events are the fundamental structure you'll be working with.

- A *Trigger* is the specific game occurrence that activates a particular event. This is the cause.

- An *Action* is the consequence an event generates in response to its Trigger. This is the effect.

Essentially, you define events so that when the Trigger happens, it triggers the Action. Note that a single Trigger can have multiple Actions associated with it, but no one Trigger can have more than one Action of the same type.

THE EVENTS FILE

Whenever you begin adding events to your scenario, the game creates a text file in the directory in which you're building the scenario. This file is named **events.txt** and must remain in the same directory as the scenario (**.scn**) file. All of the text in this file represents events you have added to your scenario.

The events file always begins with the line:

    @BEGINEVENTS

and ends with the line:

    @ENDEVENTS

These tell the ***Civilization II*** program that the file is, indeed, a valid events file.

The rest of the file consists of the definitions of the events themselves. It is extremely important that these definitions are in the correct format, and the **Events** Editor takes care of that. The point is that you should not go in and change things manually unless you know what you're doing.

CREATING EVENTS

First things first. Pull down the **Editors** menu and select the **Events Editor** option. (We're assuming that you already toggled the scenario flag on and named your scenario directory.) The EVENTS EDITOR window opens. There are two boxes in this window, one for Triggers and one for Actions.

> **Special note:** There is a gauge in the EVENTS EDITOR window that notes how much of the memory space allotted for events is unused. (There is a 32K heap dedicated to events.) As you add events, this gauge will approach zero. Do **not** allow it to reach zero, or none of your events will work (and you could experience other problems).

THE FIRST TRIGGER

This must seem obvious to most of you, but *you must create a trigger before you can create any actions.* Because every action is associated with a trigger, there can be no actions without triggers. Therefore, the first thing you should do is to click on the upper ADD button to create your first trigger.

ADD brings up a list of the valid triggers. Select one from the list, and you're prompted to select or enter any parameters that are required for that trigger. Once you've set all the parameters, the trigger is completely defined and is inserted in the box with a Trigger number assigned to it.

THE FIRST ACTION

Now, you can add an action to this event. Because there is only one trigger, it is (by default) the selected trigger. Click on the other ADD button. This brings up the list of valid actions. Select one of them just as you did the trigger, and you're prompted to select or enter any parameters that are required for that action. Once you've set all the parameters, the action is complete and is inserted as an action in the selected trigger.

That's all there is to it. You have created an event.

All The Rest

Now that there is at least one event in existence, you can ADD actions to that event in the same way as you created the first action. Note that any new actions you create are appended to the list (at the end).

Note: Although a single Trigger can cause multiple Actions, each Trigger can cause only one Action of each type. You can, for example, use MoveUnit, ChangeMoney and Create-Unit all in the same Event, but you can't use CreateUnit twice (or more times) in the *same* Event. If you wanted to create more than one unit, you would need to define another Event using an identical Trigger.

You can also make changes to any existing trigger or action using the two EDIT buttons. Make sure to select the trigger or action you want to modify before you click on EDIT.

Last, but not least, you can remove unwanted actions and triggers using the two DELETE buttons. Again, make sure to select the one you want erased before clicking on the button. One note: if you delete a trigger, all of the actions associated with it are removed automatically.

FYI: Event Definitions

The editor makes sure that every event definition follow the necessary format, but if you ever decide to edit your events by hand, it will help to know the details. There are three parts to an event:

1. The Trigger Statement (@IF) defines the Trigger for the event.

2. The Action Statement (@THEN) defines the Actions associated with that Trigger.

3. The End Statement (@ENDIF) tells the parser that there are no more Actions for this Trigger.

All put together, a valid event definition looks like this:

```
@IF
Trigger
@THEN
Action 1
Action 2
...
Action N
@ENDIF
```

Where the words *Trigger* and *Action* represent valid Triggers and Actions (as defined in the next section.)

For example, say you want to remind the player on the 16th turn that they have only four more turns before the end of the scenario. The Trigger is the beginning of turn 16, and the Action is to display some text in a pop-up box. The definition of this event should look something like this:

```
@IF

TURN

turn=16

@THEN

TEXT

You have only four more turns to meet your victory conditions!

ENDTEXT

@ENDIF
```

At the start of the player's 16th turn, a text box pops up with the message "You have only four more turns to meet your victory conditions!" displayed in it.

VALID TRIGGERS AND ACTIONS

What constitutes a "valid" Trigger or Action? Essentially, any line that is in the right place and follows the correct format. The line must begin with a recognized word—one of the trigger words or action words—and must contain the proper number of parameters and a legitimate value for each parameter. Note that, to be legitimate, a value does not have to make sense. Thus, for example, the value **Goober7** for a city name is legitimate, even if there is no city in the scenario by that name.

There is a "wildcard" value that is legitimate for certain parameters.

Anybody: If a parameter requires the name of a civilization as its value, this value sets it so that any civilization meets the requirements.

Some triggers require you to specify (as parameters) the civilization that is attacking, defending, or receiving the object of the trigger. In these cases, you can also normally use **Anybody** in place of the name of a specific civilization. For those particular triggers, there are three other "wildcard" values you can use with the **Receiver** and **Owner** parameters of the associated actions.

TriggerAttacker: This specifies the civilization that was the aggressor in the happening that triggered the trigger.

TriggerDefender: This denotes whichever civilization was the defender in the happening that triggered the trigger.

TriggerReceiver: This represents the civilization that has the technology named in the **ReceivedTechnology** trigger.

Note that case (capitalization or lack thereof) is not important for parameters. "ANYBODY" is the same as "anybody" or "anYBoDy" as far as the game is concerned.

One important thing to remember is that there should never be spaces where they are not called for. This is especially vital before and after equals signs (=). Under no circumstances should there *ever* be a space next to an equals sign.

Debugging

One of the statements available in the **Events** Editor is not an event, but rather a tool you can use.

If you add the line:

```
@DEBUG
```

immediately after the @BEGINEVENTS line, you enable the Event Parsing Debugger (EPD). This can help you find problems in your event files.

When you load the scenario and the events file, the EPD opens a window that lets you watch as each line of the event file is processed. Only valid statements that have been processed successfully appear in this window. Thus, if the parser runs into an invalid statement in your file, the display in the window will stop at the line before the problem statement. This should allow you to search out errors and repair them.

Make sure to take this line out of your events file when you're done debugging the scenario.

The Triggers

Every Trigger is a specific trigger word, which might be followed by one or more required parameters. There are *no* optional parameters. The editor puts each parameter on a line by itself, in order immediately after the trigger word. For example:

```
@IF
CityTaken
city=Rome
attacker=Anybody
defender=Romans
```

is a valid Trigger.

Each parameter is the parameter word, which might be followed by the equals sign (=), then the value for that parameter. When a value must be entered exactly as written here, it is listed in bold type. (Case still doesn't matter.)

TRIGGER WORD	PARAMETERS	LEGITIMATE VALUES
CityTaken	city=	name of a city
	attacker=	civilization name or **Anybody**
	defender=	civilization name or **Anybody**
Negotiation	talker=	civilization name or **Anybody**
	talkertype=	**Human**, **Computer**, or **HumanOrComputer**
	listener=	civilization name or **Anybody**
	listenertype=	**Human**, **Computer**, or **HumanOrComputer**
RandomTurn	denominator=	number >0 and <1001
ReceivedTechnology	receiver=	civilization name or **Anybody**
	technology=	technology index number
ScenarioLoaded		
Turn	turn=	number or **Every**
TurnInterval	interval=	number
UnitKilled	unit=	name of a unit
	attacker=	civilization name or **Anybody**
	defender=	civilization name or **Anybody**

CityTaken: This Trigger is activated when a city changes ownership. It's excellent for reacting to key cities being captured. "Attacker" is the civilization that took the city, "Defender" is the one who owned the city beforehand.

Negotiation: This is triggered when two civilizations try to talk to each other. Note that there is an automatic Action to this Trigger that stops the two civilizations from talking to each other. When using this trigger, keep in mind that many things cause negotiations in the game, especially between computer-controlled players. Although it might be tempting to add some flavor to the game with a text pop-up whenever two civilizations try to meet ("Lincoln and Davis meet face to face, but Davis is adamant," for example), this can happen so often as to make the scenario unplayable. The "talkertype" and "listenertype" parameters allow you to specifically include or exclude computer (or human) civilizations from this Trigger.

RandomTurn: Rather than a specific turn, this triggers an Event on a turn chosen at random. **Denominator** is the "one in" number. That is, for example, if **denominator** is 40, there is a one in 40 chance every turn that this Event will be triggered.

ReceivedTechnology: This one's activated when a civilization receives—through whatever means—the specified technology *and* every turn thereafter, as long as the civilization retains the advance. Note that this can cause some irregularities unless you really want the action to happen every turn for the rest of the game. (To prevent that, make sure to include the **JustOnce** action in the event.) *Receiver* is the civilization that gets the advance. The *technology index number* is the position of the particular advance in the advances list in the **rules.txt** file. Remember that the index numbers begin at zero (for Advanced Flight), and only go up to 100 (Extra Advance 7). Also, note that Future Technology (90) can be received over and over and over without limit.

ScenarioLoaded: When a scenario is first loaded, this Trigger becomes activated. Note that this Trigger only works with two Actions: **PlayCDTrack** and **DontPlayWonders**. Any other use will cause unpredictable results.

Turn: Use this to have something happen at the beginning of a specific turn (or every turn). This can be useful for creating units on specific dates in historical scenarios, reenacting troop movements, and more.

TurnInterval: This is a repeating Trigger. The value of the **interval** parameter is the number of turns between the triggering of the action(s). An interval of 4, for example, would trigger this event every fourth turn.

UnitKilled: Use this when you want to respond to a particular unit being killed in battle. This is especially good for leaders, one-of-a-kind units, and special objectives. "Attacker" is the civilization that killed the unit, "Defender" is the one who owned the unit.

THE ACTIONS

Actions, much like Triggers, consist of a specific action word, which might be followed by one or more required parameters. There are *no* optional parameters. Each parameter must be on a line by itself, in order immediately after the action word (if there is one). For example:

```
@THEN
MakeAggression
who=Romans
whom=Carthaginians
```

is a valid Action.

Each parameter is the parameter word, which might be followed by the equals sign (=), then the value for that parameter. (Note that one action word, **Text**, has a value with no parameter word, followed by a parameter word with no values.) When a value must be entered exactly as written here, it is listed in bold type. (Case still doesn't matter.)

ACTION WORD	PARAMETERS	LEGITIMATE VALUES
ChangeMoney	receiver= amount=	civilization name number
ChangeTerrain	terraintype= maprect	terrain index number (on following line) coordinates
DestroyACivilization	whom=	civilization name
GiveTechnology	technology= receiver=	technology index number civilization name
MakeAggression	who= whom=	aggressor civilization name victim civilization name
MoveUnit	unit= owner= maprect moveto numbertomove=	name of a type of unit civilization name x1,y1,x2,y2,x3,y3,x4,y4 x,y number or **All**
PlayCDTrack		a number >1 and <25 (2–24 are valid)
PlayWaveFile		file name (*.wav)
Text		text to be displayed
	EndText	

Note that, although a single Trigger can cause multiple Actions, each Trigger can cause only one Action of each type. You can, for example, use MoveUnit, Change-Money and CreateUnit all in the same Event, but you can't use CreateUnit twice (or more times) in the *same* Event. If you wanted to create more than one unit, you would need to define another Event using an identical Trigger.

ChangeMoney: This adds money to or subtracts it from a civilization's treasury. (Use a negative number for the amount to subtract.) If after the adjustment the treasury is less than zero, *Civilization II* makes it zero, instead. **Receiver** is the affected civilization.

ChangeTerrain: This changes all of the terrain in a specified rectangular region of the map (delineated by the coordinates you give) to the specified type. You specify the type using the *terrain index number*, which is the position of the desired terrain type in the terrain list in the **rules.txt** file. Remember that the index numbers begin at zero (for Desert) and only go up to 10 (Ocean).

The coordinates define the corners of the rectangular region. They must (1) be on the line immediately following the word **maprect**, (2) be separated by a comma and a single space, and (3) be listed in the following specific order to be valid. (They also must be valid map coordinates.) The first coordinate must be the upper left corner; next comes the upper right, then the lower right, and finally the lower left. Thus:

1–2

4–3

CreateUnit: Creates a new unit (at no expense) with specified characteristics and places it on the map at the first of the specified locations. If that placement is invalid for any reason, the program tries the subsequent locations (there can be up to 10), in order, until one works or it reaches the **endlocations** parameter. The x and y in these locations represent horizontal and vertical coordinates on the scenario map.

DestroyACivilization: This one is exactly what it sounds like. Cities, units, and everything else is completely wiped out. *Whom* is the civilization slated to meet its doom (as in, "for *whom* the bell tolls").

DontPlayWonders: This Action toggles off the display of the Wonder of the World videos that normally play when a new wonder is completed.

GiveTechnology: Bestows the specified advance on the named civilization. The *technology index number* is the position of the particular advance in the advances list in the **rules.txt** file. Remember that the index numbers begin at zero (for Advanced Flight) and only go up to 100 (Extra Advance 7). Also, note that Future Technology (90) can be received over and over and over without limit. *Receiver* is the civilization on which the bestowing is to descend.

JustOnce: This special Action tells the program to execute this event once and only once. If, for example, you wanted to do something special the first time a city is taken, but not afterward, you would use the **CityTaken** Trigger and include JustOnce as one of the consequent Actions.

MakeAggression: The Actions causes two civilizations to cancel their peace treaty, if one exists. Then **who** immediately declares war on **whom**.

MoveUnit: This scans a specified rectangular region of the map (**maprect**), then orders a specified number of the owner's units of the given type in that region to move to a certain location. The program only activates units that are (1) not fortified, (2) not on sentry duty, (3) not already headed for a destination, (4) not building fortifications, and (5) not nuclear weapons. **MoveUnit** does not affect units owned by the human player.

The **maprect** coordinates define the corners of the rectangular region. They must be listed in a specific order to be valid. The first coordinate must be the upper left corner; next comes the upper right, then the lower right, and finally the lower left. Thus:

1–2

4–3

PlayWaveFile: Play the specified **.wav** file. The program searches the **sound** sub-directory of the current scenario directory for the file.

PlayCDTrack: Tells your computer's CD player to play the specified audio track. On all the *Civilization II* discs, Track 1 is reserved for program information, so the first audio track is actually Track 2. Thus, the **number** value must be 2 or greater.

Text: This simply presents a pop-up text box to the player. The box includes whatever text you put between the **Text** and **EndText** lines.

Note that unit types, civilization names, and so on *must* match the names in the **rules.txt** file exactly. Mismatches cause errors.

REFERENCE: SCREEN BY SCREEN

This section details each of the menus and major screens in the game and the parts and options of each. Refer to the body of the manual for the whys and wherefores (all we're discussing here is the how-to). The screens are covered alphabetically, for ease of reference.

THE CITY DISPLAY

You can direct the operation of each city from the CITY DISPLAY. Here, you assign citizens to work in the surrounding fields, mines, forests, and fishing grounds. This display collects in one place all the critical information concerning the pictured city's status, including how many shields it produces; how much food and trade income it is generating; what it is producing and how close the item is to completion; the happiness of the population; who is defending the city; and what improvements you've already built.

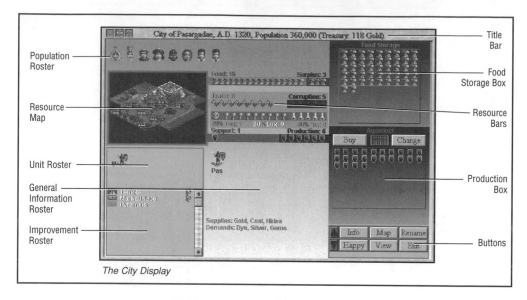

Population Roster

Resource Map

Unit Roster

General Information Roster

Improvement Roster

Title Bar

Food Storage Box

Resource Bars

Production Box

Buttons

The City Display

You can open the CITY DISPLAY in many ways.

- Position the cursor over a city in the MAP window, then click on that city.
- Pull down the KINGDOM menu and choose FIND CITY, then select the city you want.
- Position the cursor or the current active unit on a city, then press [Enter].
- Double-click on any city name in the CITY STATUS report.
- Double-click on any city name in the ATTITUDE ADVISOR's report.

You can close the CITY DISPLAY by clicking the EXIT button or the 🗵 button in the top left-hand corner of the window. If you have the ENTER KEY CLOSES CITY SCREEN option (one of the GAME OPTIONS accessible through the GAME menu) enabled, you can just press [Enter].

Civilization II has a CITY DISPLAY that is similar to, but not the same as, those in past ***Civilization*** games. Those of you familiar with ***Civilization*** or ***CivNet*** should take the time to learn the differences. We'll discuss each section of the display in turn.

Two important new features are the ZOOM buttons in the top left-hand corner of the window frame. You can click on 🔽 to contract the CITY DISPLAY and 🔼 to expand it again.

TITLE BAR

Along the top of the display is the TITLE BAR. The name of the city, the current date, the total population of this city, and the amount you have in your treasury are noted here.

POPULATION ROSTER

Near the top of the display are icons representing the city's population. Each citizen icon in the POPULATION ROSTER represents one population point. (Note that each population point represents a different number of citizens as the game progresses; the actual population is listed in the TITLE BAR.) In addition to the usual workers, a city can support three different types of Specialists.

Population Roster

Citizen icons can be happy, content, unhappy, or very unhappy. If the number of unhappy people exceeds the number of happy people (with content people and Specialists ignored), that city goes into civil disorder (see **Civil Disorder** for details).

SPECIALISTS

Citizens who are not working in the city radius are Specialists. For an example, click on a productive city radius square; the workers there become Entertainers (one citizen in the POPULATION ROSTER is replaced by an entertainer icon). Specialists no longer directly contribute to the resources a city generates. However, they might be useful in adjusting the amount of luxuries, taxes, and research the city generates. Specialists do consume food like other citizens. There are three types of Specialists: Entertainers, Scientists, and Taxmen. Cities must have a population base of five or more to support Taxmen or Scientists.

Entertainers: Citizens removed from the work force immediately become Entertainers. Each Entertainer adds two Luxury icons to the tally in the APPORTIONMENT bar. These additional luxuries are added before the effects of improvements such as Marketplaces and Banks are calculated. Creating Entertainers has the result of creating more luxuries, thus making more citizens happy.

'The King'

Taxmen: Click on an Entertainer icon in the POPULATION ROSTER to put him to work as a Taxman. Each Taxman adds three Tax icons to the APPORTIONMENT bar (instead of the two Luxuries the Entertainer used to generate). No tax collection is made if a city is in civil disorder (see **Civil Disorder** for details).

Scientists: Click on a Taxman icon to create a Scientist. Each Scientist adds three Science icons to the total in the APPORTIONMENT bar (instead of the taxes the Taxman used to generate). This additional research is added before the effects of improvements such as Libraries and Universities are calculated. As with Taxmen, Scientists are only useful if your city is not in civil disorder.

Click on a Scientist icon to return it to Entertainer status.

Food Storage Box

Any surplus food generated by your city each turn accumulates in this box. The capacity of the box expands as the city's population increases. When the box overflows, your city's population grows by one point, and a new citizen is added to the Population Roster. The Food Storage Box empties and begins to fill again the next turn.

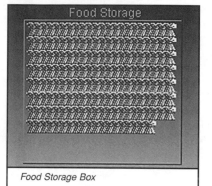

Food Storage Box

If one of your cities is not producing enough food to feed its population, the shortage is subtracted from the reserve in the Food Storage Box. If the box is empty and the city still has a food shortfall, any Settlers or Engineer units that draw food from its stores are disbanded, one per turn, until the shortfall is corrected. If there are no Settlers or Engineers, or if a shortfall still exists after they are lost, the city loses one point of population each turn to starvation, until an equilibrium is reached.

The Granary improvement has the effect of speeding population growth. When a city has a Granary, the Food Storage Box only half empties when it overflows and creates more people. The box empties only to the granary line.

The Resource Bars

The Resource bars compile all the resources generated by the city's workers each turn. Food, shields, and trade goods are collected each turn from the City Radius squares being worked by citizens. The amount of any particular resource collected might be modified by the presence of a certain improvement in the city, the form of government you choose, or by your ownership of a certain Wonder (see **City Improvements** for details).

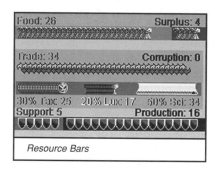

Resource Bars

Food

The top bar represents the state of the city's food harvest each turn. Each population point (citizen icon) in your city consumes two units of food each turn. Also, some units consume food as part of their support needs. Any surplus or shortfall is noted on the right side of the bar. Excess accumulates in the Food Storage Box.

Trade

The center area contains the Trade bar and the Apportionment bar. Together, these represent the state and disbursal of the city's trade income each turn. The Trade bar lists the total trade goods produced on the left, including any derived from trade routes. Depending on your type of government and each city's distance from your capital, some portion of the arrow icons might be lost as corruption; this is noted on the right side of the bar.

The Apportionment bar notes how the income from these trade goods is divided into taxes (gold), luxuries (goblets), and research funding (beakers). These numbers depend on your trade rates (see **Kingdom Menu** for details) and the assignment of the city's Specialists. The apportionment is figured after the losses to corruption have been subtracted.

SHIELDS

The bottom bar represents the state of the city's production each turn. Depending on the form of government under which your civilization operates, some of the shield icons generated each turn might be required to maintain units that a city has previously built. Support requirements are noted on the left side of the bar. Any production capacity lost to waste is noted in the center of the bar. Production is indicated on the right side of the bar and accumulates toward what the city is building in the PRODUCTION BOX.

If the city's industrial capacity is not sufficient to maintain the existing units, the shortage is indicated. If your turn ends and there is such a shortage, enough units are disbanded to make up the difference, beginning with the ones farthest from the city.

RESOURCE MAP

Immediately below the POPULATION ROSTER is a detail map showing all of the discovered terrain squares within a city's radius. The city square itself is always under production. For each population point (each citizen in the roster), you can work one

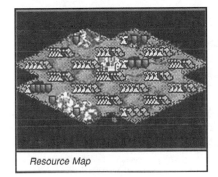

Resource Map

additional square. The maximum number of squares a city can work is the number of citizens plus one, or 21, whichever is smaller. Note that it is possible to have more citizens than there are squares to work.

Depending on the type of terrain in a map square, citizens working there can produce food, production shields, and/or trade goods. Most squares produce a combination of several resources. Clicking on any square under production (except the city square, which remains permanently under production) temporarily takes that citizen off work. Click on an unoccupied square to put the citizen back to work in a new place. You can move people from one square to another however you wish to change the mix of resources the city is harvesting. Citizens removed from work are temporarily converted into Specialists.

When the city population increases, each new citizen is automatically assigned an area to develop. You might want to review the map of a city that has just increased in size to be certain that workers have been placed as you wish.

PRODUCTION BOX

Below your FOOD STORAGE BOX is the PRODUCTION BOX. Any production (shield icons) generated by your city each turn accumulates in this box. The capacity of the PRODUCTION BOX changes to reflect the cost of the unit, improvement, or Wonder currently under construction. When the box is full, the item is complete. The box empties, and the new item is ready for use. The item being built is noted at the top. The items available for building depend on the advances your civilization has achieved.

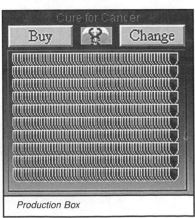

Production Box

When the discovery of a new advance makes available a unit that supersedes units currently being built, your production is automatically upgraded to the new unit. If you are building a Wonder and another civilization completes it before you can, you are reminded that you must change production in that location.

Some Wonders on the Production menu might be marked with an asterisk (*) before their name. This indicates that the Wonder's special ability has been made obsolete by someone's discovery (not necessarily yours) of the terminating advance. You may still build obsolete Wonders to gain points toward your final score (see **Scoring** for details).

CHANGE

You can use the CHANGE button to switch production to another item at any time before the production of the existing item is completed. If you have already accumulated sufficient shields to construct the new item, any excess is lost, and the item is immediately completed. Otherwise, the accumulated shield icons roll over toward the new item. Note, however, that changing the production assignment often results in a significant loss of efficiency, which is reflected as a loss of accumulated shields.

This button changes to AUTO OFF if you set the city to automatic production mode.

BUY

You can speed the completion of an item by clicking the BUY button. A dialog box shows how large a cash outlay the rush job requires (see **Rush Jobs** for why you might choose this option). If you have sufficient funds in your treasury, you are given the option to buy the item outright.

PRODUCTION MENU BUTTON

These buttons are not in the PRODUCTION BOX, but rather on the PRODUCTION menu from which you choose the next item you wish constructed.

Auto: This button allows you to hand the city's production choices off to your advisors (you get to choose the MILITARY ADVISOR, the DOMESTIC ADVISOR, or both). Each option causes your cities to be run using a different philosophy. The game automatically decides what to build next after each item is completed. To take back the responsibility for these decisions, click the AUTO OFF button in the PRODUCTION BOX.

Help: The HELP button calls up the CIVILOPEDIA entry for whatever item is highlighted.

Cheat: When the CHEAT menu is enabled, this button allows you to select a unit improvement or Wonder from the PRODUCTION menu and build it instantaneously, without interrupting your regular production in any way.

UNIT ROSTER

Below the RESOURCE MAP is the UNIT ROSTER. This shows all of the units that call this city home. The status of each unit (fortified, veteran, or whatever) is indicated on the unit's shield. Food and shield icons below these units indicate any resources

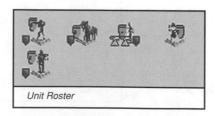

Unit Roster

required by each as support. The amount and type of support that units need depends on your civilization's chosen form of government (see **Types of Government**). Additionally, if your civilization operates a Democracy or a Republic, armies on foreign duty whose absence is causing unhappiness are noted. If the city does not generate enough resources to maintain all of the supported units, units left unsupported are disbanded, beginning with those farthest from the city. Click on any unit icon for its exact location. The SUPPORTED UNIT INFORMATION window that opens also gives you a few useful options:

- No changes
- Center map on unit
- Center map on unit and close city screen
- Order unit to return home
- Disband Unit

These are all exactly what they sound like.

IMPROVEMENT ROSTER

Below the UNIT ROSTER is a list of all of the existing improvements and Wonders of the World in the city. Each entry in the list includes the item's icon and name. If the improvement is one you can sell, there is a gold icon next to the listing. Click on the listing to sell the improvement. (You cannot sell Wonders.) Improvements are added to the roster as they are completed. Any improvements destroyed by disaster or bombardment are removed from the list, as are any improvements you sell. Note that Wonders will remain on the roster even after their special ability has become obsolete.

GENERAL INFORMATION BOX

What information is in the box in the bottom center of the CITY DISPLAY depends on what you want to see. Three of the buttons in the bottom right-hand corner of the display control this area.

CITY INFO CHART

Click the INFO button to view this chart. (This is the default display the first time you open the CITY DISPLAY.) Every unit currently in the city is represented by its icon. The three-letter abbreviation of the name of its home city appears under each unit. You can click on any of these units to give it orders. The orders available in the UNIT INFORMATION window are:

- No changes
- Clear orders
- Sleep / Board next ship
- Disband
- Activate Unit
- Activate Unit and close City Display

Each does exactly what it sounds like it does.

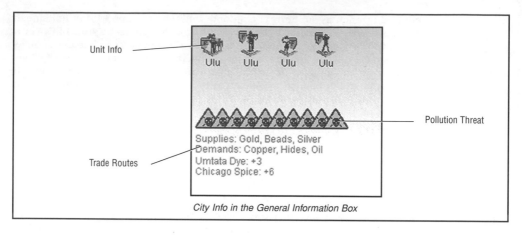

Unit Info

Ulu   Ulu   Ulu   Ulu

Pollution Threat

Supplies: Gold, Beads, Silver
Demands: Copper, Hides, Oil
Umtata Dye: +3
Chicago Spice: +6

Trade Routes

City Info in the General Information Box

Once your civilization has discovered the Trade advance, this area lists items in demand and items the city can supply. It also summarizes the income from trade routes if you have any. A city can have up to three trade routes in operation at any time. Each destination city is listed, along with the commodity traded and the income generated each turn.

The threat of pollution as a result of the industrial production and smog in the city is represented by cautionary triangles marked with skull-and-crossbones. The more of these that appear in the GENERAL INFORMATION box, the greater is the likelihood a random terrain square within the city radius will become polluted this turn.

HAPPINESS CHART

Click the HAPPY button to see this chart. The HAPPINESS chart breaks down the factors affecting the happiness of a city's population into a series of citizen icon representations. Each row encompasses the effects of the previous row and adds the results of specific measures.

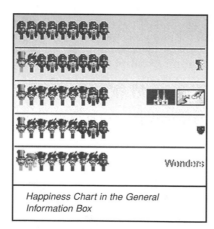

Happiness Chart in the General Information Box

The first row shows the natural happiness of a city's population before any adjustments. The number of content citizens is determined by the difficulty level at which you are playing.

The second row shows the effect luxuries have in the city, if any. Every two units of luxuries make one content person happy or one unhappy person content. Note that contented persons are made happy before unhappy persons are made content.

The third row adds in the benefits of city improvements like Temples, Cathedrals, and Colosseums.

The fourth row adds in the effects of martial law and field duty. Any units imposing martial law are shown in this row. Under a Republic or a Democracy, martial law does not work, and this row instead displays any unhappiness generated by having units in the field.

The fifth row adds in the effects of any Wonders of the World, whether in this city or elsewhere, that influence the population's happiness. Additionally, the fifth row reflects the attitudes shown in the Population Roster, since all of the adjustments have been factored in.

FOREIGN SERVICE MAP

Click the Map button to see a miniature map of the world. The city location is noted on this map, and so are the locations of all of this city's units assigned to foreign service.

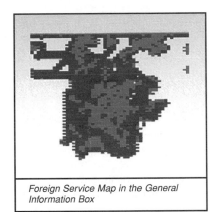

Foreign Service Map in the General Information Box

THE BUTTONS

In the bottom right-hand corner are two arrows and a few buttons. Here's what each does:

- The arrow buttons allow you to scroll through your cities one at a time, in alphabetical order. These buttons are not active when the City Display pops up in response to a report.

- Info changes the display in the General Information box to the City Info chart.

- Happy changes the display in the General Information box to the Happiness chart.

- MAP changes the display in the GENERAL INFORMATION box to the FOREIGN SERVICE MAP.

- VIEW shows you a view of the city as seen from the air.

- RENAME allows you to change the name of the city.

- EXIT closes the CITY DISPLAY.

THE MENU BAR

As is usual in Windows applications, a menu bar spans the top of the ***Civilization II*** window. There are eight menus: GAME, KINGDOM, VIEW, ORDERS, ADVISORS, WORLD, CHEAT, and CIVILOPEDIA. You can open any menu by clicking on its name or by holding [Alt] and pressing whichever letter in the menu name is underlined. Having opened a menu, double-click on any option to activate it or use the arrow keys to move the highlight to that option, then press [Enter]. Most options also have a shortcut key, which is noted next to the option on the menu. Even when the menu is not open, you can use the shortcut to activate an option. Any option that is grayed out is currently unavailable.

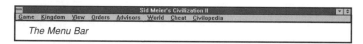

The Menu Bar

GAME

The options on this menu are what we call "meta-game functions;" that is, they affect the game as a whole.

GAME OPTIONS [Ctrl][O]

This option calls up a checklist of other options. Each of these is a toggle; those with checked boxes are currently "on," and those with empty boxes are "off." Click on an option to toggle it on or off. Note that some options, such as TUTORIAL HELP, might affect game speed. When you have these options set as you want them, click OK to return to the game. If you change your mind and wish to discard your changes, click on CANCEL instead.

Sound Effects: Includes battle noises, message alerts, and construction sounds. If you want to hear the audio cues that ***Civilization II*** provides, make sure this box is checked.

Music: Turns all the background music in the game on and off.

Always wait at end of turn: Guarantees that your turn will not end until you press [Enter] or click in the STATUS box. If this option is not checked, you need only press [Enter] to end a turn when you have no active units to move.

Autosave each turn: Automatically saves your game every turn and backs it up to a save file every four turns. If something dreadful happens and you need to restart the game, you can use one of these backup files just as you would any saved game.

Show enemy moves: Makes the progress of any enemy units within observation range of your units and cities visible. When this option is not checked, you see only those enemy moves which result in combat with your units.

No pause after enemy moves: Normally, ***Civilization II*** pauses briefly after each enemy unit moves. This gives you time to actually see every enemy move. If you turn this option on, there is no pause; enemy units will move as quickly as possible.

Fast piece slide: Increases the speed at which all units move from square to square. Checking this option will speed up the game, but might make some unit movements difficult to follow.

Instant advice: When turned on, this option allows your advisors to provide helpful hints whenever they have an opinion to proffer. Otherwise, they'll keep silent until you ask for their input.

Tutorial Help: When active, provides even more advice for novice players. This option does not have any effect during multiplayer games.

Move units w/ mouse (cursor arrows): As in the original *Civilization*, in *Civilization II* you use the keyboard controls (specifically, the numeric keypad) to move your units. If you would rather use the mouse-and-keyboard method introduced in *CivNet*, turn this option on. You will then be able to position the mouse just to the side (or top or bottom) of the active unit (the cursor will change to reflect the fact that you are giving movement orders) and click to have the unit move in that direction. The keyboard controls remain active regardless.

Enter key closes City Screen: When this option is checked, the CITY DISPLAY closes any time you press Enter. Otherwise, the CITY DISPLAY remains visible at all times once opened, unless you click the EXIT button to close it. Note that turning this option on removes your ability to use Enter (when the viewing cursor is on a city) to open the CITY DISPLAY.

GRAPHIC OPTIONS Ctrl P

This option also opens a checklist of other options. Each is a toggle; those with checked boxes are "on," and those with empty boxes are "off." Click on an option to toggle it on or off. Note that some options, such as CITY ANIMATIONS, might affect game speed. When you have these options set as you want them, click OK to return to the game. If you change your mind and wish to discard your changes, click CANCEL instead.

Throne Room: You will not be notified of the spontaneous improvements to your THRONE ROOM that your citizens offer unless you have this option turned on.

Diplomacy Screen: When this option is checked, diplomatic discussions take place on the full DIPLOMACY SCREEN, with a portrait, military and technical information, and perhaps the animated herald (see the next option). If you turn this off, diplomacy is a spartan matter carried on in text boxes.

Animated Heralds: Whenever you make contact with a representative of another civilization, the communication will include an animated Herald unless this option is turned off.

Civilopedia for Advances: Every time your civilization successfully researches an Advance, you'll see the CIVILOPEDIA entry for that technology. Turn this off when you've gotten to know the advances well enough.

High Council: An animated group of councilors will convene occasionally to offer you advice. If you'd rather not listen to them, turn this option off. You can still ask them for advice using the CONSULT HIGH COUNCIL option on the ADVISORS menu.

Wonder Movies: If you would rather not watch each Wonder of the World video every time you build that wonder, uncheck this option. Otherwise, the videos will continue to appear. (Note that you can take a look at a Wonder movie at any time by opening the CIVILOPEDIA menu, holding down the Shift key, and clicking on WONDERS OF THE WORLD.)

This option also opens a checklist of other options. Each toggles reporting of an aspect of city information. Those with checked boxes are "on," and those with empty boxes are "off." Click on an option to toggle it on or off. Note that some options might affect game speed. When you have these options set as you want them, click OK to return to the game. If you change your mind and wish to discard your changes, click CANCEL instead.

Warn when city growth halted (Aqueduct/Sewer System): When one of your cities reaches the maximum population that its current infrastructure can support, you will receive a warning of the situation only if this option is checked.

Show city improvements built: When on, this notifies you of the completion of any improvement to a city. This is especially useful when you have a city in automatic production mode.

Show non-combat units built: If on, this notifies you when a city has completed production of a non-combatant unit (a Diplomat, for instance). This is especially useful when you have a city in automatic production mode.

Show invalid build instructions: If you assign a production order to a city that is not valid (building a Wonder of the World that another city has already completed, for example), you will not receive notification of the problem unless this option is turned on. This is especially helpful when you have cities set in automatic production mode.

Announce cities in disorder: When this is on, you will be notified of any city that goes into civil disorder.

Announce order restored in city: If this is checked, you will be notified when any city in disorder has been calmed.

Announce "We Love The King Day": If the citizens of a city are particularly happy with your rule, they have a celebration in your honor. You won't know about it unless this option is turned on.

Warn when food dangerously low: Cities running at a harvest deficit can quickly deplete their stores of food. You will be warned of the impending starvation of your people only if this option is checked.

Warn when new pollution occurs: Industrial civilizations often produce waste products that are unfriendly to the environment. News of ecological damage will only reach your ears if this option is turned on.

Warn when changing production will cost shields: Changing the production assignment of a city when it has not completed its previous assignment often results in a substantial loss of production efficiency and accumulated shields. Unless this option is checked, you will not be notified or have the option to verify your orders when this is the case; you will simply have the penalty deducted.

"Zoom-to-City" NOT default action: When you are notified of one of the above situations, the notification box generally has two selections at the bottom: ZOOM TO CITY and CONTINUE. Unless you check this box, the first is always selected when the box appears.

MULTIPLAYER OPTIONS

This option calls up a checklist of other options. Each of these is a toggle; those with checked boxes are currently "on," and those with empty boxes are "off." Click on an option to toggle it on or off. When you have these options set as you want them, click

OK to return to the game. If you change your mind and wish to discard your changes, click on CANCEL instead.

Clear chat buffer at the start of a new game: When you enable this, old messages are cleared out of the CHAT window whenever you start a new game or load a saved game.

Clear chat buffer each time we boot up: Turn this on to have old chat messages cleared every time you start up the game.

Double production of each terrain type: If you're the Host, use this to propose a change in the doubling status for terrain output. If you propose to change this during the game, all of the players must agree (the vote must be unanimous) before the change goes into effect.

Double movement rate of ground units: If you're the Host, use this to propose a change in the doubling status for the movement allowance of ground units. If you propose to change this during the game, all of the players must agree (the vote must be unanimous) before the change goes into effect.

SET PASSWORD

In a multiplayer game, allows you to protect your civilization from poachers by setting a password lock on it. Whenever you load a saved multiplayer game or join a game loaded by someone else, each player reselects their civilization from those included in that saved game. Unless you have assigned a password to your civilization, an unscrupulous player could select *your* civilization as their own.

CHANGE TIMER

Allows the host player to reset the multiplayer GAME TIMER. This clock determines the length of time each player has to take a single turn. Choose one of the preset time limits or set this to any turn length between 10 seconds and 3600 (one hour). If you don't want to limit the length of turns, select *Unlimited*. The turn timer countdown is displayed in the title bar of the MAP window. If the Host proposes to change the time limit during the game, all of the players must agree (the vote must be unanimous) before the change goes into effect.

PICK MUSIC

This option is only available if you installed the music files from the CD. It allows you to choose what music plays during your game.

SAVE GAME [Ctrl][S]

Use this option to save your game. **Civilization II** suggests a name for the save file, but you can type in any name you like (as long as it is eight characters or less). The default extension for saved games is .SAV. The only limit on the number of saved games you can have is the capacity of your hard disk.

LOAD GAME [Ctrl][L]

Use this option to load a game saved previously (including autosaved games). Select one of the files listed in the window, then click OK.

JOIN GAME

This option is available only during *Hot Seat* games. Use it to add a new player to a game already in progress.

RETIRE [Ctrl][R]

Retiring is one way of ending your game. When you retire, the game shows you how your civilization did in comparison to the others (which it does not do if you simply quit). The closing displays are exactly the same as if the game had come to a conclusion on its own. First, of course, you must confirm that you want to retire.

QUIT [Ctrl][X]

Choose this option if you just want to exit the game without all the closing displays. You have a chance to confirm or cancel quitting.

KINGDOM

This menu includes options that affect not just one city, but your entire civilization.

TAX RATE [Shift][T]

Choose this option to adjust the proportion of taxes (gold icons) to science (beaker icons) to luxuries (goblet icons) that each city generates each turn. As the percentage of any one of these increases, the percentage of one or both of the others must decrease.

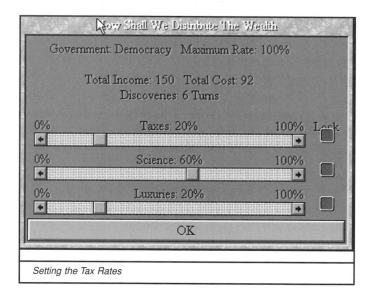

Setting the Tax Rates

VIEW THRONE ROOM [Shift][H]

As you progress through the game, your achievements and skill in management are acknowledged periodically by your people. The citizens express their favor by spontaneously adding to the grandeur of your THRONE ROOM, which is located in your Palace, which is in your capital city. (If you want to, you can relocate your THRONE ROOM and capital by constructing a new Palace in any city you control.) This option allows you to take a look at the status of the chamber from which you rule.

FIND CITY [Shift][C]

Select this to choose from a list of all your cities. The MAP window will center on the city you pick.

REVOLUTION! [Shift][R]

Choose this option when you want to switch forms of government. You must have acquired specific technological advances to choose a type of government other than Despotism. Usually, a revolution brings on a period of Anarchy. This can last for several turns. Eventually, you'll receive notification that your citizens are ready to choose a new type of government. All the options available to you are listed. Click on your choice.

Note that once the period of Anarchy ends and you have chosen a new government, you can use this option for the rest of that turn to freely switch your form of government without provoking further Anarchy.

VIEW

This menu includes options that affect the views in the various game windows.

MOVE PIECES [V]

Use this option to switch the MAP window from VIEW PIECES mode into MOVE PIECES mode. The current active unit will be centered in the MAP window, blinking.

VIEW PIECES [V]

Use this option to switch the MAP window from MOVE PIECES mode into VIEW PIECES mode. The terrain cursor unit will be centered in the MAP window, blinking. You can use the keys on the numeric keypad to move this cursor just as you would a unit.

ZOOM IN [Z]

This option incrementally increases the size of the map squares shown in the current MAP window. This functions in the same way as the [icon] button in the upper left-hand corner of each window.

ZOOM OUT [X]

This incrementally decreases the size of the map squares shown in the current MAP window. This option functions in the same way as the [icon] button in the upper left-hand corner of each window.

MAX ZOOM IN [Ctrl][Z]

This option zooms in to the maximum size map square in the current MAP window.

STANDARD ZOOM [Shift][X]

This option resets the square size in the current MAP window to the default size.

MEDIUM ZOOM OUT [Shift][X]

This option zooms to a medium size map square in the current MAP window, a size that we have found useful.

MAX ZOOM OUT [Ctrl][X]

This option zooms out to the minimum size map square in the current MAP window, showing the entire known world.

SHOW MAP GRID [Ctrl][G]

Select this to superimpose a grid on the map in the MAP window. This can help novice players become familiar with the isometric movement system used in *Civilization II*.

ARRANGE WINDOWS

This option returns the screen to its original configuration. Only the MAP window, the STATUS window, and the WORLD window remain open.

SHOW HIDDEN TERRAIN [T]

Use this to temporarily remove the improvement graphics from all terrain, so that you can clearly view the terrain underneath.

CENTER VIEW [C]

This option centers the current MAP window on the current active unit. If there is no current active unit, nothing happens.

ORDERS

This menu lists the orders you can give the current active unit. Note that orders that are not appropriate for the active unit, or not currently available, are grayed out (or not listed). Some options have different results (and different text) depending on what type of terrain the unit is standing on.

BUILD NEW CITY/JOIN CITY [B]

This option tells a Settlers or Engineer unit to create a new city where it stands. If the unit stands in an existing city with fewer than eight population points, the option reads JOIN CITY instead, and the unit adds itself to the city as a population point.

BUILD ROAD/RAILROAD [R]

This option tells a Settlers or Engineer unit to build roads across the square in which it stands. If you have discovered the Railroads advance, the option might read BUILD RAILROAD. In this case, your unit can improve existing roads to railroads.

BUILD IRRIGATION/CHANGE TO... [I]

Use this option to order a Settlers or Engineer unit to irrigate the square in which it stands. If the introduction of agriculture requires or will cause the square to change type, the option will read CHANGE TO instead, followed by the type of terrain that will result. For example, if your unit is on a Forest square, the option might read CHANGE TO PLAINS. These alternate orders tell the unit to enact the change. Note that this change does not include irrigation; you can only do that once the terrain is suitable. For details on which terrain types can be transformed to which others, please refer to the **Poster**. If your unit stands in a square that will not benefit from irrigation, the option will be grayed out.

Build Mines/Change to... Ⓜ

Use this option to order a Settlers or Engineer unit to mine the square in which it stands. If the introduction of mining requires or will cause the square to change its type, the option will read CHANGE TO instead, followed by the type of terrain that will result. For example, if your unit is on a Grassland square, the option reads CHANGE TO FOREST. These alternate orders tell the unit to enact the change. Note that this change is in place of the mining. For details on which terrain types can be transformed to which others, please refer to the **Poster**. If your unit stands in a square that will not benefit from mining, the option will be grayed out.

Transform to... Ⓞ

This option tells an Engineer unit to drastically change the terrain type of the square in which it stands. For example, if your unit stands in a Mountains square, the option reads TRANSFORM TO HILLS, and it orders the unit to do exactly that. For details on which terrain types can be transformed to which others, please refer to the **Poster**.

Build Airbase Ⓔ

This orders a Settlers or Engineer unit to build a military Airbase (*not* an airport) in the square it occupies. Once it is built, your air units can land for fuel and repairs at the Airbase.

Build Fortress Ⓕ

This orders a Settlers or Engineer unit to build defensive fortifications in the square it occupies. Once it is built, your units can occupy the Fortress to enhance their defensive capabilities.

Automate Settler Ⓚ

If you would rather not give a Settlers or Engineer unit specific commands every time it finishes a job, you can automate that unit—in effect, give a friendly AI control over it. Automated units will not build cities, but will work to improve terrain around existing ones. In some situations, such as the approach of an enemy unit, control reverts to you.

Clean up Pollution Ⓟ

Use this option to order a Settlers or Engineer unit to detoxify a polluted square.

Pillage (Shift)Ⓟ

This option tells a unit to wreak havoc on the square it occupies, which could mean collapsing mines, destroying irrigation, ripping up roads, or other destruction.

Unload Ⓤ

Give this order to a ship to activate all its passenger units, allowing them to move ashore or onto another ship. The ship must be adjacent to a land square, a city square, or another friendly ship. You can also click on the ship to bring up a box showing all of the shipboard units, then click on each one that you want to unload.

Go To [G]

This option allows you to send a unit directly to one of your cities. Select a city from the list (only those which the unit can reach on its own will be listed), and the unit will go there without further orders. (Note: the original function of this order, sending a unit to a destination square, is now a mouse function. Click-and-hold on the square to which you want the current active unit to go until the mouse cursor changes to a "GoTo" arrow, and the unit proceeds to the selected square without further orders.)

Paradrop [P]

This movement order is available only to Paratrooper units currently located in an Airbase or a city with an Airport. Choose any unoccupied square no more than 10 squares distant from the unit's current location. The unit will move immediately to that square. This order uses all but one of the Paratrooper's movement points for that turn.

Airlift [L]

Use this order to move a unit that has not yet moved this turn from any of your cities served by an Airport to any other (friendly) city with an Airport. This travel uses all of the unit's movement points for that turn. Only one unit may be airlifted from or into each city per turn.

Go Home to Nearest City [H]

Use this option to order a unit to move directly to the nearest city under your control. If the unit is already in a city, this reassigns the unit to that city for support (makes that city the unit's new Home city).

Fortify [F]

Select this option to order a military unit to dig in and fortify itself in the square in which it stands. This enhances the defensive capabilities of the unit for as long as it remains fortified.

Sleep [S]

When you order a unit to sleep (sentry), that unit is assigned the task of remaining in the square it occupies. The unit maintains this posture until you wake it (activate it) or an enemy unit approaches an adjacent square. You can click on a sleeping unit and give the Activate Unit order at any time to wake it and return it to active status. Units boarding a ship to undertake naval transport automatically assume sleeping status when they ship out.

Disband [Shift][D]

This order allows you to dismiss a unit from active duty. The unit disappears completely and irrevocably, so be careful when invoking this option. If you disband a unit in a city square, one-half of the unit's construction cost is immediately added to the Production Box in that city. This represents the redistribution of support and retraining of soldiers.

Activate Unit [A]

This orders the unit at the cursor location to become active. If there is more than one unit in that square, you can select which unit you want to activate.

Wait [W]

Use this to order the current active unit to wait for orders until you have given every other active unit something to do. Note that if you give another unit the Wait order, that unit will get in line behind the first unit you ordered to wait, and so forth.

Skip Turn [Spacebar]

Use this order to pass over a unit for a turn. The unit takes no action, but will repair itself somewhat if it has been damaged.

Advisors

These options all provide reports on the overall picture of your civilization's strengths and progress.

Consult High Council

The High Council is a video-animated meeting of all your advisors. In it, you can ask one or all of them for advice on your current situation.

City Status [F1]

This report lists vital statistics for all the cities in your empire, in the order in which they were founded. This information includes how many of each resource type (food, production, and trade) each is collecting, what each city is building, and how close it is to finishing that assignment. You can double-click on any of the listed names to open the City Display for that city.

Defense Minister [F2]

The Defense Minister reports on your military assets. This includes information on every one of your existing units, plus statistics on past performance in battle and casualties to date.

Foreign Minister [F3]

This report is a summary of everything you know about the other civilizations with whom you have made contact. This report includes thumbnail sketches of each (the name and title of the leader, your current diplomatic status with them, and their leader's current attitude toward you). If you have an embassy with a civilization, you also find out how much gold they have in their treasury.

You can double-click on any of the leaders (or the Send Emissary button) to begin negotiations with that ruler immediately.

If you have established an embassy with a particular civilization, clicking Check Intelligence opens the Intelligence Report, which gives you further details, including a complete list of their cities and notice of which Wonders (if any) they are attempting to build.

Attitude Advisor [F4]

This advisor summarizes the relative happiness of your citizens. For each city, this report details the base status of its population (happy, content, unhappy, and specialist citizens) and the effects of any influences (Temple improvements, for example) which, directly or indirectly, modify the happiness of the people. If any city is about to go into civil disorder (next turn) or will remain in civil disorder unless you do something, that city will be clearly marked. Double-click on any of the listed city names to open the CITY DISPLAY for that burg.

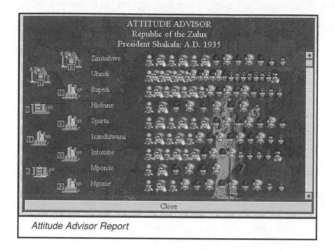

Attitude Advisor Report

TRADE ADVISOR [F5]

Your TRADE ADVISOR reports on the percentages of trade you have earmarked for luxuries, tax revenue, and scientific research funding in each city. In addition, this report covers those improvements to your cities which require maintenance payments. Comparing your total tax revenue (income) with your maintenance cost total (expenses), you can see whether the treasury of your civilization is increasing each turn, shrinking, or remaining the same. If your treasury is shrinking, this might be a good time to increase taxes or adjust individual cities to produce higher revenue. In an emergency, you might wish to sell an improvement to raise cash. In addition, your trade advisor keeps tabs on the market for every trade cargo in the game. Click the SUPPLY AND DEMAND button to see a list of commodities. Click on the commodity in which you are interested, to see a list of cities interested in that cargo. The OK button lets you choose another cargo and the CANCEL button returns you to the TRADE ADVISOR'S Report.

SCIENCE ADVISOR [F6]

Your SCIENCE ADVISOR keeps a record of the advances your civilization has already achieved and the progress of your scientists toward the next advance. (Advances that your civilization was the first to learn appear in white type.)

Click the GOAL button to see the entire list of advances and help options that are available.

Note that it is possible to continue making advances beyond the list that defines civilization up to the end of the 20th century. These continuing advances are called Future Tech, and each one you acquire adds to your civilization score.

CHAT WITH KINGS

During a multiplayer game, this opens the CHAT window, in which you can exchange messages with other players. For the detailed description of how chatting works, please read the **Chat with Kings** section in **Playing a Multiplayer Game**. Chat features are not available in *Hot Seat* games.

WORLD

This menu allows you to view statistics comparing the progress of all the world's civilizations.

WONDERS OF THE WORLD F7

This option shows the icon for each Wonder that has been built and identifies both its location and the culture that (currently) owns it. If a Wonder was built but has since been destroyed, that fact is also noted.

TOP 5 CITIES F8

This option brings up important statistics about the top five cities in the world, including their population size and citizens' attitudes, the culture to which they belong, and any Wonders present. City rank is determined on the basis of the number of happy citizens, content citizens, and Wonders of the World there. This list might even contain information on places you didn't know existed (your civilization has yet to discover them).

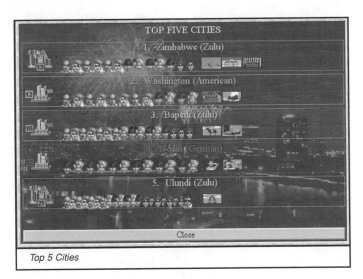

Top 5 Cities

CIVILIZATION SCORE F9

Use this option to find out your score so far. This is based on the total number of citizens in your entire civilization, Wonders you have built, bonuses for various measures like world peace, and similar penalties for negatives like pollution. If you have enabled CHEAT MODE during your game, it is noted in your score.

DEMOGRAPHICS [F11]

This option shows you a list of demographic statistics and the ranking of your civilization for each measure mentioned. If you have diplomatic relations with civilizations whose rank in a particular category is higher than yours, that culture's statistics are listed as well.

SPACESHIPS [F12]

When you contact your space advisors, they report the progress of any spaceship under construction. Select from the menu the civilization whose spaceship you wish

Apollo Program

to examine. Your advisors present a picture of the construction accomplished to date and their assessment of what the craft can carry, its estimated flight time, and its probability of success.

The space race begins once the Apollo Program Wonder of the World has been constructed. Thereafter, any civilization that has the required technologies can begin building parts of a spaceship.

Once the space race begins, it is important to maintain a watch on the spaceships of your rivals. You need to assess when they are likely to launch so that you can plan the size of your own ship and its launch date. If you conclude that your ship construction is too far behind to catch up, it might be necessary to mount a military campaign to capture the enemy capital. Capturing an enemy capital destroys a spaceship, whether it is under construction or already launched.

CHEAT

This menu contains options designed as crutches for those of you too loathsome and pathetic to be able to win on your own. No, seriously, these are aimed at novice players who might want (or need) a headstart, so that they can "jump the learning curve" and enjoy some of the more advanced portions of **Civilization II**. More experienced players might want to use these to cut out some aspect of the game that they find less than fun, so as to enjoy the rest that much more. In addition, the features on the CHEAT menu are indispensable for those of you designing and building your own **Civilization II** scenarios. Whatever your reasons for cheating, remember that using this menu goes on your permanent record.

Remember, the CHEAT menu comes with no guarantees—use it at your own risk and don't blame Customer Support if they can't help when it causes problems.

The options on the CHEAT menu are not available during multiplayer games.

TOGGLE CHEAT MODE [Ctrl][K]

Use this to toggle CHEAT MODE on and off. You cannot use any of the other options on this menu unless this one has been enabled. Once you use this option, *even if you never actually use any of the other cheat options*, the fact that you have cheated is noted permanently on your civilization score.

CREATE UNIT [Shift][F1]

This option creates a new unit at the current cursor location. You can generate any type of unit that you can currently build, or use the buttons at the bottom of the window to select from lists of Obsolete (OBS) or Advanced (ADV) units. Other buttons determine whether or not the created unit is a veteran and which civilization has control of that unit.

REVEAL MAP [Shift][F2]

Use this to view the map of any civilization (what they have discovered to date) or to have the entire world revealed to you.

SET HUMAN PLAYER [Shift][F3]

This option allows you to abandon your rule and take control of whichever civilization you would prefer to run. You can also abdicate completely and watch the game play against itself.

SET GAME YEAR [Shift][F4]

Use this to turn the calendar forward or back to whatever game year you like. You will be prompted to enter a number of "Turns Elapsed." This is the game's way of expressing years. There are several different time scales for years versus turns, depending on the difficulty level and how far the game has progressed. It might help to know that there are 550 turns in a Chieftain level game, 500 in Prince level, 450 at King level, and 400 at both the Emperor and Deity levels. After these turns, there is always a grace period of 20 years between the last turn (2000 A.D.) and the end of the game (2020 A.D.). Nothing but the year (neither your civilization nor any of your opponents') will be affected.

KILL CIVILIZATION [Shift][F5]

You can completely eliminate any civilization, including your own, with this option.

TECHNOLOGY ADVANCE [Shift][F6]

This option allows you to immediately confer on any civilization (including your own, of course) whatever advance they are currently researching.

EDIT TECHNOLOGIES [Ctrl][Shift][F6]

This option gives you the power to edit the technology of every civilization in the game. You determine what advances an empire has (asterisked ones) and does not have (not marked) by selecting them and clicking the OK button. (What technologies are available for research are marked with a dash; that's based on the tech tree, which you cannot change here.) With the GIVE/TAKE ALL button, you can give a civilization all the technologies or, if you have already given all, take them all away. Use the CANCEL button to leave when you're done; this does *not* cancel your changes.

Note that some technologies (Irrigation, for one) are known by all civilizations at the dawn of time; you cannot take these away.

Force Government [Shift][F7]

Use this to change the government of any civilization to the type you wish it to be, whether or not that form of government has been discovered.

Change Terrain at Cursor [Shift][F8]

This option gives you the ability to instantly determine the type of terrain that exists in the square that is the current cursor location—using the Terrain button. You can also add or remove any improvements appropriate to the type of terrain, with the single exception of Farmland. Note that you cannot specify special resources for any terrain square; they just happen.

Destroy All Units at Cursor [Ctrl][Shift][D]

This quite simply destroys any units at the current cursor location.

Change Money [Shift][F9]

Use this to specify the amount of funds in the treasury of any civilization.

Edit Unit [Ctrl][Shift][U]

Use this to change the attributes of any unit at the current cursor location. The veteran status, movement points, hit points, home city, and fortification status are modifiable. If you're editing a Caravan or Freight unit, you can change the type of commodity it is carrying. You cannot, however, change a unit to another type.

Edit City [Ctrl][Shift][C]

This option allows you to meddle with the status of any city on the map—as long as you position the cursor on it first. You can set the size (population) of the town, determine exactly how many shields are in the Production Box, make all the Wonders of the World in that burg suddenly disappear, or copy all of the improvements in some other city to this one. If the city is in disorder or celebrating a We Love the _____ Day, you can clear either state of affairs. Finally, you can make the city an objective of the scenario (the number in parentheses will change to '1') or remove it from the list of objectives ('0').

What good is an objective? Read about the **Scenario Parameters** option to find out.

Edit King [Ctrl][Shift][K]

No, this doesn't let you change what the rulers of other civilizations look like. You can, however, specify any ruler's treaty status with every other civilization, the most recent turn when two civilizations had contact, the ruler's current attitude toward other rulers, and any ruler's current reputation. In addition, you can clear a ruler's patience counter (making them very tolerant for a while), set or clear a research goal for any civilization, and determine how far each ruler has progressed toward the advance currently being researched. You can copy the technology of one civilization to another—quite a shortcut from doing it one advance at a time with the Edit Technologies option. Finally, you can change the name and sex of every leader in the world.

This is a catchall that includes some powerful tools for setting up scenarios. Most of these options have little or no use during a game already in progress.

TECH PARADIGM affects how long it takes to research technological advances. The default is 10/10. By lowering the numerator, you decrease the time necessary to discover new advances; the fastest you can allow research to progress is 1/10. Conversely, increasing the numerator makes scientific progress slower.

TURN YEAR INCREMENT allows you to decide how much time passes with each game turn. If you leave this at zero, *Civilization II* uses the default increment, which changes with time as described earlier in this manual. Any positive integer sets a number of years to pass per turn; a negative integer sets a number of months to pass per turn.

STARTING YEAR determines the year or month in which the scenario will begin (month if you've set the Turn Year Increment to a number of months, year if you've set it to a number of years). Any positive number is A.D., and any negative number is B.C.

MAXIMUM TURNS allows you to set the length of the game in turns.

TOGGLE SCENARIO FLAG tells *Civilization II* whether or not you want to save this game setup as a scenario. Note that the CHEAT menu option SAVE AS SCENARIO automatically sets this toggle for you.

WIPE ALL GOODY BOXES removes all of the villages of minor tribes from the world, permanently.

RESTORE ALL GOODY BOXES recreates all of the minor tribe villages in the world, except for those which were originally on a terrain square that is now occupied by a city or unit.

REVEAL WHOLE MAP makes the scenario take place in a known world. The entire map, excluding enemy units but including their cities, will be visible from the beginning of the game.

COVER WHOLE MAP makes the scenario take place in an unexplored world, the *Civilization* standard.

SET SCENARIO NAME allows you to give your scenario a title.

TOGGLE TOTAL WAR FLAG silences the senate in all republics and democracies. Set this to '1' to force the assumption that there is a war going on at the outset of the scenario, and that the usual senatorial meddling in foreign affairs has been effectively stifled for the duration. This also turns the BLOODLUST option on, eliminating the possibility of space flight.

EDIT VICTORY CONDITIONS itself contains multiple options:

- The first, TOGGLE USE OBJECTIVE VICTORY FLAG, must be set to '1'; otherwise, the game ignores the rest of these settings. Essentially, the objective victory flag tells *Civilization II* to completely ignore the usual scoring conventions. Rather, all that counts is the taking of the preset objectives in the scenario. Using the EDIT CITY option on the CHEAT menu, you can make any city a scenario objective.

- TOGGLE COUNT WONDERS AS OBJECTIVES determines whether or not captured Wonders of the World also count toward the objective score.

- Next, you decide which civilization will be the protagonist; this is not the player's civilization. This setting only determines which civilization is used as the benchmark for the four final settings.

- The last four allow you to set conditions for the types of outcome possible in an objective scenario. For each, enter the number of objectives that the protagonist civilization must control (that is, have conquered or kept) at the end of the game in order to accomplish that level of victory or defeat. Other civilizations are automatically assigned the corresponding outcome. For example, if the Romans as protagonists achieve a Marginal Defeat, all other groups win a Marginal Victory.

EDIT SPECIAL RULES also contains a few sub-options, each of which is fairly straightforward. You can prevent any civilization from ever changing its form of government, make it impossible to obtain advances by taking over enemy cities, and remove the specter of pollution from the game. One caveat is necessary; you should never use the last option—SPECIAL WWII-ONLY AI. This was put in as an aid for the game designers and will almost certainly cause your scenario to crash.

SAVE AS SCENARIO

This allows you to save the current game situation as a scenario file.

EDITORS

The EDITORS menu is filled with powerful tools for scenario builders that allow you to change nearly everything about the game. The detailed explanation of how these work is in **Scenario Building Tools**. This section includes only a brief introduction to each editor.

The options on the EDITORS menu are not available during multiplayer games.

ADVANCES EDITOR

This editor is the one you use to messing with the "schedule" of advances in the game—the Tech Tree.

CITIES EDITOR

The Cities Editor allows you to change the way all cities look. When you select this editor from the menu, the CITIES EDITOR window opens.

EFFECTS EDITOR

This one is dangerous. The EFFECTS editor lets you change most of the fundamental numbers on which many portions of **Civilization II** is built. Some of these have straightforward effects, but others have consequences that can be difficult to foresee. Be careful when messing with the universal effects.

CITY IMPROVEMENTS EDITOR

Infrastructure is what holds an empire together, and it's sloppy design work if the city improvements and Wonders of the World in your scenario don't match up with the rest of it. The CITY IMPROVEMENTS editor is the tool you use to modify these things for your scenario.

TERRAIN EDITOR

The terrain underfoot is one of the most basic elements in any scenario, and it's one that many designers never think to modify. Select this editor from the menu to open the TERRAIN editor.

Tribe Editor

A "tribe" is a potential civilization. Even though there can be only seven civilizations in play at any one time, there are 28 tribes defined in the rules. Any tribe can be placed into a scenario as a civilization. The Tribe editor allows you to define each of these 28 tribes and their salient characteristics.

Units Editor

One of the things almost every scenario designer wants to do is to modify the military and non-military units civilizations can build. The Units editor is the tool to do that.

Icon Editor

Half the fun of a new scenario is seeing all of the new art for the first time. If you enjoy creating scenarios, you'll certainly want to customize the look of many of the existing icons. This editor is what you use to do so.

Events Editor

As explained elsewhere, is possible to add *events* to any scenario. With the Events editor, you can do so with a minimum of fuss.

Civilopedia

The Civilopedia is an online encyclopedia of *Civilization II*. The entries under each topic appear alphabetically, and each includes detailed information about the item, its historical importance, and its significance in the game.

Civilization Advances

This option focuses on the advances. The Civilopedia entry describing each advance automatically appears when you acquire that advance, unless you turn that feature off using the Civilopedia for Advances toggle in the Graphic Options on the Game menu.

City Improvements

This option culls the list to include only the structures you can build in a city to improve its working.

Wonders of the World

To narrow your choices down to information about the various Wonders, use this option.

Military Units

The title of this topic might be slightly misleading, as *Civilization II* considers all units to be military, even Diplomats, Caravans, and Settlers.

Governments

If you want information on the various forms of government, this is the place.

Terrain Types

This option provides the entries for each type of terrain square and special resource that exists in *Civilization II*.

This option includes all the information not covered under any of the other focused topic lists, including things like Pollution, Disbanding, and Fortresses.

THE STATUS WINDOW

The information displayed in this window helps you keep abreast of the status of your civilization and your turn. Note that you can click anywhere in this window to toggle the Map window between VIEW PIECES mode and MOVE PIECES mode.

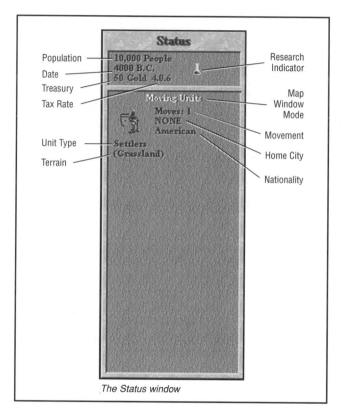

The Status window

WORLD PEACE BAR

At the top of this window is a bar indicating the accumulated turns of world peace. World peace is a situation in which *no* civilizations are at war. Each turn of peace adds to your civilization score. (This bar might not become visible for quite a while, if ever.)

SUMMARY BOX

Below the peace bar is a quick reference box summarizing data you'll find useful during the game.

POPULATION

This figure reports the current size of your civilization's population.

DATE

The date is reported in years B.C. or A.D. A normal game begins in 4000 B.C. Each turn represents the passing of a period of years. Depending on the current date, turns might be 1 year, 2, 5, 10, 20, 25, or 50 years long.

TREASURY

This figure reports the amount of gold currently in your treasury. If it increases each turn, you've got a surplus; if it decreases each turn, you're operating at a deficit.

TRADE BALANCE

The figures that appear here represent the percentages you've set for the spending of your trade income. They are, in order: taxes, luxuries, and research. (Note: multiply the number shown by 10 to get the actual percentage.) Each of these three byproducts of trade has its benefits. As time passes and cities grow, you might have to adjust the trade rates to provide a minimum amount of taxes and science research while providing more luxuries to keep the population sufficiently happy. To adjust trade rates, pull down the KINGDOM menu and select the TAX RATE option.

SCIENTIFIC RESEARCH

The research indicator is a graphic representation of your progress toward the next advance. The beaker notes your progress, and it changes as you get closer to your current research goal. Once the new discovery is reported and your scientists are sent off to study something else, this indicator is reset.

ENVIRONMENT

If there is any danger of global warming, the environment indicator graphically represents the extent of this risk. With the first case of pollution, the sun icon appears, at its lowest setting. If pollution continues, the sun changes to indicate the "progress" of pollution. If pollution is not brought under control when the indicator is at its highest, the planet suffers a bout of global warming, then the indicator reverts to a setting that reflects the new equilibrium.

Pollution and environmental problems can also be caused by nuclear reactor meltdowns and fallout from nuclear weapons. For more information on pollution and global warming, see **Planetary Caretaking**.

ACTIVE UNIT/LOCATION BOX

Below the SUMMARY BOX is an area dedicated to information on the current cursor location. This is normally the current active unit, but might also be a terrain square you have selected. Note that for the purposes of this information box, cities are ignored. The following information is included, not necessarily in this order.

MODE

Whether the MAP window is in VIEW PIECES or MOVE PIECES mode is noted.

ICONS

If there are any units at the current location, each will be represented by its icon. These icons are complete with the colored shield denoting nationality and the bar showing damage status.

NATIONALITY

If there are any rival units at the current location or if you are viewing a unit, rather than a terrain square, the name of the civilization to which each unit belongs is displayed.

HOME CITY

If there are any of your units at the current location, the name of the city from which each unit derives support is displayed. This is normally the city where the unit was built. You can transfer a unit to another city by moving it there and using the Go HOME TO NEAREST CITY order (or by clicking on the unit in the CITY DISPLAY and selecting the SUPPORT FROM THIS CITY option). This can be useful when one of your cities is threatened with capture, since all units supported by a captured city are destroyed.

UNIT TYPE

If there are any units at the current location, the type of each unit is displayed. For your units, the box also tells you whether or not it is a veteran unit.

MOVEMENT

If there are any of your units at the location, the number of movement points the active unit has remaining are noted. (If you are finished moving a unit, but it still has movement left, use the SKIP TURN order to end that unit's movement for the turn.)

Note that points are shown as fractions when the unit is moving along a road (roads triple movement, making fractional movement points necessary). The fraction indicates the lowered attack strength as well as the use of movement points. For example, a unit that begins with 1 movement point and moves one square along a road would show 2/3 movement points remaining, which also equates to 2/3 attack strength.

Also remember that units beginning on a square containing a railroad and moving along the railroad spend no movement points until they leave the railroad.

TERRAIN

This is the terrain type of the square. This terrain report disregards the presence of a city, but does mention other improvements such as irrigation, roads, and railroads. If there are special resources available at that site, they are also noted.

THE MAP WINDOW

The MAP window is the isometric map, the window in which you view and move your active units. The area shown in this window is the section of the world outlined on the map in the WORLD window. You can move and resize the MAP window just as you would any other window. (Note that, if you open so many reports, displays, and messages that you bury the MAP window, you can always close them all and bring it to the front of the heap by choosing ARRANGE WINDOWS from the VIEW menu.)

MULTIPLE WINDOWS

If, for some reason, you would like to have more than one MAP window open (to keep an eye on an especially valuable piece of real estate, for example), you can do so. Right-click anywhere in the WORLD window. The new window acts just like the default one, except that you have an additional button in the top left-hand corner. You can use this button to cycle through the viewing modes for that window. The modes are View Friendly Units, View Enemy Units, View All Units, and Static View (which centers on the map square you choose and stays there).

ZOOM BUTTONS

In the upper left-hand corner of the window frame are ZOOM IN ▨ and ZOOM OUT ▨ buttons. Use these to customize the size of your map view. There are 16 levels of adjustment. You can also use any of the ZOOM options on the VIEW menu.

MOVING THE VIEW

To reposition the MAP window so that it shows a different section of the game map, simply click on any map square in the window. *Civilization II* redraws the map, centering on the square you selected. If you want to center on a square that is not presently in the window, you can also click on a location in the WORLD window to center there.

CENTERING ON A CITY

Use the FIND CITY option on the KINGDOM menu to center the map on any known city, regardless of where or whose it is.

CENTERING ON A UNIT

To center the view on a particular one of your units, open the CITY DISPLAY for that unit's home city. In the UNITS ROSTER, click on the icon for that unit. Use the CENTER MAP ON UNIT option to center the MAP window on the unit.

WORLD WINDOW

This window shows a map of the entire known world. It is centered on the part of the world shown in the MAP window. The rectangle delineates the edges of that view. You can use the WORLD window to move around the MAP window more rapidly. Click on a location in the WORLD window, and both windows shift to center on that position.

Right-click anywhere in the WORLD window to open a secondary MAP window. (See **Multiple Windows** for the details.)

APPENDIX: SCENARIO MACRO "LANGUAGE"

We've included a new tool that experienced *Civilization II* scenario builders should find useful.

Warning: The scenario macro language is a supplementary design tool, not a part of the game. It has not been tested as well as the game itself and could cause problems if used incorrectly. If you experience difficulties in the game after creating an events file, do not immediately call Customer Support. The best solution is to delete (or at least rename) the events file. If you do so and the problems still persist, *then* call Customer Support.

Building scenarios with the original *Civilization II* tools, the designers ran into several limitations that frustrated their creativity. Their reaction was to install a primitive—but rather useful—macro language that allowed them to add "events" to the game.

TERMINOLOGY

Before we start explaining how to use this macro "language" (it's really not a full-scale language, but there's no better word for what it is), we should define a few terms.

- An **Event** is the combination of a *Trigger* and an *Action*. Each Event is a simple cause-and-effect sequence. Events are the fundamental structure of this macro language.

- A **Trigger** is the specific game occurrence that activates a particular Event. This is the cause.

- An **Action** is the consequence an Event generates in response to its Trigger. This is the effect.

Essentially, you define Events so that when the Trigger happens, it triggers the Action. Note that a single Trigger can have multiple Actions associated with it, but no one Trigger can have more than one Action of the same type.

THE EVENTS FILE

The first step in adding Events to your scenario is to create a text file in the directory in which you're building the scenario. This file must be named **events.txt** and must be in the same directory as the scenario (**.scn**) file. All of the text you put in this file represents events you want in your scenario.

The events file must begin with the line:

    @BEGINEVENTS

and end with the line:

    @ENDEVENTS

These tell *Civilization II Multiplayer Gold Edition* that the file is, indeed, a valid events file.

The rest of the file consists of the definitions of the events themselves. It is extremely important that these definitions are in the correct format. That format is covered in the next section. Before we go on, however, there is one optional statement we should mention.

DEBUGGING

One statement is not an event, but rather a tool you can use.

If you add the line:

    @DEBUG

immediately after the @BEGINEVENTS line, you enable the Event Parsing Debugger (EPD). This can help you find problems in your event files.

When you load the scenario and the events file, the EPD opens a window that lets you watch as each line of the event file is processed. Only valid statements that have been processed successfully appear in this window. Thus, if the parser runs into an invalid statement in your file, the display in the window will stop at the line before the problem statement. This should allow you to search out errors and repair them.

Make sure to take this line out of your events file when you're done debugging the scenario.

EVENT DEFINITIONS

Each event definition must follow a strict format. There are three parts to this format:

1. The Trigger Statement (@IF) defines the Trigger for the event.

2. The Action Statement (@THEN) defines the Actions associated with that Trigger.

3. The End Statement (@ENDIF) tells the parser that there are no more Actions for this Trigger.

All put together, a valid event definition looks like this:

```
@IF
Trigger
@THEN
Action 1
Action 2
...
Action N
@ENDIF
```

where the words *Trigger* and *Action* represent valid Triggers and Actions as defined in the next section.

For those of you to whom it means something, there is a 32K heap dedicated for events. This is the memory used for each internal event structure and all TEXT information.

For example, say you want to remind the player on the 16th turn that they have only four more turns before the end of the scenario. The Trigger is the beginning of turn 16, and the Action is to display some text in a pop-up box. The definition of this event should look something like this:

```
@IF
TURN
turn=16
@THEN
TEXT
You have only four more turns to meet your victory conditions!
ENDTEXT
@ENDIF
```

At the start of the player's 16th turn, a text box pops up with the message "You have only four more turns to meet your victory conditions!" displayed in it.

VALID TRIGGERS AND ACTIONS

What constitutes a "valid" Trigger or Action? Essentially, any group of lines that is in the right place and follows the correct format. The group must begin with a recognized word—one of the trigger words or action words—and must contain the proper number of parameters and a legitimate value for each parameter. Note that, to be legitimate, a value does not have to make sense. Thus, for example, the value **Goober7** for a city name is legitimate, even if there is no city in the scenario by that name.

There is one "wildcard" value that is legitimate for certain parameters.

Anybody: If a parameter requires the name of a civilization as its value, this value sets it so that any civilization meets the requirements.

Some triggers require you to specify (as parameters) the civilization that is attacking, defending, or receiving the object of the trigger. In these cases, you can also normally use **Anybody** in place of the name of a specific civilization. For those particular triggers, there are three other "wildcard" values you can use with the **Receiver** and **Owner** parameters of the associated actions.

TriggerAttacker: This specifies the civilization that was the aggressor in the happening that triggered the trigger.

TriggerDefender: This denotes whichever civilization was the defender in the happening that triggered the trigger.

TriggerReceiver: This represents the civilization that has the technology named in the **ReceivedTechnology** trigger.

Note that case (capitalization or lack thereof) is not important. "ANYBODY" is the same as "anybody" or "anYBoDy" as far as the parser is concerned.

One important thing to remember is that you must *not* put spaces where they are not called for. This is especially vital before and after equals signs (=). Under no circumstances should there *ever* be a space next to an equals sign.

Now, let's go over all the recognized trigger words and action words, their parameters, and the legitimate values thereof.

THE TRIGGERS

Every Trigger is a specific trigger word, which might be followed by one or more required parameters. There are *no* optional parameters. Each parameter must be on a line by itself, in order immediately after the trigger word. For example:

```
@IF
CityTaken
city=Rome
attacker=Anybody
defender=Romans
```

is a valid Trigger.

Each parameter is the parameter word, which might be followed by the equals sign (=), then the value for that parameter. When a value must be entered exactly as written here, it is listed in bold type. (Case still doesn't matter.)

TRIGGER WORD	PARAMETERS	LEGITIMATE VALUES
CityTaken	city=	name of a city
	attacker=	civilization name or **Anybody**
	defender=	civilization name or **Anybody**
Negotiation	talker=	civilization name or **Anybody**
	talkertype=	**Human**, **Computer**, or **HumanOrComputer**
	listener=	civilization name or **Anybody**
	listenertype=	**Human**, **Computer**, or **HumanOrComputer**
RandomTurn	denominator=	number >0 and <1001
ReceivedTechnology	receiver=	civilization name or **Anybody**
	technology=	technology index number
ScenarioLoaded		
Turn	turn=	number or **Every**
TurnInterval	interval=	number
UnitKilled	unit=	name of a unit
	attacker=	civilization name or **Anybody**
	defender=	civilization name or **Anybody**

CityTaken: This Trigger is activated when a city changes ownership. It's excellent for reacting to key cities being captured. *Attacker* is the civilization that took the city, *defender* is the one who owned the city beforehand.

Negotiation: This is triggered when two civilizations try to talk to each other. Note that there is an automatic Action to this Trigger that stops the two civilizations from talking to each other. When using this trigger, keep in mind that many things cause negotiations in the game, especially between computer-controlled players. Although it might be tempting to add some flavor to the game with a text pop-up whenever two civilizations try to meet ("Lincoln and Davis meet face to face, but Davis is adamant," for example), this can happen so often as to make the scenario unplayable. The *talkertype* and *listenertype* parameters allow you to specifically include or exclude computer (or human) civilizations from this Trigger.

RandomTurn: Rather than a specific turn, this triggers an Event on a turn chosen at random. *Denominator* is the "one in" number. That is, for example, if the denominator is 40, there is a one in 40 chance every turn that this Event will be triggered.

ReceivedTechnology: This one's activated when a civilization receives—through whatever means—the specified technology *and* every turn thereafter, as long as the civilization retains the advance. Note that this can cause some irregularities unless you really want the action to happen every turn for the rest of the game. (To prevent that, make sure to include the **JustOnce** action in the event.) *Receiver* is the civilization that gets the advance. The *technology index number* is the position of the particular advance in the advances list in the **rules.txt** file. Remember that the index numbers begin at zero (for Advanced Flight), and only go up to 100 (Extra Advance 7). Also, note that Future Technology (90) can be received over and over and over without limit.

ScenarioLoaded: When a scenario is first loaded, this Trigger becomes activated. Note that this Trigger only works with two Actions, **PlayCDTrack** and **DontPlayWonders**. Any other use will cause unpredictable results.

Turn: Use this to have something happen at the beginning of a specific turn (or every turn). This can be useful for creating units on specific dates in historical scenarios, reenacting troop movements, and more.

TurnInterval: This is a repeating Trigger. The value of the *interval* parameter is the number of turns between the triggering of the action(s). An interval of 4, for example, would trigger this event every fourth turn.

UnitKilled: Use this when you want to respond to a particular unit being killed in battle. This is especially good for leaders, one-of-a-kind units, and special objectives. *Attacker* is the civilization that killed the unit, *defender* is the one who owned the unit.

ACTIONS

Actions, much like Triggers, consist of a specific action word, which might be followed by one or more required parameters. There are *no* optional parameters. Each parameter must be on a line by itself, in order immediately after the action word (if there is one). For example:

```
@THEN
MakeAggression
who=Romans
whom=Carthaginians
```

is a valid Action.

Each parameter is the parameter word, which might be followed by the equals sign (=), then the value for that parameter. (Note that one action word, **Text**, has a value with no parameter word, followed by a parameter word with no values.) When a value must be entered exactly as written here, it is listed in bold type. (Case still doesn't matter.)

ACTION WORD	PARAMETERS	LEGITIMATE VALUES
ChangeMoney	receiver=	civilization name
	amount=	number
ChangeTerrain	terraintype=	terrain index number
	maprect	(on following line) coordinates
CreateUnit	owner=	name of a civilization or **Anybody**
	unit=	type of unit
	veteran=	**Yes, No, False**, or **True**
	homecity=	name of home city or **None**
	locations	x1,y1
		...
		x10,y10
	endlocations	

ACTION WORD	PARAMETERS	LEGITIMATE VALUES
DestroyACivilization	whom=	civilization name
DontPlayWonders		
GiveTechnology	technology= receiver=	technology index number civilization name
JustOnce		
MakeAggression	who= whom=	aggressor civilization name victim civilization name
MoveUnit	unit= owner= maprect moveto numbertomove=	name of a type of unit civilization name x1,y1,x2,y2,x3,y3,x4,y4 x,y number or **All**
PlayCDTrack		a number >1 and <25 (2–24 are valid)
PlayWaveFile		file name (*.wav)
Text		text to be displayed
	EndText	

Note that, although a single Trigger can cause multiple Actions, each Trigger can cause only one Action of each type. You can, for example, use MoveUnit, Change-Money, and CreateUnit all in the same Event, but you can't use CreateUnit twice (or more times) in the same Event. If you wanted to create more than one unit, you would need to define another Event using an identical Trigger.

ChangeMoney: This adds money to or subtracts it from a civilization's treasury. (Use a negative number for the amount to subtract.) If after the adjustment the treasury is less than zero, *Civilization II* makes it zero, instead. *Receiver* is the affected civilization.

ChangeTerrain: This changes all of the terrain in a specified rectangular region of the map (delineated by the coordinates you give) to the specified type. You specify the type using the *terrain index number*, which is the position of the desired terrain type in the terrain list in the rules.txt file. Remember that the index numbers begin at zero (for Desert), and only go up to 10 (Ocean).

The coordinates define the corners of the rectangular region. They must (1) be on the line immediately following the word **maprect**, (2) be separated by commas, and (3) be listed in the following specific order to be valid. (They also must be valid map coordinates.) The first coordinate must be the upper left corner; next comes the upper right, then lower right, and finally lower left. Thus:

1–2

4–3

CreateUnit: Creates a new unit (at no expense) with specified characteristics and places it on the map at the first of the specified locations. If that placement is invalid for any reason, the program tries the subsequent locations (there can be up to 10), in order, until one works or it reaches the *endlocations* parameter. The x and y in these locations represent horizontal and vertical coordinates on the scenario map.

DestroyACivilization: This one is exactly what it sounds like. Cities, units, and everything else is completely wiped out. *Whom* is the civilization slated to meet its doom (as in, "for *whom* the bell tolls").

DontPlayWonders: This Action toggles off the display of the Wonder of the World videos that normally play when a new wonder is completed.

GiveTechnology: Bestows the specified advance on the named civilization. The *technology index number* is the position of the particular advance in the advances list in the rules.txt file. Remember that the index numbers begin at zero (for Advanced Flight), and only go up to 100 (Extra Advance 7). Also, note that Future Technology (90) can be received over and over and over without limit. *Receiver* is the civilization on which the bestowing is to descend.

JustOnce: This special Action tells the program to execute this event once and only once. If, for example, you wanted to do something special the first time a city is taken, but not afterward, you would use the CityTaken Trigger and include JustOnce as one of the consequent Actions.

MakeAggression: This Action causes two civilizations to cancel their peace treaty, if one exists. Then *who* immediately declares war on *whom*.

MoveUnit: This scans a specified rectangular region of the map (*maprect*), then orders a specified number of the owner's units of the given type in that region to move to a certain location. The program only activates units that are (1) not fortified, (2) not on sentry duty, (3) not already headed for a destination, (4) not building fortifications, and (5) not nuclear weapons. **MoveUnit** does not affect units owned by the human player.

The *maprect* coordinates define the corners of the rectangular region. They must be listed in a specific order to be valid. The first coordinate must be the upper left corner; next comes the upper right, then the lower right, and finally the lower left. Thus:

1–2

4–3

PlayWaveFile: Play the specified *.wav* file. The program searches the **sound** subdirectory of the current scenario directory for the file.

PlayCDTrack: Tells your computer's CD player to play the specified audio track. On the *Civilization II Multiplayer Gold Edition* CD-ROM, Track 1 is reserved for program information, so the first audio track is actually Track 2. Thus, the *number* value must be 2 or greater.

Text: This simply presents a pop-up text box to the player. The box includes whatever text you put between the **Text** and **EndText** lines.

Note that unit types, civilization names, and so on *must* match the corresponding names in the **rules.txt** file exactly. Mismatches cause errors.

Due to the lead time between printing the manual and releasing the game, the designers might have made changes to the scenario macro language that are not reflected here. For the latest information, check the file **macro.txt** in the *Civilization II* directory.

EXAMPLE

Here is a hypothetical sample Event definition from an American Revolution scenario. If England takes New York from the Americans, this Event displays the text "New York captured by the Redcoats! Enraged local citizens join the fight for liberty!" Then, it creates a new American militia unit and tries to place it at map location 84,22. If that is not a legal placement (enemy units already there or whatever), it then tries 84,23 and—if that location is invalid, too—79,31.

```
@BEGINEVENTS

@IF

CityTaken

city=New York

attacker=English

defender=Americans

@THEN

Text

New York captured by the Redcoats! Enraged local citizens join
    the fight for liberty!

EndText

CreateUnit

unit=Militia

owner=Americans

veteran=false

homecity=none

locations

84,22

84,23

79,31

endlocations

@ENDIF

@ENDEVENTS
```

INDEX

1x1 brush 183
3x3 brush 183
5x5 brush 183

A

Abilities button 196
Academic knowledge 187
Accelerated Startup 25
Actions 200, 201, 202, 203, 206–208, 242, 244, 246–249
Activate Unit 72, 226
Active status 84
Active unit 71–72
Add button 201
Add to City 96
Adjective 195
ADM rating 64, 84, 87
Advances. See Civilization advances
Advances Editor. See Technological Advances Editor
Advisors menu 169, 227–229
AEGIS Cruisers 87, 89
After the Apocalypse scenario 123–124
Age, customize 23
The Age of Discovery scenario 124–125
The Age of Napoleon scenario 125–126
The Age of Reptiles scenario 126–128
Aggressive 195
AI Value 187
Air units. See Units, air
Airbase 33, 71, 73, 85, 86, 99–107, 225, 226
Airlift Orders 72, 226
Airport 29, 30, 72, 85, 226
Alexander the Great scenario 128–129
Alien Invasion scenario 129–130
All Humans Can Chat From Start 165, 173
Alliance 17, 34, 104–105
Alpha Centauri 3, 115
Alpine Troops 32
Always wait at end of turn 218
The American Civil War scenario 131–132
Analyze Map 182

Anarchy 33, 55, 56, 59, 60, 61, 62, 93, 104
Ancient epoch 187
Animated Heralds 219
Announce "We Love The King Day" 220
Announce cities in disorder 220
Announce order restored in city 220
Antechambers 102
Apollo Program 109, 230
Applied knowledge 187
Apportionment bar 211, 212
Aqueducts 31
Arrange Windows 182, 224, 239
Arrows 8, 10, 41, 54
Artillery 29
Ask to Declare War 176
Ask to Share Maps 176
Atlantis scenario 133–134
Atolon scenario 158
Attack 195, 197
Attack strength 84, 88
Attack/Defense/Movement. See ADM
Attitude Advisor 227–228
Attitudes 17, 54, 55, 56, 57, 58, 59, 102, 175, 232
Automate Settler 99, 225. See also Settlers, automated
Automobile 67
AutoPlay iv
Autosave each turn 218
Autoscroll During Paint 183

B

Bank 47
Barbarians 14, 24–25, 35, 49, 99–100
    Ransoming barbarian leaders 100
Barracks 29, 30, 50, 191
Barter 176
Battle of the Sexes scenario 159
Battleship 87
Beakers 10, 12, 46, 54, 212, 222
Bears at Play scenario 159
Begin Scenario 22, 118
Benefits box 187, 191
Best of the Net II scenarios 119, 159
Best of the Net scenarios 119, 158

D

T

U

CREDITS

MULTIPLAYER GOLD EDITION

DESIGN
William F. Denman, Jr.
David Ellis

PROGRAMMING
William F. Denman, Jr.
with John O'Neill and Steven L. Cox

SMEDS 32 PROGRAMMING
Lee Baldwin
Wayne Harvey
Paul Rowan

MANUAL
John Possidente
Marisa Ong
Caroline Crossfield

CREATIVE SERVICES
Reiko Yamamoto
Kathryn Lynch
Matthew Willis

MARKETING
Mary Lynn Slattery, U.S.
Geraldine Burke, Europe

QUALITY ASSURANCE
HUNT VALLEY

Rosalie Kofsky, Lead Tester

Chris Bowling, Lead Tester

Bob Abe

Paul Ambrose

Kevin Bane

Matt Bittman

Eleanor Crawley

Alan Denham

Michael Dubose

Ross Edwards

Grant Frazier

Mark Gutknecht

Joe Lease

Jason Lego

Tim McCracken

Steve Purdie

John Ross

Sal Saccheri

Rick Saffery

Greg Schneider

ALAMEDA

Anthony Constantino XXVII

Brian King

Bill Schmidt

PRODUCER
William F. Denman, Jr.

SPECIAL THANKS
Jeff Goodwin

Marisa Ong

Caroline Crossfield

William Salit Design

Moore & Price Design

ORIGINAL CIVILIZATION II

GAME DESIGN
Brian Reynolds
with Douglas Caspian-Kaufman
and Jeffery L. Briggs

DESIGN ASSISTANCE
Mick Uhl

ORIGINAL CIVILIZATION DESIGN
Sid Meier and Bruce Shelley

PROGRAMMING
Brian Reynolds
Jason S. Coleman
Chris Taormino

SMEDS SYSTEM DESIGN
William F. Denman, Jr.
Paul L. Rowan
with Lee Baldwin
Wayne Harvey
Jason Snyder
John O'Neill

ART
Michael Haire, Art Director
Barbara Bents Miller
Stacey Clark Tranter
Murray Taylor
Barbara Jeznach
Nicholas Rusko-Berger
Bob Kathman
Michael Bazzell
Jerome Atherholt
Frank Vivirito
Katharine Seman
Michael Bates
Betsy Kirk
Guy Sparger
Chris Tamburrino
Mike Reis

MUSIC COMPOSED & ARRANGED BY
Roland Rizzo
Jeff Briggs

SOUND DESIGN
Mark G. Reis
with Ken Lagace

SOUND RECORDING & ENGINEERING
Mark G. Reis
Roland Rizzo

SOUND PROGRAMMING
David Evans

CIVILOPEDIA
David Ellis

MULTIMEDIA
Michael Ely
Timothy Train
Jason S. Coleman
with David Evans

DOCUMENTATION
Jonatha Caspian-Kaufman
with M. Christine Manley
& John Possidente

DESIGN & LAYOUT
Cesar Novoa
Joe Morel

QUALITY ASSURANCE
Jennifer MacLean, Lead Tester
Steve Moseley
Mike Barker
Chris Bowling
James King
Tammy Talbott
Bob Abe
Russell Clark
Don Emmel
David Ginsburg
Jim Hendry

Mike Prendergast
Matt Showalter
Vaughn Thomas
Brian Vargo

MARKETING PRODUCT MANAGER
Lindsay Riehl

PRODUCER
Jeffery L. Briggs

SPECIAL THANKS
Paula Scarfone
Marcia Foster
Jonathon Buckel
Jill & Ro Reynolds

CONFLICTS IN CIVILIZATION

GAME DESIGN
Mick Uhl

PROGRAMMING
Kerry Wilkinson

ART
Barbara Bents Miller
Stacey Clark Tranter
Barbara Jeznach
Michael Bazzell

MUSIC BY
Roland Rizzo

SOUND DESIGNERS
Mark Cromer
Mark G. Reis

RECORDING ENGINEERS
Mark G. Reis
Roland Rizzo

MULTIMEDIA
Michael Ely

Documentation
John Possidente

Layout & Design
Reiko Yamamoto
Jerome Paterno
Rick Rasay

Quality Assurance
Chrispy Bowling, Lead Tester
Wm. David Possidente, Second
Robin Pole, Second
Bob Abe
Brad Christman
Guy Lamarr
Dan Mcjilton
Joe Morel
Jun Yun

Additional Testing
Kathy Abe
Jim Crawley
Dave Ellis
Steve Purdie
Don Emmel
Rick Saffery
Brandon Martin

Technical Support
Tim Goodlet

Marketing Product Manager
Kathryn Lynch

Producer
Kerry Wilkinson

Best Of The Net Scenarios
Kevin Bromer, *Persian Gulf War*
Jeppe Grue & Jan Dimon Bendtsen, *The Conquest Of Britain*
Eric Hartzell, *Cross and Crescent*
Antonio Leal, *The Cholera of Zeus* and *Atolon*
Tim Mcbride, *The Fall of the Great Kesh*

Don Melsom, *East Wind, Rain*
Mike Regan, *Native Rebellion*

SPECIAL THANKS
Tom Nichols
Chris Deyo
Derek Mcleish
Ken Allen
Janet Dickerman
Marisa Ong
Kip Welch
Anu Kirk at Desper Technologies
Murray Taylor

FANTASTIC WORLDS

EDITOR DESIGN
Mick Uhl
with Stephen L. Cox

PROGRAMMING
Stephen L. Cox

MACRO PROGRAMMING
Kerry Wilkinson

SCENARIO DESIGN
Mick Uhl
John Possidente
Ken Burd
Bob Abe
Brandon Martin
Matt Bittman

ART
(MPS Texas)
Patrick Owens, Texas Lead
Shelly Hollen
Jim Mcintyre
Judith Peterson
Sam Yeates
(MPS Hunt Valley)
Jim Crawley

Barbara Jeznach
Joe Morel
Betsy Kirk
John Cameron
Brandon Martin
Alan Denham

ADDITIONAL ART
Herb Perez
Scott Nixon
John Gallagher
Eric Martin

MUSIC
Kevin Manthei
Roland Rizzo

SOUND DESIGNERS AND RECORDING ENGINEERS
Mark Cromer
Mark G. Reis

MANUAL
John Possidente

CREATIVE SERVICES
Jerome Paterno
Rick Rasay
Reiko Yamamoto

MARKETING
Carter Lipscomb
Geraldine Burke

QA
Rosalie Kofsky, Project Lead
Steve Purdie, Project Lead
Rick Saffery, Project Lead
Bob Abe
Paul Ambrose
Kevin Bane
Matt Bittman
Brandi Boone
Jim Crawley

Alan Denham
Mike Dubose
Grant Frazier
Mike Gibbons
Jason Lego
Brandon Martin
Rex Martin
Tim McCracken
Nick Price
John Allan Ross
Dean Schwarzkopf
Mike Seal
Aron Seiler

PRODUCER
Martin De Riso

SPECIAL THANKS
Murray Taylor
Yma, Mate Of Org
Greg Harvey
Wendy White
Corky, Destin & Don
Daniel Quick (The Emperor)

STOCK PHOTOGRAPHS PROVIDED BY:
The Corel Stock Photo Library
PDI

CUSTOMER SUPPORT

If you have any questions about *Civilization II Multiplayer Gold Edition* or any of our other products, please contact MicroProse Customer Support at:

- MicroProse

  2490 Mariner Square Loop

  Alameda, CA 94501

  ATTN: Customer Support
- (510)864-4550

  9:00 AM to 5:00 PM Pacific Time

  Monday through Friday
- Fax

  (510)864-4602
- World Wide Web

  www.microprose.com
- E-mail

  support@microprose.com

INTERNET:

You can read the latest news and information about MicroProse on our World Wide Web page at www.microprose.com. Download files from our FTP site at ftp.micro-prose.com. Send electronic mail to Customer Support at support@microprose.com.

COMPUSERVE:

To reach our Customer Support board in the Game Publishers B Forum, type **go gambpub** at any "!" prompt. Then select "Section 2" for MicroProse. In addition to posting and reading messages, you can download files from the "Libraries (Files)" menu. Send electronic mail to Customer Support at 76004,2223.

How to Get Help:

If you are having problems with *Civilization II Multiplayer Gold Edition*, we can best help you if (1) you are at your computer when you call and (2) you have the following information handy:

- Version number of *Civilization II Multiplayer Gold Edition*
- Your computer's processor and its speed (such as a 166MHz Pentium)
- Your computer's brand and model
- Total RAM installed in your computer
- Version of DirectX drivers
- CD-ROM brand and model name
- Video card brand and model name
- Sound card brand and model name
- Mouse brand and version number of mouse driver
- Joystick brand and model name
- Any error message you see in the game

How to Return Defective Materials:

If your game manual or CD-ROM is damaged or defective, you can return that item to Customer Support for a replacement. Send only the item to be replaced, not the whole game package. You must also include a photocopy of your receipt showing the date of purchase, not the date when you "registered" your game with MicroProse. Your 90-day warranty period begins with the date of purchase as shown on your receipt. MicroProse is not responsible for items lost in the mail. We suggest that you insure, register or certify your mail.